THE 30-Day SUGAR ELIMINATION DIET

A Whole-Food Detox to Conquer Cravings & Reclaim Health,
Customizable for Keto or Low-Carb

BRENDA BENNETT

VICTORY BELT PUBLISHING INC.

LAS VEGAS

First published in 2023 by Victory Belt Publishing Inc.

Copyright © 2023 Brenda Bennett

ISBN-13: 978-1-628604-74-0

Cover design by Kat Lannom

Interior design and illustrations by Yordan Terziev and Boryana Yordanova

Additional recipe photos by Jo Harding

Author photos by Shawon Davis

Printed in Canada

TC 0223

This book is dedicated to you, the reader—the one who has struggled for years with a compulsion for eating sugar and refined carbs and an inability to break free from its hold. I am here rooting for you.

CONTENTS

Letter to the Reader / 7

My Story / 9

How This Book Is Set Up / 12

1: WHAT IS THE 30-DAY SUGAR ELIMINATION DIET? / 14

Why We Crave Sugar and Carbs / 17

Before You Start / 24

Low-Carb Track or Keto Track? / 29

Taking Supplements During the Detox / 31

2: PROGRAM GUIDELINES / 34

Building New Habits / 36

The Basics / 38

Prioritizing Protein / 44

Days 1–7 / 48

Days 8–15 / 58

Days 16–23 / 67

Days 24–30 / 72

3: MEAL PLAN & RECIPES / 74

About the Meal Plan and Recipes / 76

30-Day Meal Plan and Shopping Lists / 80

MEAL PLAN RECIPES / 91

Apple Pie Dutch Baby / 94

Asparagus Salad with Avocado Dressing / 96

Bacon Bourbon Burgers / 98

Breakfast Sausage Patties / 100

Brown Butter Crispy Chicken Thighs / 102

Buffalo Chicken Salad Wraps / 104

Buffalo Wings / 106

Buffalo Wing Sauce / 108

Cabbage Roll Skillet / 110

Cauliflower Rice / 112

Cheddar and Bacon–Stuffed Burgers / 114

Chicken Cauliflower Fried Rice / 116

Chicken Chili Stuffed Peppers / 118

Chicken Kiev Meatballs / 120

Chicken Mushroom Skillet / 122

Chimichurri / 124

Cloud Bread Rolls / 126

Cobb Ranch Salad / 128

Corned Beef Hash Skillet with Eggs / 130

Creamy Cilantro Lime Slaw / 132

Crispy Broccoli / 134

Crustless Ham and Cheese Quiches / 136

Crustless Skillet Supreme Pizza / 138

Dairy-Free Mini Waffles / 140

Deviled Eggs / 142

Easy Bacon / 144

Easy-Peel Hard-Boiled Eggs / 146

Egg Foo Young / 148

Egg Noodles / 150

Egg Salad / 152

Eggs Benedict / 154

Fish Taco Bowl / 156

French Onion Meatballs / 158

Garlic Butter Mushrooms / 160

Garlic Butter Steak Bites / 162

German "Potato" Salad / 164

Grilled Romaine Salad / 166

Homemade Ketchup / 168

Jambalaya / 170

Low-Carb Marinara Sauce / 172

Mashed Roasted Cauliflower / 174

Momma's Italian Dressing / 176

Monte Cristo Waffle Sandwiches / 178

Open-Face Tuna Chaffles / 180

Palmini Rice / 182

Pan-Seared Lemon Butter Salmon / 184

Philly Cheesesteak Stir-Fry / 186

Pizza Chaffles / 188

Protein Pancakes / 190

Reverse-Seared Rib Eye with Chimichurri / 192

Roasted Balsamic Vegetables / 194

Rutabaga Fries / 196

Sausage Egg Cups / 198

Sausage Zucchini Skillet / 200

Sautéed Summer Squash / 202

Scotch Eggs / 204

Sheet Pan Chicken Fajitas / 206

Sheet Pan Shrimp with Crispy Pepperoni / 208

Shirataki Rice / 210

Shrimp Linguine in Garlic Butter Sauce / 212

Simple Skillet Chili / 214

Smoked Salmon Omelet Roll-Ups / 216

Smoky Grilled Pork Chops / 218

Soft Scrambled Eggs / 220

Spicy Mayo / 222

Spicy Smoked Salmon Wrap / 224

Spring Roll Chicken Salad with Creamy Asian Dressing / 226

Stuffed Chicken Thighs / 228

Sugar-Free BBQ Sauce / 230

Sugar-Free Maple Syrup / 232

Taco Seasoning / 234

Taco Soup / 236

Tuna Salad / 238

2-Minute English Muffins / 240

Waffle Breakfast Sandwich / 242

Zucchini Noodles with Roasted Garlic Cream Sauce / 244

DETOX DESSERTS & BEVERAGES / 247

Berry Fluff / 248

Brownie in a Mug / 250

Keto Chocolate Lava Cakes for Two / 252

Keto Dalgona Coffee / 254

Deep Dish Chocolate Chip Cookie / 256

Egg Custard / 258

Keto Electrolyte Drink—Three Ways / 260

No-Churn Vanilla Ice Cream / 262

Panna Cotta / 264

Raspberry Clafoutis / 266

Scrambled Egg Chocolate Pudding / 268

Sugar-Free Whipped Cream / 270

Tiramisu for Two / 272

4: KEEPING THE MOMENTUM GOING / 274

Are You a Moderator or an Abstainer? / 276

Reintroducing Carbs / 278

What's Next? / 281

Testimonials / 284

Shopping Guide / 288

Sweetener Conversion Chart / 290

The Scale Worksheet / 291

Hunger or Habit? / 292

With Gratitude / 294

Bibliography / 296

Recipe Quick Reference / 298

Recipe Index / 300

General Index / 305

Letter to the Reader

You can do anything for 30 days—even remove sugar from your diet. In fact, you may have done it before, but for some reason, old habits crept back in, and sugar has once again become too hard for you to resist. The refined carbs and sugary treats that were once just for holidays, birthday celebrations, and other special occasions eventually spilled into your work week. Now, they may be a daily indulgence and a difficult habit to stop.

Sugar is well known for being a comfort for many people during times of stress. For those of us who are unable to "moderate" foods that contain sugar, though, it is just as controlling as cocaine is for a drug addict, and we are just as out of control as other addicts when they get a hit of their addictive substance.

You may not identify yourself as being addicted to sugar. Maybe you just feel you don't have enough willpower, and you need a little guidance to detox for a short time and get a handle on your cravings. This 30-Day Sugar Elimination Diet will help you do just that.

I was a sugar addict from the age of 12 until I turned 34. The contents of this book are how I gained independence from sugar obsession, broke the hold of intense cravings, lost weight, and have maintained my sugar freedom since 2006.

No matter why you picked up this book or how you identify yourself, one thing remains true: sugar and refined carbs can wreak havoc on our bodies, our health, our minds, our internal organs, and how we age.

The good news is that you can regain control, and you can do it within one month. With this book, you will learn how to detox from sugar without horrible withdrawal symptoms. You will learn how to balance your blood sugar, remove those intense cravings, and lose weight while enjoying delicious food that keeps you totally satisfied. The tools I share in this book provide all the support you will need to live happily free of cravings for sugar and processed carbs.

Freeing yourself from sugar isn't about willpower and whether you have enough of it. It's not about following a Paleo or low-carb or keto diet. It is about the sugar and processed foods that have taken over your life. It's time to take back control and never be enslaved to any food again.

You can do it! One day at a time. You can remove sugar for 30 days, you will feel amazing, and you will lose weight.

MY STORY

A happy child—that's how I would describe myself. I had wonderful parents who cared for me in every way. My lovely childhood involved dance classes, ice skating lessons, baton twirling, bike riding, picnic dinners on the beach at sunset, and classic Italian food. Although my parents didn't go to college, they worked hard to provide my brothers and me with what we needed. We never lacked.

My issues with sugar and refined carbs began when I was 12, when I was an innocent kid who liked to sneak potato chips. Now, as a 49-year-old woman, I cannot understand why I felt I needed to sneak food, because my parents always had an open-door policy. I was never told I couldn't eat something. No one policed what I ate or when I ate or how much I ate. I was never told I needed to go on a diet. Furthermore, my mom can moderate sugar and enjoy it once a week. My father can do the same. I tried and tried to be like them and enjoy sweets in moderation, but that approach never worked for me.

All I know is that eating brought me comfort. As time went by, I had more difficulty controlling my urges, as if my body were compelled to eat without my conscious awareness. Sometimes I would find myself in the basement with my hand in a bag of chips without even remembering that I had walked down the stairs.

As I sought control over weight gain as a teen, I discovered a new way to enjoy my binges while keeping my weight stable. I found bulimia disgusting, but the results were too convincing for me to stop because I didn't have to change anything about my other habits. I could continue to overeat and indulge in sugar and carbs without the consequence of weight gain. And this made me happy for a long time. Until it didn't anymore. My period stopped for a year. I popped blood vessels around my eyes, and I would feel sharp pains down my throat at random times throughout the day, even for a long time after I stopped purging.

I finally found some freedom when I attended an Overeaters Anonymous (OA) meeting at age 22. I learned how to eat three meals a day. The "rule" of not eating between meals really worked for me. I found freedom in discipline; however, the guidelines didn't say that any food was off-limits, so sugar was still in my life. As time went on, I learned of other OA meetings in which people were advised to stay away from flour and sugar, but I thought

I didn't need that additional restriction. I lost 35 pounds in six months, going from 159 pounds to 124, and I was happy. I continued with OA until I had my first child at 29. Then I decided I was too busy with the new baby to go back to meetings, and I felt strong enough to lose the baby weight on my own, without support.

Within six months, I was able to lose 70 pounds of the weight I'd gained during pregnancy, so I was back to 124 pounds. Life was good. I had a baby, I was working full-time as a teacher, and I was happily married. When I got pregnant again at 32, I gained 40 pounds. This time, though, I couldn't lose the last 20 pounds of baby weight. I was stuck at 145 pounds, and I was miserable. I went to Weight Watchers to see if weekly support meetings would help. They did not. I saved up my points for packaged Weight Watchers snacks instead of eating real food.

In 2004, a friend of mine joined a program that removed white sugar and flour for six weeks. I decided to give that program a try. I had a weekly phone call with a mentor and was required to mail her my food journal for the week. This program changed my life. When I began, I thought I couldn't give up sugar—even for just six weeks—but the results from sticking with it were satisfying enough for me to continue. I lost all the weight I'd gained during my second pregnancy and again was back to 124 pounds. I stayed away from refined sugars, white flours, white potatoes, white rice, and so on until I got pregnant for the third and final time. With that pregnancy, I gained 50 pounds and decided to throw all my knowledge about sugar out the window. I figured I could go back to the sugar-free lifestyle after I had the baby. I was so wrong. The pull of sugar and refined carbs was worse than ever. I felt that avoiding them was beyond my conscious control, as if I had a ravenous lion inside me who couldn't get enough.

I struggled for a year, fighting every single day to tame that lion. Having to use my weakened willpower each day was utter emotional turmoil, but finally things turned around for the better.

My fight paid off. Not giving in when I was tempted paid off. Not turning to sugar and refined carbs paid off. Praying for strength every day paid off. My new behaviors started to rewire my brain. Those behaviors became automatic, and I no longer needed to use willpower every day to fight off cravings.

That was in 2006, and I have not let sugar or refined carbs touch my lips since. I refused the lie it once told me—that it would comfort and help me. I refused to believe I could moderate and have "just a little" or indulge only on a holiday. I believed it was an addiction I could not tame unless I was 100 percent abstinent. I couldn't give it up 98 percent of the time; I needed to keep it out of my life for good. I never take for granted where I was or where I am today. I am free from cravings. I am happy in my own skin, and I maintain a healthy weight. I never wake up and have to decide whether I will eat sugar and refined carbs that day. I don't. I won't. I will never give up the food sobriety that I have today. No food containing sugar or refined carbs will ever lure me into giving in because I know the harm it did to my body and mind. I know true freedom, and I pray that my story and the contents of this book will bring you that same freedom.

I've taught my method for detoxing from sugar and refined carbs for many years now. I offered my first program in 2012; then I updated the online recorded course to make it a live six-week course with weekly intensive Zoom meetings. That course has been so successful in transforming lives that I knew I had to turn it into a book to reach more people who are suffering as I was so many years ago.

I understand what it's like to go through multiple breakups with sugar and have it be a constant struggle in your life, because I was there myself for what seemed like an eternity. Then one day I said, "Enough is enough; I cannot live like this anymore. I cannot have 'just a little' and try to moderate something I have no control over. I've tried that for years."

Abstaining from sugar is my choice, but it doesn't have to be yours. You don't even need to decide right now whether a sugar-free lifestyle will be permanent. All you need to do for this detox is commit to going 30 days without sugar.

You may not label yourself as an addict like I do, but it doesn't matter. The steps you will follow in this detox will set you free regardless of whether you choose to bring sugar back into your life afterward.

HOW THIS BOOK IS SET UP

The 30-Day Sugar Elimination Diet provides you with everything you need to know to remove sugar from your life for one month without feeling deprived. You will enjoy delicious, nutritious meals; you won't feel like you're sacrificing anything; your cravings will be reduced or even eliminated; and you will lose weight.

IN PART I of this book, you will learn what the elimination diet entails, what you need to know before beginning, how often to use this program, why we crave sugar and carbs, and how to read food labels. I also give you a pantry guide and include a section on helpful, but optional, supplements.

IN PART II, I explain why I recommend food journaling during the program. I talk about why protein is so important, whether you need to exercise, and my opinion on using the scale as a self-assessment tool. This section is where you will find all the information you need to know prior to starting each segment of the detox. You do not need to read it all at once. For example, you can read just the material for Days 1–7 and then go to Part III to find the corresponding meal plan and begin enjoying the meals. After completing the first seven days, you can read the content for Days 8–15 and then head to the meal plan for those eight days, and so on. I've found that this method works best when I teach my online course. Getting bits of information each week makes the entire process less overwhelming.

PART III features the meal plan and all the recipes. Each seven- or eight-day section of the plan has an easy-to-follow chart showing what you will eat on those days, along with its own shopping list. If you're following the low-carb track rather than the keto track (see pages 29 and 30 for more on the two tracks), look for the special notations in blue text.

The breakfast, lunch, and dinner recipes immediately follow the meal plan and shopping lists. They are listed in alphabetical order to make them easy for you to find.

Sugar-free dessert recipes follow the meal plan recipes. It is your choice whether to try some of these recipes or to abstain from all sweet foods—even sugar-free ones—during the plan. Some of the people I coach feel that foods containing any type of sweetener (low-carb sweeteners included) cause them to want to eat more and more. If you're in this group, not including any sweet foods during the 30 days may be best for you. On the other hand, you may find that making some of my dessert recipes during the plan keeps you from feeling deprived and helps you stay on the program. If that's you, please enjoy no more than three desserts weekly.

IN PART IV, you will determine whether you are a moderator or an abstainer and learn how to reintroduce carbs after the detox (if you want to). I also offer tips on how to keep the momentum going after the 30 days is complete.

AT THE BACK OF THE BOOK, I've included some amazing testimonials in this section to inspire and motivate you. I've also included a shopping guide of reputable brands of products that you can use to save time when you are too busy to make everything from scratch, along with some handy tools that you can use during the detox if you wish.

1
WHAT IS THE 30-*Day* SUGAR ELIMINATION DIET?

The 30-Day Sugar Elimination Diet is a four-part program to help you detox from sugar, eliminate cravings for sugar and carbs, balance your blood sugar to feel better, and lose weight. You will focus on eating nutrient-dense whole foods. You will learn which kinds of carbs work for your body to get to your ideal weight and end cravings for good.

Not only are you going to improve your own life by eliminating sugar for 30 days, but you'll also have the opportunity to change the lives of those you love. Your success will be very motivating for everyone around you!

Everyone is bioindividual and has unique needs, so the focus of this book is not to convince you to consume a specific amount of carbs. Instead, my goal is to help you learn what your body needs to function best. In 30 days, you will have eliminated cravings for sugar and carbs and regulated your appetite while enjoying whole, delicious foods and without feeling deprived. You're likely to lose weight, too; most of the people who follow my online course report that they lose 10 to 20 pounds in six weeks.

Before you begin, I explain exactly why you've craved sugar and carbs, how to detox from sugar, how to read ingredient lists to identify sugar, and ways to avoid sugar and carb withdrawal. I also suggest some supplements that might help you feel better during the detox, although those are completely optional.

Each segment of the detox has a different focus:

- **DAYS 1–7:** You will learn about hydration, electrolytes, and beverages allowed during the cleanse; healthy fats and oils to cook with; and natural sugar-free sweeteners. I also talk about whether and how to incorporate appropriate snacks into this first week of the plan.

- **DAYS 8–15:** You will assess your experience on the first 7 days of the plan and learn how to resolve any issues you may have had. You will also learn about intermittent fasting and how to combat cravings.

- **DAYS 16–23:** You will learn how to handle trigger foods so that you don't revert to old habits for comfort. You will also find out how to tweak the program and troubleshoot to make the most of your 30-day detox.

- **DAYS 24–30:** You'll find out how to test your blood glucose to see how your body reacts to certain foods. With that information in hand, you can carb test, which will help you reintroduce certain whole-food carbohydrates after the 30 days. Carb testing is completely optional.

You can use this program as often as you need to. It's a perfect plan to implement after holiday indulgences or a few times per year when you need to get yourself on track. With the strategies shared in Part IV, you will learn how to turn the 30-day detox into a realistic and sustainable lifestyle. When you truly commit to this program, sugar cravings become a thing of the past, and you'll never again regain the weight you've lost!

WHY WE CRAVE SUGAR AND CARBS

You may not believe this just yet, but cravings for sugar and carbs are not your fault. You may think your lack of willpower is what's getting in the way of your weight-loss goals. I don't deny that giving in to temptations is an issue when you're trying to lose weight, but the reasons you're giving in are why it's not all about a lack of willpower. Low serotonin levels, lack of quality sleep, and hyperpalatable foods are three of the most common reasons people struggle with cravings.

Low serotonin equals poor sleep, an imbalance of melatonin, high cortisol from stress, depressed mood, low energy, and irritability, all of which lead to cravings. Poor sleep increases inflammation, impairs your immune system, and increases insulin resistance, and those things are stressors that lead to cravings. Furthermore, your appetite is regulated by your brain, and your brain has been hijacked by super palatable processed foods that lack protein and are often skewed toward highly refined carbs. These types of foods produce an unnatural degree of stimulation in the brain that leaves you feeling that natural whole foods are just not appealing.

The good news is that following this 30-day detox will naturally increase your serotonin levels, improve your sleep, and regulate your appetite to end cravings, lose weight, and feel great.

Starved for Serotonin

Serotonin is a neurotransmitter or brain chemical that your body needs to feel happy and satisfied. It is essential to your body in many ways, but particularly to your mental state, because it produces feelings of joy, peace, and hopefulness.

Everyone produces serotonin, but your lifestyle, your stress level, and the amount of sleep you get can result in very low amounts in your body, which will affect all your other functions. When you have a balanced amount of serotonin, you can think positively about what you can accomplish in your life and health goals, and you are able to encourage, soothe, and comfort yourself when the going gets tough.

Chronic daily stress depletes serotonin, which causes depressed moods, low energy, poor sleep, and, of course, cravings for carbs and sugar. Stress doesn't come only from your job or family or money issues. Simply not getting quality sleep can be considered a stressor. When you're tired, you may eat more and find it harder to resist high-carb, sugar-laden treats that spike blood sugar. Your body can't tell the difference between job, family, or financial stress and stress from spikes in your blood sugar due to what you just consumed.

When you feel like the glass is half empty or you're anxious, fearful, and without hope, you may be low in serotonin, which can cause you to experience intense sugar and carb cravings. Studies show that eating carbs increases serotonin levels. Your body knows this even if you're not thinking of it consciously, so, regardless of your intentions, when your body is low in serotonin, the carbs will call to you. Unfortunately, many of us choose processed and refined carbs and sugar when stress hits and we are seeking comfort.

When you feed yourself sugar or carbs to feel better, you will feel better— temporarily. Then, minutes or even seconds later, you will feel regret. Your brain is starved for serotonin, and you will need more and more sugar or carbs to get that same amount of comfort you did the previous time. It's a vicious cycle.

When it doesn't get adequate serotonin throughout the day, your body does not produce enough melatonin to fall asleep, enter deep sleep, and stay asleep at night. Serotonin and melatonin need to be in balance. Craving carbs before bed is often the body's natural way of seeking assistance with sleep.

There are several ways you can make lifestyle and diet changes to increase serotonin to help break the craving cycle.

BOOSTING SEROTONIN THROUGH SELF-CARE

Learning how to increase and balance serotonin naturally is the key to long-lasting positive habits that will enable you to lose weight and break free from the craving cycle. When you naturally increase serotonin through diet and lifestyle, you reduce your chances of reverting to old habits of using food for comfort and minimize cravings for sugar and refined carbs. This is essentially self-care.

But does the term *self-care* stress you out? Is the reason you never take time for yourself because you're too busy? Is self-care something you think only people who have a lot of time on their hands get to enjoy? If that's the case, you may be thinking about self-care the wrong way.

Self-care involves all the things that create an environment in which your body can thrive. Eating well is one aspect, but it's not necessarily the most important one. Devoting 30 minutes of each day to doing something that brings you happiness will make it much easier to be diligent about your food choices and steer clear of sugar over the next 30 days.

I know, I know; you're thinking you just don't have time to spend 30 minutes on an enjoyable activity. But let me explain why making the time will help you make the best food choices and stick to your new habits for good. Doing something that brings you joy brings you happiness, which will increase serotonin. Find an activity that calms you—for example, talking to a friend, taking a walk during your lunch break, writing in your journal, or savoring a cup of coffee or tea. Anything that is simple enough to incorporate into each day will be exactly what you need to relieve stress without turning to sugar and carbs for comfort. This is a form of self-care, my friend.

Think about it: when you feel bad about yourself, do you feel motivated to make positive changes, or do you just feel more depressed and then turn to food for comfort after promising yourself you wouldn't? Often, when we put ourselves down or believe we're failing at sticking to a diet, the result is a continuous cycle of self-sabotage. You can break this cycle. Stop berating yourself and acknowledge that you made certain decisions in the past that have consequences. End of story. *Accept it and move on.*

25 ACTIVITIES TO INCREASE SEROTONIN THROUGH SELF-CARE

- Canoe
- Chat with a friend
- Cook a healthy meal
- Exercise
- Fish
- Go to a farmers market
- Go to a park
- Hike
- Inhale deeply through your nose and exhale through your mouth for ten breaths
- Journal
- Kayak

- Knit
- Listen to your favorite music
- Meditate
- Pet an animal
- Play a game
- Pray
- Read something encouraging
- Scrapbook
- Send a card
- Take a bath
- Take a walk

- Unplug from electronics
- Volunteer
- Watch a comedy

Self-care is the piece of the puzzle that helps you put things into perspective. It can help you realize that your struggles with sugar aren't about your self-worth; they're about your habits and decisions. Some decisions move the needle toward your goals, and others don't. Feeling like a failure time and again will never cause you to be positive and make better decisions and changes. When you practice daily self-care to feel happy, satisfied, and content, you increase your serotonin levels, which helps end those sugar cravings and gives you that hopeful boost that you can make lasting changes for your health.

For the next 30 days, I want you to focus on finding out what self-care means to you. You'll be making an investment in your future. You must look at the whole picture during this detox. Your concern is not just what you are putting into your mouth; you also need to consider *why* you are putting those foods in your mouth and how you can change that habit to reach your health goals.

BOOSTING SEROTONIN WITH SUNLIGHT

Getting enough sunlight for your body to produce vitamin D increases your production of serotonin and helps balance melatonin for sleeping. A daily minimum of 20 minutes of sunlight will give you a healthy boost of vitamin D, which can also help fight depression.

Note that your skin needs to be free of sunscreen while it's exposed to the sun for those 20 minutes in order to stimulate vitamin D production. After 20 minutes of exposure, don't allow your skin to burn; put on a natural sunscreen.

BOOSTING SEROTONIN WITH LOW-CARB WHOLE FOODS

In your body, the amino acid tryptophan, vitamins B6 and C, folate, magnesium, and zinc need to be in balance for you to produce an adequate amount of serotonin. Some low-carb whole foods that provide these nutrients will increase your production of serotonin, and the nutrient-rich foods in the following list can help your body secrete more leptin, which is your satiety hormone:

- **FOLATE:** asparagus, broccoli, Brussels sprouts, kale, lemons, mushrooms, romaine lettuce, spinach, Swiss chard

- **MAGNESIUM:** almonds, cashews, sesame seeds, broccoli, collard greens, spinach, squash, Swiss chard, halibut, salmon

- **TRYPTOPHAN:** almonds, cashews, chia seeds, flax seeds, hazelnuts, peanuts, pistachios, sunflower seeds, avocado, cod, perch, salmon, beef, eggs, plain full-fat yogurt

- **VITAMIN B:** carrots (watch portion size), spinach, pistachios, sunflower seeds, salmon, shrimp, beef, pork, turkey

- **VITAMIN C:** broccoli, Brussels sprouts, cauliflower, chili peppers, elderberries, garlic, kale, limes, parsley, red and yellow bell peppers, raspberries, spinach, strawberries

- **ZINC:** almonds, cashews, peanuts, pumpkin seeds, sunflower seeds, crab, flounder, oysters, sole, beef, bison, chicken, lamb, pork, turkey

BOOSTING SEROTONIN WITH BETTER SLEEP

I don't think anyone who has taken my online sugar detox course has said that they are satisfied with how much and how well they sleep. Poor sleep is a common problem in our society because of technology overload and the lifestyles we lead. We are all busy, and trying to fit more work and less sleep into the 24 hours we have is detrimental to us physically and mentally. Ultimately, a lack of quality sleep is one of the biggest reasons cravings happen.

Poor sleep increases inflammation, impairs your immune system, and increases insulin resistance, which stresses your body and causes cravings. Good-quality sleep reduces inflammation, reboots the immune system, restores antibodies, allows for healing in your gut, and produces anti-aging hormones.

When sleep deprivation becomes chronic, meaning you get less than seven hours of sleep more than five nights a week, your body feels stressed and adapts by seeking food the next day—most often highly processed carbs and sugar. It's a survival mechanism. The hunger hormone ghrelin increases with lack of good sleep, and temptations are just more appealing when you are sleep-deprived. Your willpower is shot.

What contributes to poor sleep? I bet you can name a few things, but did you know that artificial blue light from phones, computers, and TVs blunts the production of melatonin? Melatonin is produced from serotonin. Low serotonin equals low melatonin. As it gets darker outside, your body sends signals to your cells to prepare you for a good night's sleep. Unfortunately, melatonin is affected by light exposure, so too much exposure to light from electronics after dark reduces your body's ability to make melatonin naturally. Have you heard the term "slept like a baby"? That's what melatonin does—it helps improve quality of sleep.

Our modern 24/7 lives compromise our bodies' natural circadian rhythms. We aren't tired when we should be, and we feel wired when we should be headed for bed. Some people say they are night owls, but most of them are simply experiencing a decreased production of natural melatonin in their bodies.

Your body needs bright natural light and consistent sun exposure during the day to get back to a natural rhythm of producing serotonin during the day and melatonin for sleep.

Tips for Getting Better Sleep

★ Get some natural light outside, first thing in the morning, which will help your body get back to its natural circadian rhythm.

★ Wear blue light–blocking glasses after 7:00 p.m. if you're watching TV or using your laptop or phone.

★ Eat lunch outside.

★ Get sun exposure for 20 minutes a day. Sunscreen prevents you from producing vitamin D from sun exposure. Don't fry and get burned; just delay putting anything on your skin for 20 minutes.

★ Don't drink or eat anything with caffeine after 2:00 p.m.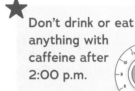

★ Get your phone away from your head while you sleep. Charge it in another room. Exposure to electromagnetic fields that come from your phone, TV, and Wi-Fi decreases melatonin production.

★ Don't eat within two or three hours of your bedtime; doing so makes it difficult for your body temperature to reduce to get ready for sleep.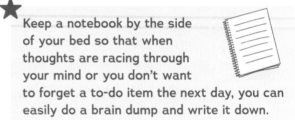

★ Sleep in a dark room where the temperature is between 64 and 68 degrees Fahrenheit.

★ Use an eye mask or blackout curtains to keep your bedroom as dark as possible. Studies show that 50 percent of melatonin is hindered with exposure to light in the room where a person sleeps.

★ Keep a notebook by the side of your bed so that when thoughts are racing through your mind or you don't want to forget a to-do item the next day, you can easily do a brain dump and write it down.

A study out of Stanford University showed that levels of the hormone leptin were significantly decreased when individuals were deprived of sleep. Leptin is your satiety hormone—the one that tells your brain you've had enough food. You want to have greater sensitivity to this hormone to help end overeating and cravings. By improving your sleep, you will become more leptin sensitive.

Addicted to Hyperpalatable Foods

The prevalence of hyperpalatable foods in the modern diet is the third cause of cravings for sugar and carbs. Food chemists create products that have the perfect balance of fat, sugar, carbs, and salt to entice the part of the brain that gives you a dopamine kick.

The excitement a drug addict feels just before a fix is the same type of excitement that can occur in response to hyperpalatable foods. That desire comes from dopamine igniting the "reward center" in the brain—the pleasure-seeking part. Even just looking at a hyperpalatable food filled with sugar and carbs raises your dopamine levels because your brain remembers past experiences with that food. Recalling that the food tasted good and made you feel good, your brain encourages you to seek that same pleasure again. Pleasure teaches your brain to repeat behaviors that made you feel good.

Low dopamine levels make you feel sad and unmotivated, so it's harder for you to resist cravings. You also may be more impulsive, which could cause you to eat "carbage" (carbohydrate + garbage = refined food), which in turn causes you to feel remorse. Consequently, you will want to eat more to comfort yourself. This is another vicious cycle that needs to end so you can establish new habits for your future health.

In his book *Wired to Eat,* Robb Wolf explains that stimulating the reward center in the brain creates a positive feedback loop and makes you want more of the thing that gave you the good feelings. If you don't continue to get the thing that triggered the release of dopamine, you may feel depressed or anxious. Put another way, according to Dr. Mike Dow, author of *The Sugar Brain Fix,* that little dopamine kick is a reward that makes it hard to resist cravings.

Think of the slogan for Lay's potato chips: "Betcha can't eat just one." It's true! The chips are highly processed using inflammatory oils and lots of salt, and they're just plain addictive. These types of foods produce an unnatural degree of stimulation in the brain that leaves you wanting *more;* unprocessed whole foods are just not exciting or desirable in comparison.

A properly functioning appetite can regulate itself when you've eaten enough to deliver the energy your body needs. The regulation of your appetite is processed in your brain. Unfortunately, the macronutrients in hyperpalatable foods are skewed toward high carbs. Those foods are full of sugar and have low nutrient density, especially with regard to protein. Highly refined carbs cause a blood sugar spike and then a crash soon afterward, and a cycle of cravings continues throughout the day. Even waking during the night can be a result of blood sugar levels spiking because of what you ate that day, especially before bed.

I hope you see that cravings are not all about willpower. If you're eating refined carbs and/or sugar, you're experiencing blood sugar spikes that make it incredibly difficult to stop the cycle of cravings. Your body craves nutrients, and it will prompt you to continue to eat—and overeat—until it gets the nutrients it needs. The lack of nutrients in hyperpalatable foods is why you feel hungry again within an hour or two of eating them. By balancing your blood sugar with the meal plan in this book, and by making the effort to build good lifestyle habits that promote healthy levels of serotonin and a good night's sleep, you can end this cycle.

BEFORE YOU START

Before you jump into the cleanse, you should do a little preparation: —————————

Visit your doctor.

If you are taking any medications, share with your doctor that you are going to be following a 30-day program using a low-carb or keto approach. Get a full blood workup. Wonderful things are about to happen, and having a benchmark to use for comparison is important for a clear evaluation for yourself and your doctor.

Clean out your kitchen.

Although you may be doing this detox on your own without support from others in your home, beginning with a cleaned-out kitchen is important. It will be a fragile time for you. Use the information on the following pages to remove anything containing sugar. If you can't toss or give away those foods, ask your family to hide them from you. Keeping trigger foods out of sight will help minimize cravings.

Purchase a digital food scale.

Whether you are going to follow the low-carb track or the keto track, you'll need a food scale to weigh and measure certain foods.

Get a food journal.

There are plenty of online journals to choose from, but I love a simple notebook for writing down food intake and thoughts during the day. You also can record any reactions to foods. I talk more about food journaling in Part II.

Take "before" and "after" pictures.

Many people are reluctant to do this, but trust me; you can never get this time back. This program is going to work for you, and you need to be able to see how much your body changes. It's best to be fully clothed in your "before" photo so you can share it publicly and compare it to an "after" shot in which you're wearing the same outfit. You will be truly regretful if you skip this step!

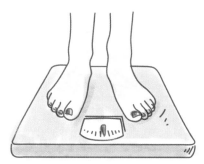

Make sure you have a bathroom scale.

If you go to a gym and there is a scale you can use to weigh yourself, great. Otherwise, you'll need a scale at home. I recommend a digital bathroom scale that also tells you your body fat percentage and can sync to your smartphone.

Purchase a fabric tape measure.

The scale tells you only one part of the weight-loss story; it leaves out details such as how many inches you are losing. Those numbers may have changed even if the number on the scale hasn't moved. Checking your measurements is much more encouraging than the scale number will ever be, I promise you!

Recruit friends to join you.

Research shows that doing a weight-loss program with a friend or other social support improves your odds for success. Recruit friends or family members to join you in this 30-Day Sugar Elimination Diet.

Making Low-Carb Swaps

During this detox and afterward, you will be eating whole foods. Your grocery shopping will focus on proteins, low-carb vegetables (or frozen alternatives for convenience), and healthy cooking fats, such as avocado oil, coconut oil, olive oil, and butter. The following table lists some of my favorite low-carb alternatives to high-carb foods such as pasta and rice, some of which are used in the meal plan recipes in Part III.

FRENCH FRIES
(3 ounces)

TOTAL CARBS	TOTAL CARBS	TOTAL CARBS	TOTAL CARBS	TOTAL CARBS
1.4g	2.9g	5.8g	8.9g	17.6g
HALLOUMI	RADISHES	RUTABAGA	BUTTERNUT SQUASH	SWEET POTATO

MASHED POTATOES
(½ cup)

TOTAL CARBS	TOTAL CARBS	TOTAL CARBS
2.5g	5.8g	6g
MASHED CAULIFLOWER	MASHED TURNIP	MASHED PALMINI (HEARTS OF PALM)

PASTA
(3 ounces)

TOTAL CARBS	TOTAL CARBS	TOTAL CARBS	TOTAL CARBS	TOTAL CARBS	TOTAL CARBS
2g	3g	3.8g	4.5g	5.5g	10g
EGG NOODLES	ZUCCHINI NOODLES	SHIRATAKI NOODLES	PALMINI NOODLES	SPAGHETTI SQUASH NOODLES	BUTTERNUT SQUASH NOODLES

RICE
(3 ounces)

TOTAL CARBS	TOTAL CARBS	TOTAL CARBS
3g	4g	4.5g
SHIRATAKI RICE	CAULIFLOWER RICE	PALMINI RICE

Eliminating packaged foods and making your own is a fun, empowering, and motivating experience that sets you up for good health. But I understand that not everyone has time to make everything from scratch. When you need a quicker alternative, prepared foods can be a good stand-in, but be sure to read the labels to avoid sugar, artificial sweeteners, and unhealthy oils (see page 52). For a list of suggested store-bought pantry essentials, see pages 288 and 289.

Reading Labels for Sugar and Artificial Sweeteners

Food companies often use multiple forms of sweetener to disguise the fact that a product contains an alarming amount of sugar. Learning all the names for sugar can be overwhelming, and it can be tricky to read food labels until you become familiar with all the varieties.

Here are some of the most common names of sugar used on food labels:

- Agave
- Aspartame
- Barley malt
- Beet sugar
- Blackstrap molasses
- Brown rice syrup
- Brown sugar
- Buttered syrup
- Cane juice
- Cane juice crystals
- Cane juice solids
- Cane sugar
- Caramel syrup
- Carob syrup
- Coconut sugar
- Concentrated fruit juice
- Confectioners' sugar
- Corn syrup
- Corn syrup solids
- Crystalline fructose
- Date sugar
- Demerara sugar
- Dextran
- Dextrin
- Dextrose
- Diastase

- Diastatic malt
- Disaccharides
- Equal
- Ethyl maltol
- Evaporated cane juice
- Fructose
- Fruit juice concentrate
- Fruit juice crystals
- Fruit puree
- Galactose
- Glucose
- Glucose solids
- Golden sugar
- Golden syrup
- Granulated sugar
- Grape sugar
- High-fructose corn syrup
- Honey
- Icing sugar
- Invert sugar
- Malt
- Malt extract
- Malt syrup
- Maltodextrin
- Maltose
- Maple syrup

- Molasses
- Muscovado sugar
- Polysaccharides
- Rated cane juice
- Raw sugar
- Refiner's syrup
- Rice extract
- Rice syrup
- Saccharin
- Sorghum syrup
- Splenda
- Sucanat
- Sucralose
- Sucrose
- Sweet'N Low
- Table sugar
- Tapioca syrup
- Turbinado sugar
- Yellow sugar

Reading labels on all store-bought items is imperative. Here is a rule that I have followed over the years that has served me well:

If sugar or artificial sweeteners are listed in any form within the first five ingredients, do not purchase the product.

As you clean out your refrigerator, freezer, and pantry, I want you to give away or throw away any packaged foods that have sugar listed within the first five ingredients. I realize you may have family members who want these foods (especially snacks), and you cannot realistically throw them all away. In that case, ask someone to move them to another place in the house so you don't have to look at anything that is tempting to you when you begin the detox.

The biggest-ticket items to replace are probably condiments. Primal Kitchen is one of the only brands I know of that uses healthy avocado oil and no sugar in its products. You can find Primal Kitchen condiments and dressings in larger stores like Walmart as well as some grocery stores. If you can't find them where you shop locally, you can order them online. See the Shopping Guide on pages 288 and 289 for my favorite Primal Kitchen products.

Ditching Other Harmful Ingredients

In addition to sugar in all forms, you need to avoid any product that includes the following:

- Artificial flavorings
- Food dyes
- Ingredients that aren't recognizable or with names that are difficult to pronounce
- Ingredients whose names include a number or an acronym (for example, red #5 or BHT)
- Monosodium glutamate (MSG)
- Preservatives

These types of ingredients are disruptive to your immune and digestive systems. Most cereals, breads, crackers, candy, multivitamins, and many snack foods marketed to children contain one or more of these ingredients.

LOW-CARB TRACK OR KETO TRACK?

Both the keto diet and low-carb diets balance blood sugar, reduce inflammation, and lead to weight loss. The biggest difference between the two is in the macronutrient ratios for protein, fats, and carbs.

There is no strict definition for what a low-carb diet should look like. People who follow a low-carb program typically keep daily carbohydrates to between 0 and 150 grams.

A ketogenic diet limits carbohydrates even further to get the body into nutritional ketosis. When you are in ketosis, you burn fat for fuel instead of burning glucose. There are many benefits to being in ketosis.

When I went to nutritional therapy school to become a practitioner, the most important thing I learned was that everyone is an individual, and no two people will react to the same foods, specifically carbohydrates, the same way. Some people might be able to get into ketosis while eating 50 grams of carbs per day, while others might need to limit their intake to 35 grams, and still others might need to go as low as 20 grams or less.

The key factor for both a general low-carb diet and the keto diet is to remove sugar and refined carbs like pasta, breads, and pastries, along with grains and high-carb veggies, such as potatoes. Focusing on nutrient-dense whole foods, like healthy proteins, low-carb veggies such as cauliflower and zucchini, and nuts and seeds seems to be the best approach no matter whether you are following a low-carb or keto diet.

WHICH DIET IS BETTER FOR WEIGHT LOSS?

Both low-carb diets and the ketogenic diet will help you lose weight and can help significantly with balancing blood sugar and reducing cravings. If you have a lot of weight to lose—more than 50 pounds—you might be able to lose weight easily with a low-carb diet. If you have less than 30 pounds to lose, you might do better and see quicker results if you follow a ketogenic diet and limit carbs to 20 grams per day.

Note

When you maintain balanced blood glucose levels and limit insulin spikes, the result is fat loss. When insulin stays high from constant snacking, fat loss does not happen.

The main factor in your success is figuring out which carbohydrates you can enjoy, and how much of them, while keeping your blood sugar balanced. You also need to know which carbs to avoid in order to prevent insulin from being raised and reduce the occurrence of cravings. Once you have these things figured out, you can adjust your carb intake to find the threshold that works best for you.

LOW-CARB VERSUS KETO: THE BOTTOM LINE

If you are simply looking to lose a few pounds, a low-carb diet may be all you need to get results. But to get lean, lose fat, build muscle, and greatly reduce cravings, a ketogenic diet is the better option. Also, if you're trying to heal any kind of inflammation, keto provides immediate results.

Ultimately, the best diet is the one that works for your body and that you will stick to. You want to follow either approach as a way of life rather than thinking of it as a "diet" simply to lose weight. Maintaining the change is the key to lasting weight loss.

ADJUSTING THE MEAL PLAN FOR THE LOW-CARB TRACK

The meal plan in this book takes a ketogenic approach, with total carbs adding up to no more than 25 grams per day. If you prefer to start with the low-carb track, in which total carbs amount to no more than 40 grams per day, simply add the additional low-carb recipes and make the recommended meal plan modifications as noted in blue type.

TAKING SUPPLEMENTS DURING THE DETOX

How wonderful it would be if we could get all the nutrients we need from food alone. Unfortunately, with modern farming practices that deplete the soil and treat crops with more and more pesticides and other hazardous chemicals, nutrient deficiency is bound to happen even with the best of diets.

With nutrient depletion comes persistent cravings that will not go away on their own, even for someone who follows this program carefully. Your body will crave sugar and refined carbs, and you may overeat as your body tries to acquire the nutrients it needs.

Supplementation is optional during these 30 days, but I do recommend it if you experience intense cravings, have had a blood test that indicates you are low in vitamin D, suffer from low moods or irregular bowel movements, or have trouble falling asleep.

In this section, I talk about the supplements I recommend in my online course and to many of my clients. You can certainly follow this plan without taking supplements and still have success, but adding some to your daily regimen may very well help you feel better as you detox from sugar and refined carbs.

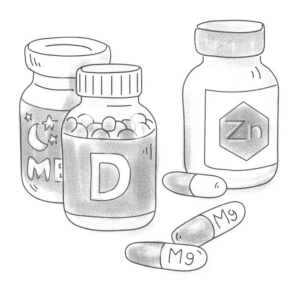

Disclaimer
Check with your primary healthcare provider before starting any supplement regimen. If you are taking medication for diabetes, thyroid issues, high blood pressure, or other health conditions, it is critical to monitor your numbers/levels to ensure things stay in balance.

Bifidobacterium

Ninety percent of your serotonin is produced in your gut. Artificial sweeteners are known to hinder the gut bacteria that help produce serotonin. A healthy gut means a healthy production of serotonin, and a healthy gut is greatly influenced by your diet, lifestyle, and exposure to natural sunlight.

Taking a probiotic supplement that contains Bifidobacterium can help keep your gut healthy and promote that desirable serotonin production. This supplement can also help keep your bowels running smoothly. Take the supplement before a meal to allow the good bacteria to travel to your gut quicker.

Magnesium Glycinate

Stress depletes your magnesium levels. If you suffer from muscle cramps, headaches, or migraines and/or you have trouble falling asleep because your mind is racing, magnesium glycinate is the supplement to take. Chronic insomnia is often a sign that you are deficient in magnesium. Magnesium helps relax your muscles, so it makes sense that it alleviates headaches and muscle cramps, but it is also naturally calming, so it relaxes your mind as well.

Magnesium is helpful for maintaining bowel regularity. However, magnesium oxide and magnesium citrate are not the most bioavailable varieties for your body, and taking them can cause diarrhea. Instead, choose magnesium glycinate, which is the most absorbable form to supplement with. Take anywhere from 200 to 800 milligrams one hour before bedtime.

Another option is topical magnesium. Because the skin absorbs ingredients quickly, a topical application works faster for assistance in falling asleep. Follow the manufacturer's dosage directions for sprays or creams.

Melatonin

If magnesium glycinate doesn't help you fall asleep and stay asleep, consider adding melatonin to your regimen. Melatonin levels decrease as we age, and its production in the body is highly affected by how much sun exposure we get during the day. Start with a small dose of 1.5 milligrams to see if it helps. If not, you can increase the dose to 3 milligrams. Take it as needed, and use only as much as necessary to be effective. On nights when you are clearly exhausted and think you can fall asleep easily, skip the melatonin.

Vitamin D

Earlier, I recommended that you get at least 20 minutes of sunlight a day to increase serotonin production, but where you live can play a big role in how much access you have to sunlight. In winter, you may have only a small window during the day. One way to deal with this is to use the dminder app (available for Apple and Android devices), which takes your latitude and longitude into consideration and factors in how much of your skin is exposed and then suggests the best time for you to get that sun exposure.

Many people are low in vitamin D just because their jobs and other obligations make it hard for them to spend time in the sun. Others (like me) have genetic variations that make it more difficult for their bodies to produce vitamin D from sun exposure. I make sure to get my daily sunlight, but I also take a vitamin D supplement. You may need to take one as well, especially if you can't make a habit of getting outside each day.

A blood test run by your doctor can confirm the range in which your vitamin D levels fall; it should be between 50 and 70 ng/mL. If you have a number lower than 45, get some sun exposure and consider a supplement. Having vitamin D levels below this range means that your serotonin will also be low. Low serotonin decreases the production of melatonin, which will cause sleep issues. On the flip side, vitamin D levels that are too high can also lead to a disruption of sleep. While vitamin D toxicity is rare, it is not usually caused by diet or sun exposure, but often by supplementation. Always check with your doctor before trying a new supplement.

Vitamin D is fat-soluble, which means you need to take the supplement with a meal containing healthy fat; otherwise, your body won't be able to absorb the vitamin.

Zinc

If you're experiencing acne, hair loss, diarrhea, or cravings for salty or sweet foods after a meal, or if you've had a blood test that shows you have a low-functioning thyroid, the reason could be that you're deficient in zinc. Zinc is another nutrient your body needs to make serotonin.

When you add a zinc supplement to your regimen, it's important to start slowly; taking too much can cause nausea. Begin with 5 milligrams a day for one week, then add another 5 milligrams each week until you reach 40 to 50 milligrams a day without any stomach upset. Always take the zinc supplement with a meal to prevent nausea.

2
PROGRAM
Guidelines

THE *30-Day* SUGAR ELIMINATION DIET

I hope you are as excited to begin this cleanse as I am to share it with you. This detox from sugar is going to be life-changing for you—I mean this sincerely! I believe in this method, and 30 days from now, you are going to believe in the program and in yourself. You will have broken free from sugar, carb cravings, and addiction!

BUILDING NEW HABITS

Let's start by talking about habits and how you build them. That's what this detox is really about: creating good habits that stick despite any kind of stress or turmoil you're experiencing so that you don't go running back to sugar and refined carbs when the going gets tough. You'll conserve self-control and willpower when you have established solid habits.

A *habit* is defined as a recurrent behavior that is cued by a specific context. You acquire habits through frequent repetition until they happen without much awareness or conscious intent on your part. For example, you don't decide to brush your teeth each day; you do it because it's a habit.

A well-established habit removes the need for daily decision-making. I don't eat sugar and refined carbs. I don't have to make this decision every day because I made my choice in 2006 and formed a habit.

Change is possible when you have great habits. Your brain loves the routine that habits provide because then you don't need to use brain energy to make decisions. There is comfort in habits, and that is the reason we tend to fall back to habits that bring us comfort when we are anxious or upset.

When a habitual behavior is repeated, the habit is strengthened. The way to establish a good habit is to be consistent and repeat, repeat, repeat.

Some habits are almost unbreakable, such as the teeth-brushing example. Others will always be fragile, even after years of repetition, and must never be taken for granted. Guard against anything that would weaken your habit, and never get too comfortable.

You may already have all the knowledge and know-how I share in this book, but for some reason you do well for only a short time before something triggers you, and you return to your old habits of sugar and refined carbs. Or maybe you're just beginning this lifestyle and will soon see how easily you might want to turn to sugar and refined carbs for comfort during the day. No matter which camp you're in, I want you to commit to not turning to sugar for the entire 30 days of this detox. Don't worry about what you will do after it ends. For now, the only thing you need to commit to completely and diligently is *no sugar or refined carbs* for 30 days. This is a boundary you should not cross for any reason.

You might feel quite angry for a few days and be wondering why you decided to do this. That is just sugar withdrawal telling you that you can't change. *Don't listen!* If you touch sugar to your lips and your taste buds embrace that sweetness again, you'll have to start over. I can tell you from personal experience that each new attempt is even harder than the first one, *so just don't let yourself slip.* Do not cross that line. Learning new habits is hard at first, but I promise you that it does get easier.

As I said, for now, you don't need to make any decisions about what you'll do after this detox is done. Just commit to the program, and do not let sugar or refined carbs touch your lips for these 30 days.

THE BASICS

I want you to live by these eight basic guidelines for the next 30 days. ─────────

Eat three meals a day unless you have already been doing intermittent fasting.

In that case, continue with that routine. During your first week, you may also include snacks if needed.

Remove temptations.

I hope you have already cleaned out your pantry, fridge, and freezer, as outlined in Part I, and you're on board with eliminating grains, sugars, and processed and packaged foods.

No packaged or processed foods.

The only exceptions are the items on the approved snack list (see page 57).

Engage in at least 30 minutes of self-care daily.

Eat no more than three low-carb or keto desserts during Days 1–7.

If you are truly addicted to sugar, this approach may be too difficult to follow, and three times a week may be too much to handle while detoxing from sweet desserts. If you feel you need a dessert every night rather than only three times a week, it is in your best interest to remove all desserts during this detox.

No second helpings.

None. One plate per meal. You plan your food, prioritize protein, and eat from the plan—end of story.

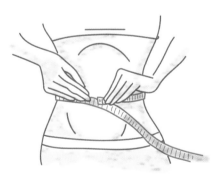

Weigh yourself weekly.

Also take measurements of your chest, waist, hips, and thigh.

Weigh and measure your food.

Write down your daily food intake in a journal or track it with an app.

Food Journaling

Daily food journaling may be a new habit for you, but it's an important part of this detox and beyond. You can no longer fool yourself about how much you are truly eating when you have the evidence in black and white. Journaling solidifies honesty and takes away the guessing game of which foods and how much of them are beneficial for your body.

Keeping a written record of what you ate and how you felt after eating those things can also shine a light on which foods might trigger you to overeat. Knowledge is power.

Low dopamine is associated with impulsiveness (you can read more about dopamine in Part I), so it's important to plan your food ahead of time, either the night before or the morning of your day. Thankfully, this book has done the planning for you! When you make a plan, you're using the part of your brain that has your best interests at heart. This area of the brain is neither tempted by the trials of the day nor prone to making impulse decisions based on emotion.

After you've decided on a plan and written it down in your journal, there's nothing to think about when it's time to eat. That means you will be less likely to succumb to impulsiveness.

Once you've written out your plan, commit yourself to it—or, better yet, share it with your partner or a buddy. Having external accountability is very important, especially if you tend to have trouble being accountable to yourself.

Write down everything you eat in the journal, especially if you diverge from your plan or have extra bites or second helpings. Track it all. I repeat, *write down everything you put in your mouth;* also record any physical symptoms or mood issues you have prior to or after eating.

Note that journaling is different from using an app to track macros. In a journal, you can include details about why you may have overeaten. It helps you track trends to figure out whether a certain food might affect you negatively, such as by causing bloating, hives, or gastrointestinal distress. You can use an app for tracking macros if you are following the keto track of this meal plan, but it is not required; the appropriate macros are already built into the plan.

Journaling is a brain dump. It clears your thoughts and gives you a fresh perspective, helping you understand how your thinking might be getting in the way of your progress.

Choose one or more of the following prompts to begin a journal entry:

Your food plan for the day. If needed, give yourself options for snacks, but if you're not hungry, don't eat between meals.

Statements of gratitude or a list of what you are grateful for on that day.

Statements of what you love about yourself and why you are worthy. Negative self-talk will never change your habits; you must feel good about yourself in order to create change.

Your goals. It's good to write your goals daily so that you don't forget what you are pushing toward.

A statement of why you are proud of yourself.

Reflections on what you wish was different and why. Try to see things more clearly and question why the situation is the way it is.

Your worries. Think about what is in your control and what is not.

After you've journaled, let it go! You've written it down, so you can move on with your day.

Exercise: Yea or Nay?

I exercise on the regular, but it is not a requirement for the 30-Day Sugar Elimination Diet. That said, you may want to incorporate some exercise into your routine because it's a wonderful stress reliever and a great habit to establish—not only for your physical health but also for your mental health.

One reason your mental health will improve through physical exercise is because dopamine is released within just 20 minutes of exercise. As I've already mentioned, dopamine, like serotonin, is a brain chemical that you need to feel excitement, take on new challenges, or meet work deadlines with stamina. It gives you the motivation to push forward and reach your goals. It provides you with an exciting rush of pleasure and satisfaction from winning at something.

If you exercise, don't do it in the evening too close to bedtime. Exercise can raise your body temperature and make it harder to fall asleep because your body is struggling to bring down your core temperature. (Refer to Part I for more on the importance of good sleep.)

When you focus on your strengths and celebrate the small wins each day, you're setting yourself up for success and happiness because you start feeling good about yourself. A short walk outside, a dance party in your kitchen, or some simple stretching is an easy way to chalk up a small win. Each small win is a little dopamine kick. It's not really about all the things you can't have or can't do; it's about getting what you are really seeking so that the impulse to self-medicate with food falls to the wayside and is not part of your everyday life.

Here are some simple ways to incorporate exercise into your day:

- Dance to your favorite music while prepping meals
- Weed the garden
- Talk on the phone outdoors as you walk around the yard or neighborhood
- Walk the dog
- Walk in the morning to get that early-morning sunshine and vitamin D
- Walk during your lunch break
- Take the stairs
- Park in the spot farthest from the door
- Jump rope
- Hula hoop
- Lift hand weights at your desk between meetings
- Try a quick high-intensity interval training (HIIT) workout

The Scale

Is the scale friend or foe? Does the number you see on the scale affect how you feel that day? Does it dictate your mood? For example, when the scale says you've lost weight, do you feel like it's a great day, but when you've stayed the same or gained, do you feel unhappy or even pissed off? Does the number on the scale leave you with questions and guilt? If any of these things ring true, the scale might have a strong hold on your well-being.

I've had to work for years not to allow the scale to be an idol for me or let it control my emotions. I've learned to accept the number on the scale for exactly what it is: a tool for measurement. It is not going to tell me the whole story. It can neither read the number of inches I've lost nor determine how my jeans fit me. It can tell me about water weight but not about lean muscle mass, and it cannot differentiate changes in body fat and lean muscle. It can only tell me how effective some of the things I did in the last week have been.

If you tend to allow the scale to control your mood and your sense of self-worth, I suggest weighing yourself only once during each seven- or eight-day period of the meal plan. The only way to determine the validity of the number on the scale is to review your food journal and evaluate what you did right and what you still need to tweak. There are too many daily fluctuations in the amount of water and sodium in the food you're eating, your bowel movements, and so on for daily weigh-ins to give you an accurate picture of your progress. On page 291, you'll find the worksheet that I created for weekly weigh-ins. This questionnaire helps you take an honest look at your eating from the previous week and removes emotion from the number on the scale.

With your food journal in hand, you can evaluate what worked for you and where you might have struggled. This is a key part of turning the scale into a tool for measurement rather than a mood enhancer or self-worth destroyer. The information in the journal works with the number on the scale to show you in an unbiased way what you need to work on.

Having more than the scale as a method of measurement is important. Using a fabric tape measure to measure your waist, hips, chest, and thigh is a better tool for tracking your progress than the number on the scale alone.

If you have access to a DEXA scan in your area, you can go one step further. This type of scan, which typically costs $150 or less, can determine your body composition at the start of the detox. At the end of the 30 days, a second scan would reflect the changes that have occurred in your body fat and muscle distribution.

Another method is the "honesty pants" test. Use a pair of pants that used to fit you perfectly but doesn't anymore, or purchase a new pair that will fit at the weight you'd like to be. Each week, try them on to see how well they fit. You can even take regular photos of yourself wearing your honesty pants so you can see the difference your efforts are making as the pants start to fit differently.

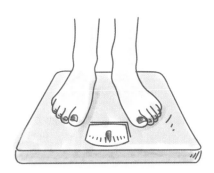

PRIORITIZING PROTEIN

Most of the women and some of the men I've coached through my online 30-Day Sugar Detox think they eat enough protein, but they quickly discover they are not eating nearly enough to support their bodies through detoxing from sugar and carb cravings. Once I explain that they need to increase their protein intake, their cravings are diminished. I think the tendency to eat too little protein is due to bad nutrition advice from the FDA and the infamous food pyramid that has failed so many people. Some of the symptoms of a low-protein diet include decreased muscle mass, thyroid issues, fatty liver, hair loss, inability to lose weight, increased cortisol, hormonal imbalances, and, of course, cravings!

Grains and carbs are not essential to life, and humans do not need them in their diets. However, protein and healthy fats are essential. Protein is made up of small units called amino acids, and your body can make 20 of them; there are nine essential amino acids that you must get from food because you can't make them. The best way to get complete proteins that contain all nine essential amino acids is to focus on animal protein. Similarly, your body needs glucose (the technical term for sugar) to survive, but that glucose does not need to come from carbohydrates. If you consume adequate amounts of protein, your body can make glucose from noncarb sources.

Don't misunderstand me: I'm not advocating for removing *all* carbs from your diet. I'm advocating an approach that is right for your body that includes whole carbohydrate foods like vegetables and fruits rather than refined, packaged, processed carbs.

Cravings happen because your body is seeking the nutrients it needs and won't stop until it gets what it's looking for. If you don't eat enough protein throughout the day, you may spend your time opening and closing the fridge and cupboards as you try to calm a craving because you aren't satisfied with what you ate, especially if it was a high-carb meal or snack.

Protein is very satiating, even more satiating than fat, and is very helpful for reducing cravings. It's nutrient dense, and it's hard to overeat protein. Including quality animal protein in your diet can help reduce your appetite and trigger leptin, which is the hormone that signals that you are satisfied and have eaten enough.

Protein not only helps you feel satiated and eliminates cravings, but is necessary for muscle growth and repair. Every day, your muscles break down protein and rebuild to create new muscle and prevent muscle loss. Furthermore, adequate protein promotes healthy skin, hair, and nails as well as immune function. People

need to be especially aware of getting enough protein as they get older because muscle protein synthesis declines with age, and the rate of decline increases past the age of 60.

In the 30-Day Sugar Elimination Diet, you can decide whether to follow the low-carb or the keto track (see pages 29 and 30 for more about these two options), but one thing that is consistent to both approaches is that the meal plan prioritizes protein.

Dr. Ted Naiman advocates a high protein intake for people who follow low-carb or keto, especially those interested in weight loss. He recommends consuming 1 gram of protein per pound of lean mass. For a person who weighs 150 pounds, this would be about 125 to 130 grams of protein daily.

An alternative recommendation from ketogenic researchers Drs. Stephen Phinney and Jeff Volek is 1.5 to 1.75 grams of protein per kilogram of reference weight, or "ideal" body weight, for most individuals. For a person who has an ideal body weight of 125 pounds, this would be around 180 grams of protein per day.

If you are sedentary, I suggest that you consume 0.8 gram of protein per pound of lean body mass for your ideal weight. For the hypothetical 150-pound person with an ideal body weight of 125 pounds, this would be around 100 grams daily. If you're strength training or looking to build muscle, consume 1.0 to 1.5 grams of protein per pound of ideal body weight. Every person's protein needs vary depending on many factors, such as physical activity, stress level, injury, illness, and hormonal issues, but by prioritizing protein, you will be providing your body the essential amino acids it needs to function optimally.

Grass-Fed and Pasture-Raised Proteins

Most animals raised in feedlots are fed corn and grains, which produces an unfavorable ratio of omega-6 to omega-3 fats in the animal. You will learn more about fats and oils in the Days 1–7 section later in this part; for now, you just need to know that you want a healthy balance of omega-6 and omega-3 fats.

Grass-fed means that the animal has been fed grass for some part of its life, but the animal also could have been fed grains. It's best to look for meat that's labeled grass-fed and grass-finished or 100 percent grass-fed. Beef that's 100 percent grass-fed has a perfect ratio of omega-6 to omega-3 fats.

Pasture-raised refers to where an animal eats, not exactly what it eats. Pasture-raised animals may be fed grains, but they spend most of their time outside.

Local farmers often offer quality proteins. Beef, bison, pork, and venison are all great options if you can get them from a local provider. You can also purchase quality proteins from some online vendors. ButcherBox, for example, offers a meat subscription service.

If your local grocery store sells grass-fed meats, choose that option if it fits within your budget. Including some grass-fed meat in your meals is better than none, and it helps you avoid the added hormones and antibiotics in most animal products sold in supermarkets today.

Cage-Free Versus Free-Range Poultry

Cage-free means that the birds are not confined to cages, but they could be living in very tight quarters without ever seeing the sun or having access to fresh air. *Free-range* birds have access to the outdoors, although we don't know how much time they actually spend outside.

Eggs produced from chickens that have been free-range for most of the day have 25 percent more vitamin D in the yolks than any other eggs you can buy. If you can't raise your own chickens (as I do), find someone who does, or shop at a farmers market where you can source local free-range eggs and poultry.

Wild-Caught Versus Farm-Raised Fish and Seafood

When you see the term *wild-caught* on a seafood label, it indicates that the fish, crustacean, or mollusk was caught in its natural habitat. *Farm-raised* seafood is raised in manufactured enclosures and sometimes fed a diet that is not natural for that species. Also, farm-raised fish and other sea creatures are often given antibiotics to prevent disease, which you shouldn't be ingesting; antibiotics have negative effects on the gut, killing the healthy bacteria that are present.

That said, wild-caught seafood has some potential drawbacks too, including exposure to industrial pollutants and mercury contamination. The Monterey Bay Aquarium Seafood Watch is an excellent source of information about choosing healthy and sustainable seafood.

Processed and Packaged Proteins

Processed meats, like deli meats, hot dogs, and salami, frequently include toxic additives like nitrates, sulfites, preservatives, and food coloring. Remember what I said in Part I about cleaning out your kitchen before beginning this detox? You should limit chemical additives as much as possible. I'm not saying you can't occasionally enjoy some packaged protein, but I recommend you limit them to a couple of times a week rather than eating them daily. In the recipes, you will see that I include corned beef and deli ham, but just once or twice; again, limiting your consumption of such foods is the key to a balanced lifestyle.

Here are some of the proteins you should limit:

- Bacon processed with sugar and/or nitrates
- Corned beef
- Deli meats
- Fast food
- Hot dogs
- Jerky
- Salami
- Sausages

You've now learned all the basic guidelines, and you're ready to begin the first seven days of your detox! My easy meal plan has you covered by prioritizing protein each day, so you should feel very satiated with tasty meals that keep your blood sugar balanced and your cravings in check.

DAYS 1-7

Welcome to the first seven days of the 30-Day Sugar Elimination Diet! In this section, you will learn about hydration, electrolytes, beverages, fats and oils, natural sweeteners, and snacks for this first week. Please read this information prior to beginning the meal plan.

Hydration, Electrolytes, and Beverages

Water, which is one of the most beneficial nutrients, is totally underrated. It plays numerous roles in your body. It lubricates your joints, cushions your bones, regulates your body temperature, transports nutrients to your cells, removes toxins and waste, helps break down the food you consume, and even moistens oxygen for effortless breathing. Yet so many people take water for granted and rarely drink enough each day for their bodies to function their best.

Participants in my online sugar detox course are often shocked at how much water I recommend, which is half your body weight in ounces per day, and many have trouble drinking that amount. Once they begin drinking the recommended amount, however, many of them can't believe what a difference it makes in their hunger levels throughout the day, including reduced cravings for sugar and carbs. It also promotes better digestion and bowel regularity. Many people even experience a reduction in headaches and joint and muscle pain!

Common symptoms of dehydration include fatigue, muscle cramps, migraines or headaches, anxiety, cravings, constipation, heartburn, joint pain, and exercise-induced asthma. You are at a higher risk of dehydration if you live at a high altitude, work outdoors in the heat, have a chronic condition like diabetes, exercise (especially if you're a runner), or are older (thirst signals decrease with age).

Caffeine is a diuretic, so if you drink two to four cups of coffee a day, you need to drink more than half your body weight in ounces—at least another 8 ounces.

Drinking too much water *with a meal,* however, dilutes your stomach acids, which you need to break down and properly digest your food. Consequently, hydrating between meals is better. Avoid drinking more than 4 ounces with a meal.

ELECTROLYTES

It is important not only to drink enough water, but also to know whether your body is absorbing the water you drink. Electrolytes facilitate the proper absorption of water and help maintain the right mineral balance in your body for homeostasis. Homeostasis is your body's ability to maintain stability in all internal functions, like body temperature, blood pressure, and blood glucose regulation, as well as defend itself against viruses, bacteria, and so on.

During this 30-Day Sugar Elimination Diet, you will avoid almost all packaged and processed foods, which typically contain a lot of sodium. When you start eating whole foods and lower your carb intake, your body is better able to balance your blood sugar, which lowers your insulin levels. As your insulin levels decline and inflammation in your body goes down, your body begins releasing fluids. As fluids are excreted, minerals like sodium—a critical electrolyte—are also removed from your body.

Replenishing sodium is the key to avoiding carb withdrawal during your first week of this detox. However, I do not recommend that you increase your intake of table salt because it is highly processed and refined. The better choice is sea salt, which is a combination of sodium chloride, magnesium chloride, and potassium chloride. (Magnesium and potassium are also electrolytes.) I recommend 1 to 2 teaspoons of Redmond Real Salt, Celtic sea salt, or Himalayan pink salt daily. You can add the salt to your food and/or water to prevent carb withdrawal symptoms.

APPROVED BEVERAGES

In addition to plain water, the following beverages are allowed on the 30-Day Sugar Elimination Diet. With the exception of coffee, all these beverages contribute to your total water intake for the day. (Remember: If you drink two to four cups of coffee per day, you will need to drink at least 8 additional ounces of water.)

Bone broth

Coffee, but only with approved sweeteners *(see "Natural Sugar-Free Sweeteners" on page 52 for options)*

Herbal tea

Homemade electrolyte drinks *(see page 260)*

Sparkling water *(no sugar added)*

Avoid diet soda because of the artificial sweeteners used in most brands. Those sweeteners make some people crave sugar and carbs.

I know that drinking plain water can be boring. Here are some recommendations to make it easier to get sufficient hydration:

- **Everly** makes a wonderful line of drink mixes for enhancing the flavor of water without sugar.

- **Kettle & Fire** is an organic brand that makes the tastiest bone broth I've tried.

- **LMNT** has an incredible electrolyte mix of sodium, potassium, and magnesium in flavors like citrus salt, orange salt, raspberry salt, and chocolate salt.

- **Pique Tea** is an instant tea that you mix into hot or cold water. It's very convenient for taking on the go. Tea is one of the most pesticide-laden crops and is commonly farmed in areas with high industrial pollution. Teabags, which have unnaturally long shelf lives, can also accumulate toxic mold in harmful quantities. Pique Tea, however, has a triple toxin screening process for pesticides, heavy metals, and toxic mold commonly found in plants.

- **SweetLeaf Water Drops** are delicious, and you need just a few drops to flavor your water.

- My **Keto Dalgona Coffee** (page 254) will make you feel like you've taken a trip to your local coffee shop for a treat.

- **Zevia** is a natural soda sweetened with stevia. It comes in many flavors, like cream soda, grape, ginger ale, and black cherry. My kids and I love the creamy root beer flavor!

A WORD ON ALCOHOL

Alcohol cannot be stored in the body and is treated as a toxin; therefore, your body must burn off all alcohol you consume before it uses any other fuel source, like glucose or ketones.

Alcohol, like sugar, blocks your body's serotonin receptors, which leads to cravings. Have you ever gotten the munchies after drinking? It reduces your inhibitions and often awakens impulsive behavior, making eating for comfort easier and cravings harder to ignore.

Most types of alcohol are also high in sugar and carbs. Although some have fewer carbs than others, drinking alcohol is not advised during the 30-Day Sugar Elimination Diet.

Fats and Oils

Contrary to popular belief, dietary fat does not make you physically fat. Healthy fat is nothing to fear. Eating a low-fat diet is neither the key to weight loss nor the way to eliminate sugar cravings. Learning which fats and oils to consume is one of the most important things you can do for your health, longevity, and quality of life.

Fats are essential to a well-functioning body and critical for many purposes, and they're necessary for certain hormones to function properly. They also act as building blocks for cell membranes, protect the linings of your organs, and help you absorb the fat-soluble vitamins A, D, E, and K. Plus, fats make food delicious. Enjoying healthy dietary fat can increase your satiety levels and help regulate the speed at which you digest your food.

There are three kinds of dietary fats (fatty acids): saturated, monounsaturated, and polyunsaturated. Cooking fats and oils are combinations of these types.

SATURATED FATS are the safest for cooking because they don't oxidize when heated, and they don't cause inflammation in the body. Saturated fats are solid or semisolid at room temperature and don't go rancid easily. Animal fats, such as butter and tallow, and tropical oils, such as coconut oil, are high in saturated fat.

MONOUNSATURATED FATS are relatively stable and can be used for cooking at lower temperatures. They are usually liquid at room temperature. They don't go rancid easily, but they are susceptible to damage from light and should be stored in dark-colored containers. Avocado oil and olive oil are primarily monounsaturated fat.

POLYUNSATURATED FATS include two essential fatty acids: omega-3 and omega-6. Good whole-food sources are fatty fish, walnuts, and flaxseed. The plant-based oils that are mainly polyunsaturated are easily affected by light, heat, and oxygen, making them too unstable for cooking, and they can be inflammatory. Turn the page for a list of polyunsaturated oils to avoid.

Your body requires a healthy balance of omega-3 and omega-6 fats. Unfortunately, omega-6 is abundant in vegetable oils and meat from grain-fed animals, which makes it easier to come by than omega-3. A dominance of omega-6 can cause inflammation. You want to avoid anything inflammatory because inflammation leads to a host of other issues, especially with keeping your blood sugar balanced and losing weight.

The following fats contain small amounts of polyunsaturated fat but are high in saturated fat and safe for cooking:

- Butter
- Coconut oil
- Duck fat
- Ghee
- Lard
- Tallow

Note _____

My Sicilian family has been cooking with extra-virgin olive oil for as long as I can remember, and I'm sure our ancestors did as well. Contrary to popular belief, cooking with olive oil is safe, and it will not oxidize when heated. Olive oil is made up of 70 percent oleic acid, a monounsaturated fat. As mentioned previously, monounsaturated fats can be used for cooking at moderate temperatures, like sautéing.

According to a post on functional medicine expert Chris Kresser's website, "While the fact that olive oil contains mostly monounsaturated fatty acids is important, researchers believe that it is actually the phenolic compounds that stabilize the oil as it's heated. That being said, it's vital that you purchase extra-virgin olive oil versus pure olive oil. Extra-virgin olive oil goes through less processing—it's simply pressed and does not go under any heat or chemical treatment.... Pressing the olives retains many more nutrients, including phenolic compounds, which we know serve to protect olive oil from heat. Even better is extra-virgin olive oil that hasn't been filtered—the particles that cause the oil to be cloudy also act as antioxidants and buffers against acidity, thus protecting the oil from oxidation."

Here is a list of omega-6 oils to avoid; not only are they inflammatory, but they can also lower your dopamine levels:

- Canola oil
- Flax oil
- Peanut oil
- Soybean oil
- Corn oil
- Grapeseed oil
- Safflower oil
- Sunflower oil
- Cottonseed oil
- Margarine
- Sesame oil
- Vegetable oil

Natural Sugar-Free Sweeteners

There are many sugar-free sweeteners on the market today; figuring out which is the best to use for one purpose or another can be quite confusing. Unfortunately, product labels can be misleading, and not all sugar-free sweeteners are created equal.

When I first went sugar-free in 2004, I didn't know of any sugar-free sweeteners beyond aspartame, Splenda, and stevia. I tried several artificial sweeteners, and I believed I could still include natural sugars like honey and maple syrup in my diet because they weren't as refined as white sugar. However, after two years of being sugar-free, my sugar cravings were just as bad, if not worse.

Anything that is a form of sugar, including coconut sugar, dates, honey, and maple syrup, is still sugar. It doesn't really matter if it is less refined than white sugar; it can and will spike your blood glucose. When glucose is spiked, insulin spikes. When your insulin is high, you're not going to lose fat, because insulin causes you to store and hold onto body fat. If you want to balance your blood sugar and lose weight, you should avoid anything that spikes your blood sugar.

In 2006, I decided to start creating recipes with natural sugar-free sweeteners and nothing artificial. The most natural sugar-free sweeteners are allulose, erythritol, monk fruit, stevia, and xylitol, but there are some big differences among them when it comes to use in recipes. For example, in no-bake recipes like mousses, liquid sweeteners work best so you won't have a grainy texture. For baked goods like muffins and cakes, using a confectioners'-style sweetener combined with a liquid sweetener helps mask any aftertaste. Cookies need a granulated sweetener, which helps create a nice crunchy texture.

The following natural sweeteners are wonderful regardless of whether you want to be sugar-free or eat low-carb or keto. None of them will spike your blood sugar, but there are some differences in their sweetness levels and applications:

- Allulose occurs naturally in only a few foods, such as wheat, raisins, and figs. The body can't metabolize allulose. Instead, nearly all of it passes into the urine without being absorbed, so it contributes negligible carbs and calories. It works wonderfully in ice cream to keep the texture smooth and soft after freezing.

- Monk fruit extract comes from the monk fruit (luo han guo), a cousin of the cucumber and melon that's native to China and Thailand. Monk fruit is rarely used fresh but is dried and used as a sweetener. It is 300 percent sweeter than sugar but is calorie-free and does not raise blood sugar levels. It is sold as a pure liquid concentrate and also can be found combined with erythritol, which makes it possible to swap it cup for cup with sugar. I love the Lakanto brand.

- Stevia comes from the stevia plant, which is typically grown in Paraguay. Its leaves are boiled down to produce the liquid form that's on the market today. Stevia leaves are also dried and sold as pure concentrated extract with no fillers. It's a calorie-free option that's 300 times sweeter than sugar and doesn't cause digestive issues, raise blood sugar, or spike insulin. The taste depends on the extraction process used, so some brands are sweeter or more bitter than others. The type I use the most in my recipes is the SweetLeaf brand liquid.

- Stevia glycerite is a plant-based sweetener like liquid stevia. The difference is in the extraction process. Dried stevia leaves are processed using glycerin instead of alcohol. Many people prefer this form over liquid stevia because they think it has no aftertaste. I've tried it and liked it just as much as my flavored liquid stevia. Stevia glycerite is much thicker than regular liquid stevia, and you don't need as much. My favorite brand is Now Foods.

Note ————————————————————————————

Liquid monk fruit can be swapped one-for-one with liquid stevia because they have the same level of sweetness.

- **Yacón syrup** is extracted from the yacón plant that grows in Peru and Brazil. It looks and tastes much like molasses. It does contain some fructose, but when used in very small amounts, it should not raise blood sugar levels. This sweetener is perfect for adding a molasses flavor to recipes like caramel sauce or BBQ sauce.

In addition, you can try the following two sugar alcohol sweeteners:

- **Erythritol** is a sugar alcohol that occurs naturally in small quantities in fruits like grapes and melons as well as mushrooms. It is *not* an artificial sweetener because it occurs naturally in plants. It is only partially absorbed and digested in the intestinal tract. It has no calories and does not spike blood sugar. It registers zero on the glycemic index, and it is non-GMO. Erythritol measures cup for cup like sugar, but it's only about 70 percent as sweet. That is why it is often combined with stevia, which is 300 times sweeter than sugar. Erythritol is most often used in chewing gums, mouthwash, cough drops, and mints.

Note ———————————————————————————

Don't confuse erythritol with xylitol, sorbitol, and maltitol, which can cause gas and bloating and have laxative effects.

- **Xylitol** is a sugar alcohol that occurs naturally in some plants. Although it looks and tastes like sugar, it has 40 percent fewer calories. It can raise blood sugar or insulin slightly, but not nearly as much as white sugar does. It also causes digestive issues in some people. Xylitol measures cup for cup like sugar and is easy to bake with.

Note ———————————————————————————

Dog owners beware! Xylitol can be fatal to dogs, so keep it where they can't accidentally ingest it. I have a dog, so I don't use xylitol in my recipes.

REDUCING AFTERTASTE

I've learned over all these years of perfecting my sugar-free dessert recipes that using two kinds of sugar-free sweeteners helps them balance each other and reduces any aftertaste. My recipes often use erythritol as the primary sweetener, but to bring up the sweetness, I add liquid stevia.

On page 290, I've included a conversion chart that I created from my vast experience in experimenting with all these sweeteners. You may find many conversion charts online, but they are not all the same, and I've seen some I greatly disagree with. You can trust that my sweetener conversion chart is the most accurate and precise one and the last one you will ever need for low-carb and keto baking.

SUGAR-FREE DESSERTS

I have not included desserts in the meal plan; they are optional. If you begin to feel like you might fall off the wagon toward sugar and refined carbs, make one of the sugar-free desserts from pages 246 to 273 to help you overcome that craving. Admittedly, during the first several days of the detox, when you're adjusting to a sugar-free lifestyle, you may need the crutch of a keto or low-carb dessert. That's okay! But please note that during these 30 days, the rule is no more than three desserts per week. I want you to work on discipline and self-control by setting some limits and incorporating delayed gratification into your life.

Later, after this detox, you can decide what will work for you as an ongoing habit. If you think having a sugar-free dessert every day will help you sustain this lifestyle, then that is totally your choice. That said, limiting your consumption of sweets is one of the best habits to establish for maintaining weight loss and living your best life.

From personal experience, and the experience of my clients, I've found that switching to keto or low-carb desserts simply replaces the sugar you once were having with a sugar-free alternative. You won't really be progressing if you're just replacing your "fix," your habit, with a sugar-free sweet treat.

Vegetables, Fruits, and Snacks

Before you launch into the first week of the plan, you should know some basics about recommended vegetables, fruits, and snacks.

LOW-CARB VEGETABLES

The following vegetables, some of which I use in the recipes in Part III, fit well with a low-carb or keto approach:

- Artichoke hearts
- Arugula
- Asparagus
- Avocado
- Bok choy
- Broccoli
- Brussels sprouts
- Cabbage
- Cauliflower

- Celery
- Chard
- Collard greens
- Cucumber
- Eggplant
- Endive
- Fennel
- Green beans
- Kale

- Kelp
- Leeks
- Lettuce
- Mushrooms
- Olives
- Onions
- Peppers
- Radishes
- Romaine

- Sauerkraut
- Spinach
- Watercress
- Zucchini

HIGH-CARB VEGETABLES

The following vegetables are higher in carbs than those listed on the previous page. Are these dense carbohydrates a better option than processed carbohydrates? Absolutely! But you don't want to overload on them. If you're following a keto diet, you should avoid these vegetables altogether; if you're following a low-carb diet, you can enjoy them occasionally, but not more than three times per week. Be aware that of the vegetables listed here, corn, potatoes, and green peas have the most carbs and should be consumed very infrequently, if at all, depending on your goals.

- Acorn squash
- Carrots
- Corn
- Green peas
- Parsnips
- Potatoes
- Spaghetti squash
- Sweet potatoes
- Tomatoes
- Yams
- Yuca

LOW-CARB FRUITS

It's a personal choice whether to include fruit in your diet. If you find that having berries daily does not cause you to crave more sweet foods, then continue to eat them, but enjoy a small serving once daily and no more. The following are the best fruits to eat whether you opt for the low-carb track or the keto track because they are low in carbs and won't spike blood sugar:

- Blackberries
- Blueberries
- Cranberries
- Raspberries
- Strawberries

SNACKING

Snacking has probably gotten in your way more times than you can count. You're on a new diet, you decide on a healthy snack, and then you've opened the door to wanting more. Why does this happen? Why is it so hard to stick to the plan? You just cued your hunger hormone—ghrelin—and it's not satisfied with your little snack.

Every time you eat, your insulin levels rise. Depending on your food choices, insulin will rise a lot or a little. Sugar and refined carbs are the biggest culprits in a high insulin spike.

When insulin is high, fat loss can't happen. Keeping insulin low is the best tool for weight loss and reducing cravings. Have you ever eaten a sugary food and then shortly after felt hungry again? Your insulin spiked, and then your blood sugar lowered to compensate, which then caused more hunger and/or cravings.

Your brain does not like blood sugar swings; that's why balancing your blood sugar is the key to avoiding crashes and cravings. To do so, add a bit more protein to your next meal. If that doesn't help, add more healthy fat as well. If these adjustments aren't enough to stave off hunger between meals during Days 1–7, you can enjoy a snack (see the list of approved snacks below).

In fact, it's possible you may need to snack to avoid feeling *hangry*—that is, when you're so hungry you feel angry. Symptoms of hanger include nervousness, agitation, foggy-headedness, and shakiness. If you feel this way when you start this detox, it's a sign that your blood sugar isn't balanced yet. But don't worry; within the first week, these symptoms will subside, and you will be well on your way to balanced blood sugar and reduced (or maybe even eliminated!) cravings.

The course of action that makes the most sense is to avoid this roller coaster of blood sugar and insulin rising and falling. Snacking between meals gets in the way of keeping insulin low; therefore, snacking is not recommended after the first seven days of the 30-Day Sugar Elimination Diet. During the first week, you'll be getting more comfortable with eating low-carb foods and not eating packaged and processed foods, and you may need snacks to satisfy your hunger, balance low blood sugar, and adjust to your new habits.

After the first week, you should be able to go many hours between meals. The ability to go without eating for long periods is a sign of a healthy metabolism and an indicator that you're eating the right mix of protein, carbs, and fat for your body.

Use the Hunger or Habit? self-assessment tool on page 292 to decide if you're truly feeling hunger.

APPROVED SNACKS FOR DAYS 1–7:

- Almonds or unsweetened almond butter
- Bacon strips
- Beef sticks (no sugar added)
- Cheese
- Cheese crisps
- Coconut butter
- Dill pickles
- Hard-boiled eggs
- Jerky (no sugar added)
- Macadamia nut butter (unsweetened)
- Macadamia nuts
- Olives
- Pecans
- Pepperoni
- Pili nuts
- Pork rinds
- Pumpkin seeds
- Sunflower seeds
- Walnuts

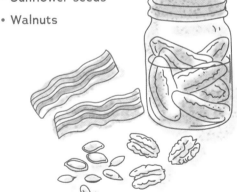

 Note ————————————————————————————

If you experience intense cravings during the first seven days of the detox, please jump ahead to the section "Combating Cravings" on page 63.

DAYS 8-15

Congratulations on completing the first seven days of the 30-Day Sugar Elimination Diet! You've been reading labels for sugar and inflammatory oils, not having second helpings, getting out in the sunlight, working in some self-care, and learning the right balance of protein, fat, and carbs by following the meal plan.

As you head into Days 8–15, remember the ongoing goals: detoxing from sugar, balancing your blood sugar, increasing serotonin through self-care and sunlight, and reducing stress through the practice of daily habits. All these small steps should help improve your sleep as well. In this part of the detox, you will learn about intermittent fasting and why snacking is no longer an option for the rest of the 30 days. I also explain blood glucose testing and how to handle those pesky cravings. Please read the information I've provided here before you jump into the meal plan for Days 8–15.

Assessing Your Experience on Days 1–7

Before I get into details about the next eight days, think about Days 1–7. Did you experience dizziness, bloating, gas, heartburn, or constipation? If you're having any of these issues, the following suggestions may help address them.

DIZZINESS

Dizziness can be related to not getting enough sodium. You can resolve this issue by consuming a little more salt. Many participants in my online course are reluctant to increase their salt intake. However, sea salt (such as my favorite kind, Redmond Real Salt) has dozens of minerals in addition to sodium, including electrolytes like calcium, magnesium, and potassium, and it is essential to have the right balance of these minerals in your body. When you add salt to your drinking water, the minerals in it help you absorb and utilize that water. Make sure to get at least 2 milligrams of sodium per day by sprinkling it on your food or dissolving it in your water.

Sodium is not something to fear. When you are no longer eating packaged and refined foods, you are not taking in as much sodium you once did. Pure protein and vegetables contain very little to no sodium. Your body needs sodium to make hydrochloric acid, which helps break down proteins. When you're low in hydrochloric acid, you will have acid reflux, heartburn, and bloating.

Dehydration is another common reason for dizziness. The necessary amount of water varies from person to person based on factors such as climate, exercise habits, and stress levels. Try to follow your thirst. Drink a minimum of 72 ounces per day by filling up a 24-ounce water bottle three times. Another good measure is to drink at least half your body weight in ounces. However, never drink more than 1 gallon (128 ounces) of water in a day.

Note ——————————————————————————

If you are taking any medication, please consult with your doctor before adding more salt to your diet.

BLOATING AND GAS

Bloating and gas are often related to digestion. The stomach's main jobs are to break down dietary protein and liberate nutrients from food. You need stomach acid to perform these functions. If you don't make enough stomach acid, you can experience problems with digesting your food. For example, undigested protein can cause leaky gut, which allows toxins to get into your bloodstream.

Bloating and gas can also be reactions to dairy, nuts, and/or gluten (although, if you are following the meal plan, you won't be eating gluten anyway).

Low stomach acid can be caused by not eating enough protein, drinking alcohol, not drinking enough water, immune responses to certain foods (like nightshades or histamines from fermented foods), and chronic stress. Drinking anything with a meal dilutes your stomach acid and can get in the way of properly breaking down your food. A few sips at the meal are OK, but the key is to hydrate *between* meals, not *with* meals.

HEARTBURN

Heartburn is often triggered by an immune response to alcohol, caffeine, chocolate, citrus, mints, tomato products, spicy foods, garlic, and onions. Taking 1 tablespoon of apple cider vinegar mixed with 2 tablespoons of water before a meal may help prevent heartburn.

CONSTIPATION

Constipation can occur with a higher-protein diet. Taking a magnesium glycinate supplement before bed (see page 32) is one way to prevent constipation. Another helpful ingredient that can get things moving is MCT oil. Add about 1 tablespoon to coffee or tea or drizzle it on a salad. If neither of these works for you, other options are magnesium citrate and vitamin C. Once you begin having loose stool, you can cut back to taking a supplement every other day.

IMPROVING GUT HEALTH

You need a healthy gut that produces good bacteria and can absorb the nutrients from the food you are eating into your cells. Serotonin is produced in the cells of your colon. You can improve the health of your gut lining by drinking bone broth, which contains the amino acid glycine. The results of a study published in *Endocrinology* show that glycine helps regulate blood sugar levels and stimulates the release of glucagon to remove insulin from the blood. Glycine has also been shown to improve sleep and cognitive function.

Now that you've examined how you feel after the first week of the detox and you know what to do to counteract any issues you've been having, you can move on to Days 8–15!

Intermittent Fasting

Intermittent fasting gives your body breaks from food. There are many other benefits to it and many ways to incorporate it into your routine. Starting with Day 8 of the meal plan, you will no longer eat any snacks between meals, which is a good start in learning how to intermittent fast. Although abstaining from food between meals might be an uncomfortable new habit to acquire, it is a worthwhile and effective strategy to incorporate during these 30 days.

A key factor in being ready for intermittent fasting is that you don't feel hungry for at least four to six hours after a meal. I'm talking true hunger, not habit hunger. (If you're not sure whether you're feeling true hunger or habit hunger, use the Hunger or Habit? self-assessment tool on page 292 to help you decide.) Some hunger is normal, but not having strong cravings is a clue that you've balanced your blood sugar and you may be ready to ditch the snacking.

Fasting is simple, free, convenient, and flexible. There are many ways to go about it to reap the power of its effectiveness.

Fasting's most obvious benefit is weight loss, but there are many other benefits you may not know about. Fasting also has the following effects:

✓ Improves mental clarity and concentration

✓ Reduces blood sugar levels

✓ Improves insulin sensitivity

✓ Increases energy

✓ Improves fat-burning

✓ Lowers blood cholesterol

✓ Decreases inflammation

✓ Contributes to longevity

When you eat, some food is converted to energy and some is stored for later. The key hormone in storage and food energy is insulin. Insulin production is triggered by the protein and carbs in the food you eat. Carbs that are absorbed turn into glucose and raise your blood sugar, but the degree to which blood sugar levels rise varies from person to person. Protein also triggers insulin production, but eating protein doesn't necessarily raise your blood sugar; again, it's bioindividual. Fat has a minimal effect on insulin.

Regular fasting improves insulin sensitivity because when you go longer between meals, insulin is lower, which signals to your body to start burning stored fat for energy. If you are constantly eating between meals and never give your body a break from digestion, you are just burning the fat you're eating rather than burning the fat on your body. Consistently high insulin also leads to health issues such as type 2 diabetes, high cholesterol, high blood pressure, gout, sleep apnea, heart disease, and Alzheimer's disease.

Lipolysis is the body's process of using stored fat for fuel, and it shuts off whenever insulin is elevated. Fasting helps increase the amount of time your body spends in lipolysis, which increases the amount of fat you may lose.

Human growth hormone (HGH) plays a key role in cell growth and repair, body composition, muscle growth, and metabolism. Some studies, such as one published in the *Western Journal of Medicine,* have found that fasting boosts HGH production by as much as 300 percent. Normally, we produce less and less HGH as we age, but your body will produce it in a fasted state.

Another benefit of fasting is that it boosts the regenerative capacity of stem cells, which are part of the body's repair system. A decline in stem cells is thought to be a major factor in the aging process. Biologists at the Massachusetts Institute of Technology (MIT) found that age-related loss of stem cell function could be reversed by a 24-hour fast.

I hope I've provided enough reasons for you to fast between meals for the rest of the time you spend on this detox. I promise that this simple step of not snacking will lead to amazing results.

WHAT IS ALLOWED BETWEEN MEALS WHEN FASTING?

Most definitions of fasting allow for noncaloric drinks only, meaning water, tea, and black coffee. No sugars are allowed, of course, but there is some debate surrounding low-carb sweeteners.

Dr. Jason Fung, author of *The Complete Guide to Fasting,* feels that artificial sweeteners such as aspartame and sucralose defeat the purpose of a fast, which is to cleanse or purify the body. However, natural sugar-free sweeteners like stevia are fine.

Fat fasting is a newer variation that permits you to have some butter, coconut oil, or cream in your coffee or tea during your fasting window. This method is not a true fast, but some people believe including a little fat during the fasting period helps with weight loss; others say it helps moderate cravings. I've tried drinking butter coffee while fasting, and it never made me feel full or satiated. I also wasn't able to fast longer, and technically I was breaking my fast with the amount of butter and cream I was consuming. Once I made the switch to true fasting, using only 1 teaspoon of cream in the morning and again between lunch and dinner, I was able to experience the full benefits of fasting, including weight loss.

Dr. Fung's clinic also allows bone broth during fasts; again, technically this is not a true fast. However, drinking some bone broth diminishes hunger pangs for many people and helps them fast longer. Bone broth also provides a good amount of sodium, which you need during this detox to compensate for the sodium you're removing when you eliminate processed and packaged foods. Dr. Fung says that adding natural flavors like lemon to your water or mint or cinnamon to your coffee is fine, too. He also states that adding 1 to 2 teaspoons of cream or coconut oil to coffee seems to make no difference in the outcome of a fast.

INTERMITTENT FASTING OPTIONS

For the 30-Day Sugar Elimination Diet, you do not need to skip meals; you will simply fast between meals. But doing a true fast as discussed above will make your fasting time easier because you won't be triggering a glucose response, so you won't be hungry. If you decide you'd like to skip meals and fast, you certainly can, but be sure to increase your protein intake in the meals you do eat.

If you are currently fasting or are ready to try more hours of fasting, here are the most common options:

- **Skip breakfast or dinner** so that you're fasting for a period of 16 to 20 hours. Here's an example: work out in a fasted state in the morning, eat at noon, and have another meal 5 to 6 hours later. With this model, your eating window is between noon and 6:00 p.m. Another option is to work out in a fasted state at 7:00 a.m., have breakfast at 9:00 a.m., eat a second meal 4 to 6 hours later, and end your eating window at 3:00 p.m., skipping dinner.

- **One meal a day (OMAD)** is a 22-hour fast. You eat during a 2-hour window—say, 5:00 p.m. to 7:00 p.m.—and don't eat again until the same time the next day. I'm not a fan of this option because I don't believe you can get enough protein during such a short eating window.

- **Full single-day fasting** is having no food from the evening of Day 1 to the morning of Day 3—a period of about 36 hours. I do this type of fast weekly, from Sunday night to Tuesday morning.

- **5:2 intermittent fasting** involves restricting yourself to 500 to 600 calories two days per week, either on consecutive days or on two days separated by one or more days of regular eating. I find this type of fasting very hard to do.

- **Alternate-day fasting** is basically doing a full single-day fast every other day.

Regardless of the method you choose, the most important thing is to consume no more than 45 calories during your fast.

Keep the following tips in mind as you begin to incorporate intermittent fasting into your routine:

 Hunger is like riding a wave, and it will pass. Staying busy is the key. As you get used to fasting, your body will begin using stored fat for fuel, which will help suppress hunger.

 You can try some natural appetite suppressants. Staying hydrated with water is helpful. Green tea has powerful antioxidants that can stimulate your metabolism. Cinnamon has been shown to slow gastric emptying, may help suppress hunger, and can help lower blood sugar. Coffee (or the caffeine in coffee) may raise your metabolism and boost fat burning; a study published in the *Journal of the American College of Nutrition* has shown that both decaf and caffeinated coffee suppress hunger.

 If you experience dizziness while fasting, you're likely dehydrated. To prevent dehydration, increase your salt and water intake or drink some bone broth.

 To prevent heartburn after a fast, avoid eating a large meal. Break your fast with a small portion of a nutrient-dense whole food, such as an egg. Drinking water with lemon can help, as can the dose of apple cider vinegar recommended on page 59.

 Headaches are common the first few times you fast. It's believed that they're caused by the transition from a relatively high-salt diet to very low salt intake on fasting days. The headaches are likely to go away as your body gets used to fasting.

Constipation is common because you're taking in less food. A magnesium glycinate supplement at bedtime will help.

Combating Cravings

Sugar and refined carb cravings are among the hardest things to overcome when detoxing from sugar. Cravings are inevitable, but there are ways to ward them off during this cleanse.

Cravings occur because your body is having withdrawal from the foods you once provided and will push you to try to increase your serotonin and dopamine by going back to refined carbs and sugar. Your brain remembers which foods made you feel good and will encourage you to succumb. Your brain may even throw a fit to try to get what it wants, like a toddler having a tantrum. The severity and duration of your cravings are dependent on how long you've been eating sugar and refined carbs and how long it takes your body to balance your blood sugar.

The number one way to reduce cravings is to eliminate the culprits, which is exactly what you are doing on this 30-Day Sugar Elimination Diet. (If you cleaned out your pantry prior to starting this cleanse, then most of those culprit foods are out of sight, which makes it harder for you to seek them out.) Within the first week, you should notice considerable relief from cravings because you are no longer consuming the kinds of foods that were causing your blood sugar spikes. That being said, most people who take my online course experience some cravings by the end of the first week and leading into Days 8–15, so you should expect that this may happen to you, too.

To figure out the best way to address your cravings, ask yourself some questions to determine where those cravings are coming from:

? Have I been taking in enough sodium?

? Have I been hydrating between meals?

? Am I eating all my protein on the plan?

? Have I been giving in to sugar and refined carbs during this cleanse?

? Am I following the meal plan exactly, or am I fudging it by eating seconds or snacking?

THE SALT TRICK

If you've been reluctant to salt your food or add salt to your water, you are missing out on one of the easiest ways to combat cravings. Often, your body seeks sodium when you aren't getting it from the foods you're eating. Whole, unrefined foods do not contain enough sodium to meet the body's needs. Trust me on this and begin adding sodium daily. If you have a craving, sprinkle some sea salt on your tongue. Drink a glass of water and wait 20 minutes, which is the amount of time it usually takes for a craving to subside.

Distract yourself for 20 minutes and then see how you feel. I'm willing to bet that the craving will be gone! I've seen it happen time and again with participants in my online course, who are shocked by how well this salt trick works.

DISTRACTION AND MOVEMENT

When a craving hits, the best way to fight it is to find a way to distract yourself. Remove yourself from the kitchen, pantry, or office break room. Call a friend, go outside, or run an errand. In other words, get physical in some way.

Cravings usually produce a spike in glucose, and if you get some exercise, you can use that extra glucose in your muscles in a productive way. Clean the shower, mop the floor, pull some weeds in the garden, do some jumping jacks, or take a walk. Whatever you can do to get moving will not only help offset that blood sugar spike but make you feel better, too, especially because you're not giving in to that craving!

HYDRATION

If you have been reluctant to drink at least half your weight in ounces of water daily, you are doing a disservice to yourself. Hydrating helps flush toxins from your system while you follow this cleanse. Removing toxins from your body is going to help you feel better, reduce inflammation, make you less susceptible to viruses, and help you lose weight.

Studies show that many people mistake thirst for hunger. So, when you feel hungry, first try giving your body what it truly needs: water!

COMMIT TO THE HIGH-PROTEIN MEAL PLAN

There is a reason my meal plan for this 30-Day Sugar Elimination Diet is higher in protein than other meal plans you may have tried. Protein works to satiate you like no other macronutrient. If you've been eating a low-protein, high-carb diet for most of your life, your body has been seeking the nutrients it needs. Always prioritize protein in your meals, especially if you feel the urge to snack. Remember:

Protein is the goal you should always hit; fat and carbs are limits to stay under.

If you are eating from the meal plan and decide to go back for "a little more," you may be setting yourself up for cravings. Overeating can raise your blood sugar, causing cravings for more food. It's a vicious cycle. Stick to the plan, and don't go back for seconds.

DON'T MAKE EXCEPTIONS

There will be parties, holidays, and birthdays to celebrate as you follow this 30-Day Sugar Elimination Diet. If you think, "I can make an exception because it's *[insert occasion here]*," you are falling into a trap for continued cravings. I know— I've been there and done that many times, hoping and praying I could "cheat" a little on those special days and then get right back to my sugar-free lifestyle. It doesn't work, my friend.

If you truly want to break free from cravings and lose weight, you have to commit to this plan for 30 days without exception. Every time you cheat, *with even one bite,* you trigger that dopamine response in your brain, which gets your excitement roaring like a lion. I can tell you, it will be so much harder to get back on track afterward.

Starting over is worse than simply following through on the commitment. Recommitting takes even more willpower than committing in the first place. **Don't let sugar or refined carbs touch your lips for even one bite during these 30 days.** I promise you, you will not regret it. As Angie, one of the alumni of my online course, said, "I've tasted that before, I know what it tastes like, and I just don't need it right now."

JOURNALING

When a craving hits, write in your food journal the time of day, who you are with, and some details about the circumstances you're in. These are important clues to what triggers you, and having notes to look back on will help you overcome future cravings. Cravings often occur due to emotional stressors, so writing down why you feel upset or disappointed is a way to process those emotions. Learning new habits for dealing with emotional stress is a step in the right direction to learning how to deal with life without succumbing to eating for comfort.

This may sound hokey, but congratulating yourself for making it through uncomfortable feelings without eating through them is important for lasting change. Reward yourself with a sticker in your journal, tell a good friend about your success, or add money to a mason jar and use that money to buy yourself something new at the end of the month. Being proud of all the small wins is going to increase your confidence and motivate you to continue.

BREATHING

Has a craving ever caused a noticeable rise in your heart rate? Your body reacts to stress using your sympathetic nervous system—your fight-or-flight response. If the craving is coming from a place of extreme upset, your heart rate might be elevated. This is not the time to stuff food in your mouth; this is the time to figure out a strategy to get yourself back to a rational state of mind so you don't make impulsive decisions, which is often how cravings win.

Whatever the cause of the craving, you need to find a way to calm yourself. Breathing techniques are easy to do anywhere, they cost you nothing, and they work quickly to get you back to a parasympathetic state of calm.

Practice this 4-5-7 breathing technique anytime you find yourself in an uncomfortable situation that turns your mind to food for comfort: take a long, deep breath in through your nose for a count of 4; hold it for a count of 5; and then open your mouth and make a swishing sound as you exhale for a count of 7. Repeat until you feel calmer.

BE CONSISTENT

If you can consistently ignore the cravings that tempt you and learn new habits and strategies that bring you peace, you will find those cravings rearing their ugly heads less and less often. Be patient with yourself, but be persistent about resisting. I repeat, do not give in to cravings, because doing so will only perpetuate the cycle. Consistency is the key to learning new habits that will last a lifetime.

DAYS 16-23

I hope you are feeling fantastic! You have tackled many obstacles in the last 15 days, and you should be super proud of all you have accomplished.

You have learned how to take care of yourself and your stress levels by making time each day for self-care, because you realize that this daily practice will help reduce sugar cravings.

You have been working diligently to get out in the fresh air and sunlight, and you're working on decreasing blue light exposure to help with your sleep. You know that better sleep also helps reduce sugar cravings.

You've worked hard on not helping yourself to seconds and being satisfied with what's on your plate. By now you're feeling the positive effects of balanced blood sugar, which makes it easier to ditch snacking between meals. If you've been abstaining from snacks, you've also had to figure out how to fill the gaps.

Consistency is key because these new habits are fragile, and you need to guard and protect them. Although 15 days isn't long enough for the habits to have become second nature, the habits may be set by the end of these 30 days as long as you repeat them consistently. (But please remember that some habits will always be tenuous.)

Days 16–23 of the meal plan include some new recipes that mimic high-carb favorites, such as low-carb bread. You need to be really careful in deciding whether you'll eat them or whether they might be trigger foods you should avoid for the rest of this cleanse. Getting into the habit of constantly needing low-carb bread with a meal is a slippery slope toward reverting to old habits that can hinder your success.

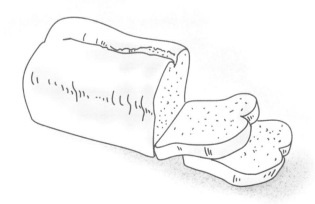

Identifying Trigger Foods

A trigger food is any food—keto, low-carb, or not—that makes you feel out of control. When you eat a trigger food, you cannot stop at a reasonable serving; you will eat until the bag, carton, or container is empty. There seems to be no off switch for these foods. You feel guilt or shame after eating them. In the past, you may have thought, "One bite won't hurt," yet it always does.

Trigger foods are bioindividual—everyone has different ones. Also, it's important to note that eating a trigger food may have nothing to do with the food itself. Instead, it has everything to do with *how that food makes you feel* while you are eating it. So your response has a lot to do with your personal history with that food.

Here's an example from my life: When I was 12 years old, my parents told me they were going to have another baby. I was devastated because I already had two younger brothers and felt like I was doing all the things to help out with them. I felt out of control of my own life and very responsible as the eldest child.

As I stated in the introduction to this book, snacks were never limited in my home. We had an open-door policy and could snack on anything we wanted, whenever we wanted. So I'm not sure why I chose to sneak snacks. There was extra storage in the basement for anything that didn't fit in the pantry upstairs. One day, I saw a bag of potato chips there, and I thought, *Who would ever know it was me who opened the bag?* So I tore it open and continued to eat until it was empty. This snack brought me joy, and I felt satisfied with being sneaky. I felt like I was in control for once. So that's how it began: my first binge and my first experience with my personal trigger food.

When I went low-carb back in 2012, the cravings for potato chips were difficult to avoid. I would make an exception at every party I attended and then regret it because a few chips were never enough for me. I wanted to finish the bag. When I decided to try keto in 2015, I finally allowed myself the healthy fats that I had avoided for a long time because I feared that fat would cause weight problems. Being in ketosis has eliminated my cravings for potato chips, and consuming more fat has not caused me to gain weight.

That said, I have to be careful with foods that have a crunch factor. I can put away pork rinds like nobody's business. I must measure them out, or I will succumb to eating more than one serving.

Your trigger food might be something sweet. Although the low-carb sweeteners called for in my recipes do not cause spikes in insulin or glucose, a little bit of sweetness is enough to set some people off on a binge. I don't think these sugar-free sweeteners provide the same dopamine hit that sugar does, but some individuals can't handle them.

Keto sweets do not cause me to binge or overeat the way I used to when I ate white sugar. You may be different, and if cake—even keto cake—causes you to feel out of control, like you can't have just one piece, it's probably a trigger food for you. No matter the food, even if it's low in sugar and carbs, you need to question whether you can include any trigger food in your life right now.

I haven't crossed my boundaries of eliminating sugar, refined carbs, and gluten since 2006, but I have had to work super hard on my triggers so I don't overeat or turn to food for comfort. When something is really good, it can be difficult to eat just one serving!

Putting an End to Comfort Eating

I know I'll never again be beholden to any food, and I want that for you, too. I'm going to share a philosophy that has helped me avoid overeating—even keto foods. Keeping the following mantra in mind helps stop me from turning to any food for comfort:

When I'm upset, I don't eat.
No matter what, I don't eat when I'm upset.

I'll give you an example of putting this idea into practice. My husband and I went out for sushi with our youngest son. We had reservations for 6:00 p.m. and quickly received the appetizers we'd ordered by 6:30. We then ordered our meals—sushi for them and sashimi (which is served without rice) for me. I was quite content until almost 45 minutes had passed and we still had no food. We did not receive our entrées until 7:45!

One hour and 15 minutes for entrées that weren't even cooked! By that time, I was *hangry.* Also, I had ordered 12 pieces of sashimi, but there were only 9 pieces on my plate when it arrived. We did enjoy the food, but when we got home at around 8:30, I was still hungry. I could have chosen to eat more, but I realized that I was more angry than anything else. I repeated my mantra and used the time to call a friend who needed some support. I made it a point to listen to her without sharing anything about our dinner fiasco. I comforted her and got out of my own head, and then I went to bed.

Moral of the story: If you can recognize your true motive and create a new habit that does not involve eating through your feelings, life becomes simpler. You begin to use food as fuel and not for comfort. You establish boundaries and become stronger when things don't go your way.

Serving others when you are struggling is just one way to remind yourself that even though you may have some hard things to work on, someone else may be going through something much worse. It's all about perspective, and being willing to get out of your own way to comfort someone else is a huge step in the process of learning to cope with life without sugar for comfort.

If you practice this and avoid your trigger foods, even keto-friendly ones, you will feel so much more confident and in control of your eating. Don't let any food or emotion be the boss of you!

Troubleshooting

If you stumbled during the first 15 days, looking back at your food journal is the best way to start learning what you may be doing to hinder your progress. This is how you troubleshoot and continue on even after your 30-day detox is done.

Acknowledging victories that aren't determined by the scale is also important. As I said at the beginning of Part II, the number on the scale does not give you the whole picture. Here are some other measures of success:

✓ Your sugar cravings have lessened or gone away.

✓ Your clothes are fitting you better.

✓ When you measure your chest, stomach, hips, and thigh, you see inches coming off.

✓ You are noticing more brain clarity and mental focus.

✓ You are waking from sleep feeling rested.

✓ You are less bloated.

Your progress may not be as significant as you had hoped or as significant as your friend's who is doing this cleanse at the same time, but everyone is different. Many years of eating sugar and refined carbs can take a toll on our bodies, and it takes time to heal from the inside out. You need to trust the process!

If you haven't experienced any of those successes, or just one of them applies to you, then something may be going on that you're not recognizing. Ask yourself these questions:

? Are you taking extra bites while preparing your meals?

? Are you eating a sugar-free dessert three times a week or more?

? Are you finishing off the leftovers as you put them away?

? Are you skipping one meal a day and not increasing your protein intake at your other meals?

? Are you snacking frequently between meals?

? Are you adding fat to your coffee or tea?

There is always a reason for a lack of progress. For example:

• You could be insulin resistant.

• You could have underlying thyroid conditions.

• You may need to be on the keto track rather than the low-carb track.

• You may need to consider intermittent fasting.

I don't know why things aren't progressing for you, and maybe you don't know the reason just yet either, but it's important to follow through with this cleanse. When you can say you truly have committed to the process for the full duration and show your doctor what you've done in 30 days, you and your doctor can discuss your ongoing issues and determine whether you need to have some tests done to get to the root cause.

Remember that you can't keep doing the same thing and expect different results. You must change something to effect a change. What can you do differently this week to get closer to your goal? That is a question only you can answer. I've given you the tools and the program that have helped hundreds of people lose weight, balance their blood sugar, and end their cravings; it's up to you to put them into action.

DAYS 24–30

Woot woot! You have completed three-quarters of the 30-Day Sugar Elimination Diet! This has probably been a huge change from your previous lifestyle, and it likely hasn't been easy. Even if you messed up a few times, getting back up and on board is what counts.

Please allow yourself grace. You don't have to be perfect, but you must always be making progress and learning. If you slip up, but you get back on track quicker than you did before and avoid the "what the hell" attitude that can ruin a whole day or weekend, you're making progress. Never stop recognizing the small wins that you're building upon.

Blood Glucose and Ketone Testing

Blood sugar (glucose) testing isn't just for people with diabetes. It is an effective method for understanding how certain foods, particularly carbohydrates, affect you. Regardless of whether you've been following the low-carb track or the keto track, testing will help you determine whether a certain food spikes your blood sugar. Remember, when your blood sugar spikes, insulin rises. And when insulin is high, you stop burning fat.

Although testing your blood sugar isn't required to complete the 30-Day Sugar Elimination Diet, I highly recommend it. It might not be something you're totally comfortable with, but it is one of the most accurate measurements available. Of course, there are times when you know a particular food did not agree with you. In those cases, the glucose number is evidence that the symptoms you experienced were not in your imagination.

If you're on the low-carb track, you only need to test your blood sugar. If you're following the keto track, you also should do a blood ketone test to determine whether you have ketones in your blood and if a particular food might have kicked you out of ketosis.

You can find blood glucose and ketone monitors at most pharmacies. Neither type of monitor is particularly expensive, but both kinds of test strips are. Not all pharmacies carry the strips, so you may need to purchase them online. Also, the strips for testing glucose are different from the strips for testing ketones, so you'll need two different kinds of strips if you're going to test both.

To check your glucose or ketones, you prick your finger and draw a drop of blood onto a test strip. You then insert the strip into the monitor, which gives you a blood glucose or ketone reading within ten seconds.

Blood glucose for someone who does not have diabetes should be less than 100 mg/dL; 70 to 99 mg/dL is considered normal before a meal or after fasting. About one to two hours after eating, blood glucose under 140 mg/dL is considered "normal" or "healthy" and indicates the food you consumed was a good match for your body. A reading higher than 140 mg/dL tells you that you should avoid that food or consume it only occasionally. With blood ketone monitoring, the goal is to see ketone levels at 0.5 mmol/L or higher.

You can test whenever you like, especially if you feel shaky or "off" after a meal or when you're fasting. Any information you can learn about how your body reacts is helpful, and you should record it all in your food journal.

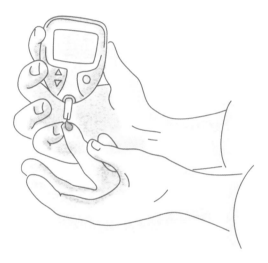

Note ——————————————

My goal with this sugar detox is to help you reach your goals, and testing your blood glucose and ketone levels is just another tool for finding what works for you. It is completely optional.

OTHER RESPONSES

In addition to noting your blood sugar readings, jot down any other responses you have after eating, such as joint pain, skin rash or hives, low energy, "hanger," digestive issues, or poor mental clarity. Even if you don't have a spike in your blood glucose, any of these symptoms might indicate a sensitivity or an intolerance, and you may not want to eat that food very often.

3
MEAL PLAN
& Recipes

Breakfast

Lunch

Dinner

If you've turned to this chapter, you're ready to go shopping and get cooking. Before getting started, however, please read the practical orientation to the plan on the following pages.

ABOUT THE MEAL PLAN AND RECIPES

Whether you're following the low-carb or the keto track, the high-protein meals I've included in this plan should keep you satiated throughout the day.

Unlike the family-friendly recipes I create for my website, www.sugarfreemom.com, which serve eight people or more, the recipes you will make for this detox yield one to four servings, and many of them make just one or two servings. This gives you the flexibility to follow the plan if you are the only one in your household doing so. Some of the recipes simply aren't practical to make in small amounts of one or two servings; in those cases, the leftovers can be stashed in the freezer and enjoyed after you've completed the plan. Or you can offer them to family members or friends!

The meal plan and shopping lists assume that you'll be feeding one person and eating one serving at a time as defined in the recipes. If you would like to use one of the smaller-yield recipes to feed your whole family, feel free to double or triple the ingredients as needed.

Optional Ingredients and Condiments

Some recipes include optional ingredients, most of which are suggested toppings or garnishes. These optional ingredients are not factored into the nutrition information; if you wish to include them, remember to recalculate the nutrition accordingly in your food tracker app or journal. Optional ingredients aren't included in the shopping lists for the meal plan, either; before heading to the grocery store, take a look through the recipes to decide if there are optional ingredients or components that you want to add to your list.

You will notice that some recipes do not call for condiments like mayonnaise, ketchup, mustard, relish, or butter. The only fats or oils you will see are for preparing the recipe. Because condiments are a personal choice, please use them as you see fit and calculate the additional nutrition information yourself.

Dairy

Dairy can be a hidden problem in weight loss. Some people have no issues with dairy, but for many looking to lose weight, dairy can be the culprit behind stalls or digestive issues. While I have not entirely eliminated dairy from the meal plan, it is not used in two-thirds of the meal plan recipes, and in many cases where it is called for, it is easily swapped with dairy-free options.

Nuts

Just like dairy, nuts can be a reason people experience stalls or lose weight more slowly than they'd like. Ninety-nine percent of the recipes in the meal plan are free of tree nuts of any kind; exceptions are the rare use of almond butter, almond flour, and almond milk, all of which can be swapped with nut-free substitutes. Nuts are included as a snack option during Days 1–7, but please enjoy them with caution. They are a calorie-dense food, and some people have trouble sticking to just a small serving. Salted nuts in particular tend to be highly addictive, causing in some people that same dopamine hit that hyperpalatable sugar and refined carb foods can (refer to pages 22 and 23).

Desserts

You will notice that the meal plan does not include desserts. Eating sugar-free, low-carb desserts is your choice, and only you can decide whether it is right for you. Since I don't know how you personally react to sweetness, even in keto desserts that won't raise your blood sugar, choosing to have dessert during the detox is ultimately your call.

If you experience sugar cravings and feel that enjoying a low-carb, keto dessert will help keep you from falling off the program, please enjoy, and do so without guilt! Anything that keeps you from letting sugar and refined carbs touch your lips is a win in my book. If, on the other hand, you worry that having any bit of sweetness on your taste buds will unleash a demon you can't control, I highly recommend sticking to the three meals a day in the meal plan and avoiding desserts. Be careful of fruit as well, which could trigger you to want more and increase your cravings for sweet foods.

The dessert chapter includes easy recipes that make perfectly portioned servings. I have found that when you are just beginning this program, having a large item like a cheesecake in the refrigerator is not helpful; it can cause you to want a piece daily, and that is going to hinder your weight loss. The sugar-free desserts in this book yield just one to four servings.

Intermittent Fasting

If you have experience with intermittent fasting and following a ketogenic approach, you can skip any meals you like during the meal plan. Feel free to skip breakfast or even dinner a few times a week. The total carbs for the keto track are between 20 and 25 grams per day. Just keep in mind that skipping a meal and eating only two meals each day will reduce the nutrition info listed. If you are hungry between meals, you may increase the amount of protein in the two meals you are eating to compensate.

On the low-carb track, your goal after Days 1–7 is to avoid snacking between meals, allowing your body to adapt to intermittent fasting with this approach. If you are having difficulty eliminating all snacks, I would not advise skipping any meals on the plan; stick with the three meals listed for each day.

For either track, do not eat if you don't feel hungry. Delay eating until you do feel hungry. This is the start of intermittent fasting. You never want to push yourself to the point of ravenous hunger, however, or you may experience those hangry symptoms discussed earlier (see page 57).

But hunger is a good thing, and it's totally normal. You should feel hungry after four to six hours; you do not need to be scared of it and stuff a snack in your mouth to make the feeling go away. This will help your body regulate its hunger and satiety hormones and learn when you've truly had enough. It begins with avoiding snacking and focusing on how you feel after eating a satiating nutrient-dense meal.

You also do not need to be part of the "clean your plate" club. If you are full, but not to the point of feeling stuffed, wait 15 minutes before taking another bite. Distract yourself with another activity and come back to the plate in 15 minutes. This will allow your brain some time away from the food to think reasonably about whether you've had enough. If, after 15 minutes, you truly feel like you want more, go ahead and eat, and then analyze how you feel. Did eating the rest of the meal make you feel stuffed to the point of discomfort? Now you know, and you can learn from the experience. If, after 15 minutes, you feel satisfied with what you ate previously, cover the plate and place it in the fridge for another day. The more practice you have at learning those feelings of eating enough but not too much, the more successful you will be in achieving lasting weight loss and good health.

Kitchen Equipment

With few exceptions, you can make all the recipes in the meal plan with everyday kitchen equipment. Here, I've listed a couple of required tools that may not be found in every kitchen but are needed for the detox. Following that are a few optional items—nice to have but not required.

MINI WAFFLE MAKER. This small appliance is used for several recipes in the book, including the Open-Face Tuna Chaffles (page 180), Pizza Chaffles (page 188), and Dairy-Free Mini Waffles (page 140), which serve as a meal on their own and also as the basis of other meals in the plan (think breakfast sandwich). I use a Dash brand mini waffle maker; whichever brand you use, be sure it's nonstick to ensure your waffles release easily.

QUICHE DISHES (5 or 4 ounces) or ramekins (7 ounces). You will need two of these to make the 2-Minute English Muffins on page 240. The larger circumference of a quiche dish works better to give you the classic shape of an English muffin, but a ramekin also works. Note that the recipes in this book were tested in ceramic quiche dishes and ramekins; if you use glass dishes, you may get a different outcome.

OPTIONAL ITEMS:

AIR FRYER. An air fryer does a great job of mimicking the crispy texture of deep-fried foods, without the fat or the mess. Almost any food that is grilled, roasted, baked, or fried can be cooked in this helpful device, and usually in about half the time. I have the Philips Essential Airfryer XL, which is large enough to prepare family-size dishes. You have the option to use an air fryer to make Cheddar and Bacon–Stuffed Burgers (page 114), Easy Bacon (page 144), Rutabaga Fries (page 196), and other recipes; in each case, however, I also provide grilling or oven directions.

INSTANT POT (6 quarts). This appliance allows you to hard-cook eggs that are easy to peel every time. If you don't have an Instant Pot, however, you can always boil eggs on the stovetop, the old-fashioned way.

SILICONE HAMBURGER BUN PAN with eight or more cavities. This pan is helpful when making the Cloud Bread Rolls on page 126, but you can also form the rolls by hand.

30-DAY MEAL PLAN AND SHOPPING LISTS

Before you head to the grocery store to buy the ingredients you will need to make the recipes in this book, please note the following:

- Because many pantry items are used multiple times throughout the 30-day meal plan, I've organized the shopping lists so that you will do one large initial shop, including all the pantry items for the entire plan (opposite) along with the fresh produce, dairy, and protein needed for Days 1–7 of the plan (pages 82 and 83). For subsequent shopping trips, you'll need to buy only the fresh ingredients for the next part of the plan.

- Ingredients required for the low-carb track appear in blue type. If you are following the keto track, you can ignore these notations.

- For some staple components used in the recipes, such as marinara sauce, you have the choice to buy a sugar-free or low-carb version or to make it yourself. Note that the ingredients required to make the homemade versions are not included in the shopping lists; if making a component yourself, you will need to review the recipe and add the required ingredients to the list.

- As noted previously, the shopping lists do not include optional ingredients, such as garnishes or toppings, or secondary ingredient choices. So please do a quick read through the recipes before heading to the store; otherwise, you may find that you wish you'd bought some sour cream to top your bowl of Simple Skillet Chili (page 214), or that you didn't need to buy pepper Jack cheese after all because the Monterey Jack that you have in the refrigerator is a perfectly good alternative.

- Finally, and very importantly, please read the program guidelines specific to each section of the meal plan before beginning. Even if you've already read the guidelines, I recommend you reread them as a quick refresher. The guidelines for Days 1–7 can be found on pages 48 to 57, for Days 8–15 on pages 58 to 66, for Days 16–23 on pages 67 to 71, and for Days 24–30 on pages 72 and 73.

Shopping List for the Entire 30 Days

PANTRY

almond butter, unsweetened, 2 tablespoons

almond flour, blanched, ¼ cup plus 2 tablespoons

almond milk, unsweetened, 1 tablespoon

avocado oil mayonnaise, 2½ cups

baking powder, 1½ tablespoons

BBQ sauce, sugar-free, 1 cup *(see page 288 for brand recommendations; if making homemade, see page 230 for ingredients)*

beef bone broth, 5 cups plus 2 tablespoons

bourbon, 2 tablespoons

chicken bone broth, 1⅓ cups plus 2 tablespoons

cocoa powder, unsweetened, 1 tablespoon

coconut aminos, ½ cup plus 1 tablespoon

coconut flour, 3 tablespoons plus ½ teaspoon

Dijon mustard, 5 tablespoons

dill relish, 1 tablespoon

egg white protein powder, 1 cup

flaxseed, ground, ¼ cup

Frank's RedHot Original hot sauce, 1 cup

gelatin powder, unflavored, 3 tablespoons

glucomannan, 1½ teaspoons

liquid allulose, ¼ cup

marinara sauce, low-carb, 3½ cups plus 2 tablespoons *(see page 288 for brand recommendations; if making homemade, see page 172 for ingredients)*

mild green chiles, chopped, 1 (4-ounce) can

Palmini rice, 3 (12-ounce) packages

pork rind crumbs (aka pork panko), 2 cups

prepared yellow mustard, 2 tablespoons

salsa, mild, 1 cup

shirataki linguine, 8 ounces

shirataki rice, 3 (8-ounce) packages (omit 1 package for low-carb track)

Sriracha sauce, 1 tablespoon

sunflower seed butter (or tahini or nut butter of choice), 1 tablespoon plus 1 teaspoon

Swerve confectioners'-style sweetener, ½ cup

Swerve granular sweetener, ¼ cup

tomato paste, 2 tablespoons

tomatoes, diced, 2 (14½-ounce) cans

tuna, packed in water, 2 (5-ounce) cans

whey protein powder, unflavored, 2 scoops

OILS AND VINEGARS

apple cider vinegar

avocado oil

balsamic vinegar

red wine vinegar

white vinegar

white wine vinegar

SEASONINGS AND EXTRACTS

apple pie extract

apple pie spice

black pepper

cayenne pepper

celery salt

chili powder

chipotle powder

cream of tartar

dried dill weed

dried minced onion

dried onion flakes*

dried oregano leaves

dried parsley

garlic powder

ground cumin

ground dried oregano

ground dried rosemary

ground dried sage

ground dried thyme

ground fennel seeds

ground nutmeg

mustard powder

onion powder

paprika

red pepper flakes

sea salt, fine

smoked paprika

vanilla extract

white pepper

*Dried minced onion can be used in place of onion flakes.

Days 1–7

	DAY 1	DAY 2	DAY 3	DAY 4
BREAKFAST	**220** **100** Soft Scrambled Eggs with 2 Breakfast Sausage Patties	**140** LEFT-OVER Dairy-Free Mini Waffles with 2 Breakfast Sausage Patties *(add 1 fried egg)*	**216** LEFT-OVER Smoked Salmon Omelet Roll-Up with 1 Breakfast Sausage Patty	**242** **144** Waffle Breakfast Sandwich with 1 piece Easy Bacon
LUNCH	**238** Tuna Salad *(add ⅓ cup fresh blueberries)*	LEFT-OVER LEFT-OVER Chicken Mushroom Skillet with Mashed Roasted Cauliflower	LEFT-OVER LEFT-OVER LEFT-OVER Sheet Pan Shrimp with Crispy Pepperoni and Shirataki Rice *(replace Shirataki Rice with Palmini Rice)*	LEFT-OVER LEFT-OVER LEFT-OVER Cheddar and Bacon–Stuffed Burger on a Cloud Bread Roll *(add 1 serving of Rutabaga Fries)*
DINNER	**122** **174** Chicken Mushroom Skillet with Mashed Roasted Cauliflower *(have 2 servings of cauliflower)*	**208** **210** **182** Sheet Pan Shrimp with Crispy Pepperoni and Shirataki Rice *(replace Shirataki Rice with Palmini Rice)*	**114** **126** **196** Cheddar and Bacon–Stuffed Burger on a Cloud Bread Roll *(add 1 serving of Rutabaga Fries)*	**206** **112** Sheet Pan Chicken Fajitas with Cauliflower Rice

NUTRITION INFO

	KETO TRACK	LOW-CARB TRACK		KETO TRACK	LOW-CARB TRACK		KETO TRACK	LOW-CARB TRACK		KETO TRACK	LOW-CARB TRACK
CALORIES	1674	1812	CALORIES	1316	1407	CALORIES	1594	1727	CALORIES	1742	1857
FAT	132g	141g	FAT	96g	101g	FAT	122g	130g	FAT	135g	143g
PROTEIN	103g	105g	PROTEIN	87g	95g	PROTEIN	106g	109g	PROTEIN	111g	113g
TOTAL CARBS	18g	30g	TOTAL CARBS	24g	26g	TOTAL CARBS	20g	33g	TOTAL CARBS	22g	33g
DIETARY FIBER	6g	9g	DIETARY FIBER	11g	10g	DIETARY FIBER	12g	14g	DIETARY FIBER	8g	11g
NET CARBS	12g	21g	NET CARBS	13g	16g	NET CARBS	8g	19g	NET CARBS	14g	22g

SHOPPING LIST

PRODUCE

avocado, Hass, 1 medium

bell peppers, mix of colors, 3 small

blueberries, 6¾ ounces (about 1 scant cup) (for low-carb track only)

butter lettuce leaves, 2 large

cauliflower, 1 large head (about 2¼ pounds)

cauliflower, riced (fresh), 1 pound

cherry tomatoes, 4 ounces

garlic, 6 cloves (add 1 clove for low-carb track)

lime, 1

mushrooms, cremini, 4 ounces

parsley, 1 small bunch

red onion, 1 small

romaine lettuce leaves, 2

rutabagas, 1 pound (for low-carb track only)

scallion, 1

thyme, 3 sprigs

yellow onion, 1 small

	DAY 5	DAY 6	DAY 7
BREAKFAST	Smoked Salmon Omelet Roll-Up with 2 Breakfast Sausage Patties	2 Easy-Peel Hard-Boiled Eggs with 2 pieces Easy Bacon *(add ½ cup fresh blueberries)*	Soft Scrambled Eggs with 1 Breakfast Sausage Patty
LUNCH	Sheet Pan Chicken Fajitas *(add 1 serving of Cauliflower Rice)*	Spicy Smoked Salmon Wrap *(add 1 serving of Rutabaga Fries)*	Egg Salad on 2 lettuce leaves and 2 pieces Easy Bacon *(add 1 Cloud Bread Roll)*
DINNER	Garlic Butter Steak Bites with Mashed Roasted Cauliflower	Garlic Butter Steak Bites with Mashed Roasted Cauliflower	Cheddar and Bacon–Stuffed Burger on a Cloud Bread Roll

NUTRITION INFO

	KETO TRACK	LOW-CARB TRACK		KETO TRACK	LOW-CARB TRACK		KETO TRACK	LOW-CARB TRACK
CALORIES	1497	1592	CALORIES	1337	1494	CALORIES	1806	2003
FAT	101g	108g	FAT	99g	107g	FAT	158g	173g
PROTEIN	121g	123g	PROTEIN	95g	98g	PROTEIN	89g	103g
TOTAL CARBS	20g	27g	TOTAL CARBS	16g	38g	TOTAL CARBS	10g	11g
DIETARY FIBER	10g	12g	DIETARY FIBER	7g	12g	DIETARY FIBER	6g	6g
NET CARBS	10g	15g	NET CARBS	9g	26g	NET CARBS	5g	5g

DAIRY AND EGGS

butter, salted, 2 sticks

cheddar cheese, ½ cup shredded plus 2 slices (about 1 ounce)

cream cheese, full-fat, 2 tablespoons

eggs, 22 large *(add 1 egg for low-carb track)*

heavy cream, 1 (8-ounce) carton*

sour cream, 2 tablespoons

You will use 6 tablespoons of heavy cream during Days 1–7. Save the remainder for Days 8–15.

PROTEIN

bacon, uncured, thick-cut, 9, 15, or 24/25 slices *(for exact number, see the Easy Bacon Meal Prepping Chart on page 145)*

chicken breasts, boneless, skinless, 1 pound

chicken tenderloins, 8 ounces

deli ham, 2 slices (about 1 ounce)

ground beef, 1¼ pounds

ground pork, 1 pound

pepperoni, 6 slices

shrimp, large, 8 ounces

sirloin steak, boneless, 1 pound

smoked salmon, 7½ ounces

Days 8–15

	DAY 8	DAY 9	DAY 10	DAY 11
BREAKFAST	154 — Eggs Benedict	190 / 144 — Protein Pancakes with 2 pieces Easy Bacon	136 — Crustless Ham and Cheese Quiche	220 / LEFTOVER — Soft Scrambled Eggs with 2 pieces Easy Bacon *(add ½ cup fresh strawberries)*
LUNCH	226 — Spring Roll Chicken Salad with Creamy Asian Dressing *(add ½ cup fresh strawberries)*	LEFTOVER / LEFTOVER — Taco Soup with 2 ounces diced avocado *(add 1 serving of Grilled Romaine Salad)*	LEFTOVER / LEFTOVER — Sausage Zucchini Skillet *(add 1 serving of Cauliflower Rice)*	LEFTOVER — Spring Roll Chicken Salad with Creamy Asian Dressing
DINNER	236 / 166 — Taco Soup *(add 1 serving of Grilled Romaine Salad)*	200 / LEFTOVER — Sausage Zucchini Skillet *(add 1 serving of Cauliflower Rice)*	102 / 194 — Brown Butter Crispy Chicken Thighs with Roasted Balsamic Vegetables	130 / 134 — Corned Beef Hash Skillet with Eggs *(add 1 serving of Crispy Broccoli)*

Nutrition Info

	KETO TRACK	LOW-CARB TRACK		KETO TRACK	LOW-CARB TRACK		KETO TRACK	LOW-CARB TRACK		KETO TRACK	LOW-CARB TRACK
CALORIES	1233	1387	CALORIES	1402	1537	CALORIES	1744	1839	CALORIES	1290	1415
FAT	82g	91g	FAT	117g	125g	FAT	144g	151g	FAT	99g	106g
PROTEIN	90g	95g	PROTEIN	67g	73g	PROTEIN	89g	91g	PROTEIN	76g	79g
TOTAL CARBS	23g	40g	TOTAL CARBS	20g	33g	TOTAL CARBS	19g	26g	TOTAL CARBS	20g	34g
DIETARY FIBER	8g	16g	DIETARY FIBER	8g	13g	DIETARY FIBER	5g	7g	DIETARY FIBER	6g	11g
NET CARBS	15g	24g	NET CARBS	12g	20g	NET CARBS	14g	19g	NET CARBS	14g	23g

SHOPPING LIST

PRODUCE

avocado, Hass, 1 small

bell pepper, any color, 1 medium

bell pepper, green, 1 small

bell pepper, red, 1 small

broccoli florets, 3 ounces (about ½ cup) (add 8 ounces [1 medium head] for low-carb track)

cabbage, green, 1 medium head (about 1½ pounds), or 1 (16-ounce) bag prepared coleslaw mix

cauliflower florets, 5 ounces (about 1 cup)

cherry tomatoes, 2½ ounces (about 6 tomatoes) (add 1¾ ounces [2 to 3 tomatoes] for low-carb track)

coleslaw mix, prepared, 6 ounces (about 2 cups)

cucumber, 1 small

daikon radish, 8 ounces (add 6 ounces for low-carb track)

garlic, 2 bulbs

lemon, 1

lime, 1

parsley, 1 small bunch

raspberries, ⅓ cup (about 1¾ ounces) (add 1¾ ounces for low-carb track)

romaine lettuce, 1 large or 2 small heads (for low-carb track only)

scallions, 4

strawberries, 1½ cups (about 8 ounces) (for low-carb track only)

yellow onions, 6 large and 1 small (add 1 small for low-carb track)

zucchini, 1 large and 1 small to medium

DAY 12	DAY 13	DAY 14	DAY 15
BREAKFAST Protein Pancakes with 2 slices pan-fried Canadian bacon *(LEFTOVER)*	Crustless Ham and Cheese Quiche *(add ⅓ cup fresh raspberries)* *(LEFTOVER)*	Deviled Eggs with 2 pieces Easy Bacon *(142)* *(LEFTOVER)*	2-Minute English Muffin, 2 pieces Easy Bacon, 1 fried egg *(240)* *(LEFTOVER)*
LUNCH Brown Butter Crispy Chicken Thighs *(add ½ cup fresh strawberries)* *(LEFTOVER)*	French Onion Meatballs with Roasted Balsamic Vegetables *(LEFTOVER)* *(LEFTOVER)*	Monte Cristo Waffle Sandwich *(add 1 serving of German "Potato" Salad)* *(178)* *(164)*	Monte Cristo Waffle Sandwich *(add 1 serving of German "Potato" Salad)* *(LEFTOVER)* *(LEFTOVER)*
DINNER French Onion Meatballs with Mashed Roasted Cauliflower *(158)* *(LEFTOVER)*	Corned Beef Hash Skillet with Eggs *(add 1 serving of Crispy Broccoli)* *(LEFTOVER)* *(LEFTOVER)*	Cabbage Roll Skillet *(110)*	Shrimp Linguine in Garlic Butter Sauce *(212)*

NUTRITION INFO

	KETO TRACK	LOW-CARB TRACK		KETO TRACK	LOW-CARB TRACK		KETO TRACK	LOW-CARB TRACK		KETO TRACK	LOW-CARB TRACK
CALORIES	1834	1857	CALORIES	1415	1538	CALORIES	1315	1470	CALORIES	1602	1757
FAT	147g	147g	FAT	110g	117g	FAT	100g	111g	FAT	119g	131g
PROTEIN	109g	110g	PROTEIN	76g	79g	PROTEIN	79g	84g	PROTEIN	107g	110g
TOTAL CARBS	18g	23g	TOTAL CARBS	25g	38g	TOTAL CARBS	24g	34g	TOTAL CARBS	22g	32g
DIETARY FIBER	5g	7g	DIETARY FIBER	6g	12g	DIETARY FIBER	8g	10g	DIETARY FIBER	7g	8g
NET CARBS	13g	16g	NET CARBS	19g	26g	NET CARBS	16g	24g	NET CARBS	15g	24g

SHOPPING LIST

DAIRY AND EGGS

butter, salted, 3 sticks

cream cheese, full-fat, 4 ounces

eggs, 21 large*

Gruyère cheese, 2 slices (about 1 ounce)

heavy cream, 1 (8-ounce) carton**

mozzarella cheese, 1 cup shredded

Parmesan cheese, 1 tablespoon grated (for low-carb track only)

*If planning to cook a full batch of Easy-Peel Hard-Boiled Eggs for meal prepping purposes on Day 6, increase the number of eggs to 23.

**If you saved the heavy cream left over from Days 1–7, you will not need to purchase more for Days 8–15.

PROTEIN

bacon, uncured, thick-cut, 8 slices (add 2 slices for low-carb track)*

Canadian bacon, 3 slices

chicken thighs, bone-in, skin-on, 4 small (about 1 pound)

corned beef brisket, ready to cook, 1 pound

deli ham, 6 slices (about 5 ounces)

ground beef, 2 pounds

ground Italian sausage, 1 pound

ground pork, 1 pound

ham, cooked, 2 ounces

rotisserie chicken (white meat only), 8 ounces, or 10 ounces raw boneless, skinless chicken breasts

shrimp, large, 1½ pounds

*If you cooked the full amount of Easy Bacon needed for the entire plan during Days 1–7, you'll need just 2 slices for this part of the plan; if you cooked a double batch of bacon during Days 1–7, you'll need 4 slices. If you wish to cook a double batch of bacon during this plan to make enough for the rest of the detox, add an extra 7 slices.

Days 16–23

	DAY 16	DAY 17	DAY 18	DAY 19
BREAKFAST	**94** Apple Pie Dutch Baby	**154** Eggs Benedict	**146** 2 Easy-Peel Hard-Boiled Eggs *(add 2 slices pan-fried Canadian bacon)*	**140** Dairy-Free Mini Waffles, 2 fried eggs, 2 slices pan-fried Canadian bacon
LUNCH	LEFT-OVER Shrimp Linguine in Garlic Butter Sauce	LEFT-OVER / LEFT-OVER Smoky Grilled Pork Chops with Sautéed Summer Squash *(have 2 servings of squash)*	LEFT-OVER / LEFT-OVER Pan-Seared Lemon Butter Salmon with Crispy Broccoli	**104** Buffalo Chicken Salad Wraps
DINNER	**218** / **202** Smoky Grilled Pork Chops with Sautéed Summer Squash *(have 2 servings of squash)*	**184** / **134** Pan-Seared Lemon Butter Salmon with Crispy Broccoli	**192** / **160** Reverse-Seared Rib Eye with Chimichurri and Garlic Butter Mushrooms *(have 2 servings of mushrooms)*	**214** Simple Skillet Chili *(have 2 servings)*

NUTRITION INFO

	KETO TRACK	LOW-CARB TRACK		KETO TRACK	LOW-CARB TRACK		KETO TRACK	LOW-CARB TRACK		KETO TRACK	LOW-CARB TRACK
CALORIES	1530	1644	CALORIES	1597	1711	CALORIES	1507	1798	CALORIES	1276	1726
FAT	111g	121g	FAT	108g	118g	FAT	109g	132g	FAT	102g	137g
PROTEIN	103g	105g	PROTEIN	124g	126g	PROTEIN	113g	128g	PROTEIN	72g	95g
TOTAL CARBS	22g	28g	TOTAL CARBS	23g	29g	TOTAL CARBS	25g	36g	TOTAL CARBS	25g	37g
DIETARY FIBER	5g	7g	DIETARY FIBER	9g	11g	DIETARY FIBER	8g	10g	DIETARY FIBER	10g	15g
NET CARBS	17g	21g	NET CARBS	14g	18g	NET CARBS	17g	26g	NET CARBS	15g	22g

SHOPPING LIST

PRODUCE

bean sprouts, 2 cups (about 5 ounces)

bell peppers, green, 1 large and 1 small

bell pepper, red, 1 small

broccoli, 1 medium head (about 8 ounces)

cabbage, green, 3 ounces (about 1/4 small head)

cabbage, red, 3 ounces (about 1/4 small head)

celery, 1 stalk

chili pepper, Fresno, 1

cilantro, 1/2 bunch

garlic, 2 medium to large bulbs (add 1 small bulb for low-carb track)

iceberg lettuce leaves, 5 large

jalapeño pepper, 1 small

lemon, 1

lime, 1

mushrooms, cremini, small, 12 ounces

parsley, 1 small bunch

raspberries, 2/3 cup (about 3 1/4 ounces) (for low-carb track only)

red onion, 1 small

rosemary, 1 sprig

scallions, 5

shallots, 2 large

thyme, 1 sprig

tomato, 1 small to medium

yellow onions, 4 medium and 2 small

yellow squash, 1 large

zucchini, 1 large (add 1 medium for low-carb track)

	DAY 20	DAY 21	DAY 22	DAY 23
BREAKFAST	144 — 2-Minute English Muffin, 1 fried egg, 1 piece Easy Bacon *(omit bacon)*	Protein Pancakes with 2 slices pan-fried Canadian bacon *(add 1/3 cup fresh raspberries)*	242 — Waffle Breakfast Sandwich	142 — Deviled Eggs with 2 slices pan-fried Canadian bacon *(omit Canadian bacon)*
LUNCH	138 / 244 — Crustless Skillet Supreme Pizza *(add 1 serving of Zucchini Noodles with Roasted Garlic Cream Sauce)*	Buffalo Wings *(add 1 serving of Creamy Cilantro Lime Slaw)*	Buffalo Chicken Salad Wrap *(add 1/3 cup fresh raspberries)*	Crustless Skillet Supreme Pizza *(add 1 serving of Zucchini Noodles with Roasted Garlic Cream Sauce)*
DINNER	106 / 132 — Buffalo Wings with Creamy Cilantro Lime Slaw	170 — Jambalaya	148 / 182 — Egg Foo Young *(add 1 serving of Palmini Rice)*	228 — Stuffed Chicken Thighs with Garlic Butter Mushrooms

NUTRITION INFO

DAY 20

	KETO TRACK	LOW-CARB TRACK
CALORIES	1571	1824
FAT	128g	152g
PROTEIN	85g	85g
TOTAL CARBS	24g	29g
DIETARY FIBER	7g	9g
NET CARBS	17g	20g

DAY 21

	KETO TRACK	LOW-CARB TRACK
CALORIES	1237	1494
FAT	80g	104g
PROTEIN	103g	106g
TOTAL CARBS	25g	37g
DIETARY FIBER	8g	14g
NET CARBS	17g	23g

DAY 22

	KETO TRACK	LOW-CARB TRACK
CALORIES	1376	1417
FAT	114g	114g
PROTEIN	70g	70g
TOTAL CARBS	25g	34g
DIETARY FIBER	8g	13g
NET CARBS	17g	21g

DAY 23

	KETO TRACK	LOW-CARB TRACK
CALORIES	1538	1820
FAT	107g	139g
PROTEIN	116g	108g
TOTAL CARBS	25g	30g
DIETARY FIBER	5g	7g
NET CARBS	20g	23g

DAIRY AND EGGS

butter, salted, 2½ sticks (add 3 tablespoons for low-carb track)

cheddar cheese, 2 slices (about 1 ounce)

eggs, 19 large*

heavy cream, 1 (8-ounce) carton (add 1 [8-ounce] carton for low-carb track)

mozzarella cheese, 1½ cups shredded

Parmesan cheese, ½ cup grated (for low-carb track only)

If you made a full batch of Easy-Peel Hard-Boiled Eggs for meal prepping purposes on Day 14, you'll need just 17 eggs. If planning to make a full batch of Easy-Peel Hard-Boiled Eggs for meal prepping purposes on Day 23, increase the number of eggs to 21.

PROTEIN

bacon, uncured, thick-cut, 4 or 5 slices (depending on number of chicken thighs purchased)*

Canadian bacon, 7 slices

chicken thighs, boneless, skinless, 1¼ pounds (4 or 5 small thighs)

chicken wings, 2 pounds

deli ham, 2 slices (about 1 ounce)

ground beef, 1 pound

ground chicken, 4 ounces

ground pork, 10 ounces

ham, cooked, 8 ounces

pepperoni, sliced, 1 ounce

pork loin chops, bone-in, 2 (6-ounce) (about 1½ inches thick)

rib-eye steaks, boneless, 2 (8-ounce) (about 1½ inches thick)

rotisserie chicken, 1, or 10 ounces raw boneless, skinless chicken thighs

salmon fillet, skin-on, 1 pound

shrimp, jumbo, 8 ounces

For Days 16–23, you will need 3 pieces of Easy Bacon if following the keto track or 2 pieces if following the low-carb track. If you didn't cook the full amount of bacon needed for the entire plan during Days 1–7, or a double batch on Day 15, add 2 or 3 slices to the shopping list according to the track you're following.

SHOPPING LIST

Days 24–30

	DAY 24	**DAY 25**	**DAY 26**	**DAY 27**
BREAKFAST	Scotch Eggs with 1 piece Easy Bacon (204, 144)	Sausage Egg Cups (198)	Scotch Eggs (add 1 piece Easy Bacon) LEFTOVER	Sausage Egg Cups with 1 piece Easy Bacon LEFTOVER
LUNCH	Open-Face Tuna Chaffles (add ½ cup fresh strawberries) (180)	Egg Foo Young (add 1 serving of Palmini Rice) LEFTOVER	Pizza Chaffle (188)	Spicy Smoked Salmon Wrap (add 1 serving of Asparagus Salad with Avocado Dressing) (224, 96)
DINNER	Simple Skillet Chili LEFTOVER	Stuffed Chicken Thighs with Egg Noodles LEFTOVER (150)	Fish Taco Bowl (156)	Chicken Chili Stuffed Peppers (118)

NUTRITION INFO

	KETO TRACK	LOW-CARB TRACK		KETO TRACK	LOW-CARB TRACK		KETO TRACK	LOW-CARB TRACK		KETO TRACK	LOW-CARB TRACK
CALORIES	1777	1800	CALORIES	1811	1838	CALORIES	1654	1772	CALORIES	1403	1678
FAT	136g	136g	FAT	126g	126g	FAT	113g	125g	FAT	111g	135g
PROTEIN	121g	121g	PROTEIN	138g	139g	PROTEIN	137g	141g	PROTEIN	83g	89g
TOTAL CARBS	24g	29g	TOTAL CARBS	23g	28g	TOTAL CARBS	24g	25g	TOTAL CARBS	25g	38g
DIETARY FIBER	9g	11g	DIETARY FIBER	6g	8g	DIETARY FIBER	10g	10g	DIETARY FIBER	10g	17g
NET CARBS	15g	18g	NET CARBS	17g	20g	NET CARBS	14g	15g	NET CARBS	15g	21g

SHOPPING LIST

PRODUCE

asparagus, medium-thick, 1 pound (for low-carb track only)

avocado, Hass, 1 medium (reserve 2 ounces for low-carb track)

bell pepper, green, ½ small

bell pepper, red, ½ small

bell peppers, any color(s), 4 medium

blueberries, ½ cup (about 3½ ounces) (for low-carb track only)

butter lettuce leaves, 2 large

cabbage, green, 2 ounces

carrot, 1 small

cauliflower, riced, fresh, 1 pound

cherry tomatoes, 1 ounce (2 or 3 tomatoes)

garlic, 1 bulb (reserve 2 cloves for low-carb track)

ginger, 1 (2-inch) piece

lemon, 1 (for low-carb track only)

limes, 1 large or 2 small

mushrooms, cremini, 1¼ ounces

onion, red, 1 small

onions, yellow, 1 large, 1 medium, and 1 small

parsley, 1 bunch

radishes, 2 (about 1 ounce) (for low-carb track only)

romaine lettuce, 2 ounces

scallions, 5

spinach, 1 ounce

strawberries, 1 cup (about 5½ ounces) (for low-carb track only)

tomato, 1 medium

	DAY 28	**DAY 29**	**DAY 30**
BREAKFAST	**142** Deviled Eggs *(add 2 slices pan-fried Canadian bacon and ½ cup fresh blueberries)*	**220** Soft Scrambled Eggs *(add 2 slices pan-fried Canadian bacon)*	**94** Apple Pie Dutch Baby *(add ½ cup fresh strawberries)*
LUNCH	**98** Bacon Bourbon Burger with Egg Noodles	**128** Cobb Ranch Salad	**LEFT-OVER LEFT-OVER LEFT-OVER** Bacon Bourbon Burger on a Cloud Bread Roll *(add 1 serving of Egg Noodles)*
DINNER	**120 LEFT-OVER** Chicken Kiev Meatballs with Mashed Roasted Cauliflower	**116 LEFT-OVER** Chicken Cauliflower Fried Rice *(add 1 serving of Asparagus Salad with Avocado Dressing)*	**186** Philly Cheesesteak Stir-Fry

NUTRITION INFO

	KETO TRACK	LOW-CARB TRACK		KETO TRACK	LOW-CARB TRACK		KETO TRACK	LOW-CARB TRACK
CALORIES	1525	1649	CALORIES	1281	1638	CALORIES	1382	1710
FAT	108g	112g	FAT	99g	127g	FAT	94g	125g
PROTEIN	97g	109g	PROTEIN	75g	92g	PROTEIN	91g	101g
TOTAL CARBS	23g	34g	TOTAL CARBS	25g	39g	TOTAL CARBS	24g	32g
DIETARY FIBER	7g	9g	DIETARY FIBER	9g	16g	DIETARY FIBER	5g	7g
NET CARBS	16g	25g	NET CARBS	16g	23g	NET CARBS	19g	25g

SHOPPING LIST

DAIRY AND EGGS

butter, salted, ½ stick

cream cheese, full-fat, 2 ounces

eggs, 25 large*

eggs, 6 small or medium

heavy cream, 1 (8-ounce) carton**

mozzarella cheese, 2 cups shredded

pepper Jack cheese, ½ cup shredded

*If you made a full batch of Easy-Peel Hard-Boiled Eggs for meal prepping purposes on Day 23, you'll need just 17 eggs.

**If following the keto track, omit the heavy cream; you should have enough left over from Days 16–23 for this meal plan.

PROTEIN

bacon, uncured, thick-cut, 8 slices (add 1 slice for low-carb track)*

Canadian bacon, 4 slices (for low-carb track only)

chicken breasts, boneless, skinless, 2¼ pounds

cod fillets, wild-caught, skinless, 8 ounces

ground beef, 1 pound

ground chicken, 1 pound

ground pork, 1 pound

pepperoni, 6 slices

rotisserie chicken (white or dark meat), 2½ ounces, or 3½ ounces raw boneless, skinless chicken breasts or thighs

smoked salmon, 4 ounces

sirloin steak, boneless, 8 ounces

*If you cooked the full amount of Easy Bacon needed for the entire plan during Days 1–7, or a double batch during Days 8–15, you'll need just 4 slices for this part of the plan.

MEAL PLAN RECIPES

The recipes that follow are presented in alphabetical order to make them easy for you to find as you prepare them during the meal plan. On pages 302 to 306, you'll find a recipe index that categorizes the recipes by type—breakfast, beef and pork, sides, and so on—which you might find useful as you continue to make these recipes after the plan.

I've included icons along with the recipes to help you identify those that are free of common allergens, including dairy, eggs, and nuts, as well as those that require only one cooking vessel or make use of an air fryer (see page 79). Here's a rundown of those icons:

Dairy-free		Made in an air fryer	
Egg-free		Made in only one pot	
Nut-free			

At the end of each recipe, you'll find the nutrition information per serving. Note that these numbers are based on the first ingredient choice listed (when more than one option is given) and do not include any optional toppings or garnishes. If you decide to add any of those optional items, make sure to recalculate the nutrition to ensure that you are meeting your goals.

Apple Pie Dutch Baby / 94

Asparagus Salad with Avocado Dressing / 96

Bacon Bourbon Burgers / 98

Breakfast Sausage Patties / 100

Brown Butter Crispy Chicken Thighs / 102

Buffalo Chicken Salad Wraps / 104

Buffalo Wings / 106

Buffalo Wing Sauce / 108

Cabbage Roll Skillet / 110

Cauliflower Rice / 112

Cheddar and Bacon–Stuffed Burgers / 114

Chicken Cauliflower Fried Rice / 116

Chicken Chili Stuffed Peppers / 118

Chicken Kiev Meatballs / 120

Chicken Mushroom Skillet / 122

Chimichurri / 124

Cloud Bread Rolls / 126

Cobb Ranch Salad / 128

Corned Beef Hash Skillet with Eggs / 130

Creamy Cilantro Lime Slaw / 132

Crispy Broccoli / 134

Crustless Ham and Cheese Quiches / 136

Crustless Skillet Supreme Pizza / 138

Dairy-Free Mini Waffles / 140

Deviled Eggs / 142

Easy Bacon / 144

Easy-Peel Hard-Boiled Eggs / 146

Egg Foo Young / 148

Egg Noodles / 150

Egg Salad / 152

Eggs Benedict / 154

Fish Taco Bowl / 156

French Onion Meatballs / 158

Garlic Butter Mushrooms / 160

Garlic Butter Steak Bites / 162

German "Potato" Salad / 164

Grilled Romaine Salad / 166

Homemade Ketchup / 168

Jambalaya / 170

Low-Carb Marinara Sauce / 172

Mashed Roasted Cauliflower / 174

Momma's Italian Dressing / 176

Monte Cristo Waffle Sandwiches / 178

Open-Face Tuna Chaffles / 180

Palmini Rice / 182

Pan-Seared Lemon Butter Salmon / 184

Philly Cheesesteak Stir-Fry / 186

Pizza Chaffles / 188

Protein Pancakes / 190

Reverse-Seared Rib Eye with Chimichurri / 192

Roasted Balsamic Vegetables / 194

Rutabaga Fries / 196

Sausage Egg Cups / 198

Sausage Zucchini Skillet / 200

Sautéed Summer Squash / 202

Scotch Eggs / 204

Sheet Pan Chicken Fajitas / 206

Sheet Pan Shrimp with Crispy Pepperoni / 208

Shirataki Rice / 210

Shrimp Linguine in Garlic Butter Sauce / 212

Simple Skillet Chili / 214

Smoked Salmon Omelet Roll-Ups / 216

Smoky Grilled Pork Chops / 218

Soft Scrambled Eggs / 220

Spicy Mayo / 222

Spicy Smoked Salmon Wrap / 224

Spring Roll Chicken Salad with Creamy Asian Dressing / 226

Stuffed Chicken Thighs / 228

Sugar-Free BBQ Sauce / 230

Sugar-Free Maple Syrup / 232

Taco Seasoning / 234

Taco Soup / 236

Tuna Salad / 238

2-Minute English Muffins / 240

Waffle Breakfast Sandwich / 242

Zucchini Noodles with Roasted Garlic Cream Sauce / 244

APPLE PIE DUTCH BABY

option

YIELD: 1 serving

PREP TIME: 2 minutes

COOK TIME: 15 minutes

When you're sick of eggs for breakfast, this is a wonderful alternative. The texture is a cross between a custard and a pancake and is quite delicious. Feel free to change out the apple pie extract and spice for either almond, banana, or vanilla extract and ground cinnamon. To make this recipe nut-free, simply replace the almond flour with sunflower seed flour.

1 tablespoon salted butter, for the pan

2 large eggs

¼ cup heavy cream

½ teaspoon apple pie extract

¼ cup Swerve confectioners'-style sweetener, or ½ teaspoon cinnamon- or vanilla-flavored liquid stevia

2 tablespoons blanched almond flour

½ teaspoon apple pie spice

Pinch of fine sea salt

FOR SERVING (OPTIONAL)

Swerve confectioners'-style sweetener, sugar-free maple syrup, and/or chopped apple

1. Put the butter in a 6-inch cast-iron skillet and place the skillet in the oven on the middle rack. Preheat the oven to 400°F.

2. Put the remaining ingredients in a blender and blend until combined. Once the oven is hot, swirl the melted butter all around the skillet. Pour the batter into the skillet and return the pan to the oven.

3. Bake for 15 minutes, or until puffed around the edges and still slightly jiggly in the center.

4. If desired, top with a dusting of confectioners'-style sweetener, a drizzle of sugar-free maple syrup, and/or a handful of chopped apple. Best served fresh.

NUTRITION INFO:
calories **411** | fat **35g** | protein **16g** | total carbs **4g** | dietary fiber **1g** | net carbs **3g**

ASPARAGUS SALAD WITH AVOCADO DRESSING

option

YIELD: **2 servings (8 ounces per serving)**

PREP TIME: **15 minutes**

COOK TIME: **3 minutes**

I must be honest: I have never been a fan of asparagus, especially when it's too soft. I love this recipe because the asparagus still has a nice crunch to it and holds up well in the refrigerator for several days without getting mushy.

FOR THE DRESSING

¼ ripe Hass avocado

2 tablespoons water

1 tablespoon extra-virgin olive oil

1½ teaspoons fresh lemon juice

1 small clove garlic, chopped

Generous pinch of fine sea salt

FOR THE SALAD

1 pound medium-thick asparagus

2 tablespoons extra-virgin olive oil

1 tablespoon fresh lemon juice

1 clove garlic, grated

½ teaspoon fine sea salt

1 ounce thinly sliced radishes (about 2 radishes)

¼ cup crumbled feta cheese (optional)

1. Make the dressing: Scoop the avocado flesh into a single-serving blender, mini food processor, or jar large enough to fit an immersion blender. Add the rest of the dressing ingredients and blend on high speed until smooth. Taste and adjust the salt if needed.

2. Prepare the asparagus: Trim and discard the bottom couple of inches off the asparagus spears, then cut the spears into 1-inch pieces.

3. Bring a pot of salted water to a boil. Set a bowl of ice water nearby. Drop the asparagus into the boiling water and blanch for 2 to 3 minutes, until just tender but still bright green.

4. Transfer the asparagus to the ice water for 1 minute. Drain and place on a clean kitchen towel to soak up the excess water.

5. In a medium serving bowl, whisk together the oil, lemon juice, grated garlic, and salt. Add the drained asparagus and toss to coat. Top with the radishes and the feta cheese, if using.

6. Serve with the dressing on the side.

7. Store leftover salad, dressed, in an airtight container in the refrigerator for up to 5 days.

96

NUTRITION INFO:
calories **275** | fat **24g** | protein **6g** | total carbs **13g** | dietary fiber **7g** | net carbs **6g**

BACON BOURBON BURGERS

option

YIELD: **4 burgers (1 per serving)**

PREP TIME: **8 minutes**

COOK TIME: **25 minutes**

Make these tasty burgers with or without the hot peppers—it's up to you!

1 cup sugar-free BBQ sauce, store-bought or homemade (page 230)

2 tablespoons bourbon

4 slices thick-cut bacon

1 pound ground beef

4 ounces sliced yellow onions (about 1 medium-large onion)

¼ cup sliced Fresno or jalapeño peppers (optional)

½ teaspoon fine sea salt

½ teaspoon ground black pepper

4 slices cheddar cheese (about 2 ounces) (optional)

FOR SERVING

4 Cloud Bread Rolls (page 126), sliced in half horizontally, or 4 servings Egg Noodles (page 150)

1. In a small saucepan over low heat, stir together the BBQ sauce and bourbon. Keep on low heat, stirring occasionally.

2. Cook the bacon in a large cast-iron skillet over medium-high heat until it reaches the desired doneness. Remove and set aside, leaving the fat in the pan. Once it's cool enough to handle, chop the bacon.

3. Put the ground beef in a large bowl. Add 1 tablespoon of the chopped bacon and 2 tablespoons of the bourbon BBQ sauce and mix together. Divide into 4 portions weighing about 4 ounces each, then form into patties about 4 inches in diameter. Set aside.

4. In the same skillet with the bacon fat, cook the onions over medium heat until golden brown, about 5 minutes. Add the hot peppers, if using, and heat until just warmed, about 1 minute. Remove the onions and peppers from the pan and set aside.

5. Season the burger patties on both sides with the salt and pepper. Increase the heat under the skillet to medium-high. Place the patties in the pan and cook without moving for 3 to 4 minutes, then flip the patties over and lower the heat to medium-low. Cover and cook for 5 minutes, or until the internal temperature reads 145°F for medium doneness.

6. If using cheese, add a slice of cheese to each patty, turn off the heat, and cover the pan for 1 to 2 minutes, until the cheese is melted.

7. To serve, place a patty on the bottom of a roll or alongside a serving of egg noodles. Top with the onions and peppers, the remaining bacon and bourbon BBQ sauce, and the top of a roll, if using.

8. Store leftovers in an airtight container in the refrigerator for up to 3 days or in the freezer for up to 1 month.

NUTRITION INFO (WITH 1 CLOUD BREAD ROLL):
calories **510** | fat **35g** | protein **30g** | total carbs **11g** | dietary fiber **1g** | net carbs **10g**

NUTRITION INFO (WITH 1 SERVING EGG NOODLES):
calories **537** | fat **39g** | protein **29g** | total carbs **11g** | dietary fiber **1g** | net carbs **10g**

BREAKFAST SAUSAGE PATTIES

YIELD: 8 patties (1 to 2 per serving)

PREP TIME: 15 minutes

COOK TIME: 16 minutes

Prepare these delicious sausage patties at the start of the week so that you can enjoy them all week or freeze some for later!

1 pound ground pork

1½ teaspoons chopped fresh parsley, or ½ teaspoon dried parsley

1 teaspoon fine sea salt

½ teaspoon ground fennel seeds

¼ teaspoon ground dried rosemary

¼ teaspoon ground dried sage

¼ teaspoon ground dried thyme

¼ teaspoon ground black pepper

¼ teaspoon garlic powder

Red pepper flakes (optional)

1½ tablespoons avocado oil, for the pan

Chopped fresh parsley, for garnish (optional)

1. Mix together all the ingredients, except the oil and the parsley garnish, until well combined.

2. Divide the mixture into 8 balls weighing about 2 ounces each, then flatten into patties about 3 inches in diameter, gently pressing in the center of each patty to form an indent. This will help the patties keep their shape.

3. Heat the oil in a large skillet over medium-high heat. Once the oil is hot, place half of the patties in the pan. Cook for 3 to 4 minutes on each side, until the outsides are browned and the internal temperature reaches 165°F. Remove from the skillet and repeat with the remaining patties. Serve garnished with chopped parsley, if desired.

4. Store leftovers in an airtight container in the refrigerator for up to 3 days or in the freezer for up to 1 month.

For the meal plan

You'll be eating four patties total on Days 1 and 2; freeze the remaining four patties for later in the plan.

NUTRITION INFO (PER PATTY):
calories **158** | fat **13g** | protein **9.5g** | total carbs **0.5g** | dietary fiber **0.5g** | net carbs **0g**

BROWN BUTTER CRISPY CHICKEN THIGHS

YIELD: **2 servings (6 ounces per serving)**

PREP TIME: **5 minutes**

COOK TIME: **25 minutes**

This comforting dinner is on the table in under 30 minutes. For the meal plan, you'll be eating the first serving with a side of Roasted Balsamic Vegetables (page 194); the second serving you'll enjoy straight up, or with some strawberries if you're on the low-carb track. If this dish becomes a staple of yours after the detox—and I hope it does—try serving it with Mashed Roasted Cauliflower (page 174), low-carb rice, such as cauliflower or Palmini (pages 112 and 182), Crispy Broccoli (page 134), or Egg Noodles (page 150).

4 small bone-in, skin-on chicken thighs (about 1 pound)

Salt and pepper

4 tablespoons salted butter, divided

1 tablespoon minced garlic

2 tablespoons chicken bone broth

1 tablespoon fresh lime juice

Chopped fresh parsley, for garnish (optional)

Lime wedges, for serving (optional)

1. Place the top rack of the oven about 8 inches from the heating element. Set the oven to broil.

2. Pat the chicken dry with paper towels and generously season both sides with salt and pepper.

3. Melt 1 tablespoon of the butter in an 8-inch cast-iron skillet over medium-high heat. Sear the chicken thighs skin side down; do not move them for 5 minutes. Flip over and sear until golden, another 5 minutes. Transfer to a plate and set aside.

4. Melt the remaining 3 tablespoons of butter in the same skillet over medium-low heat. Scrape up the bits left in the pan as the butter melts. Continue to scrape and stir until the butter settles and begins to turn golden brown. Add the garlic and sauté for 1 minute, or until fragrant.

5. Add the broth and lime juice and stir well.

6. Return the chicken to the pan, skin side up, and cook for another 5 minutes, basting the skin with the liquid in the pan. Cover, reduce the heat to low, and cook until the internal temperature in the thickest part of a thigh near the bone registers 165°F, another 5 minutes or so.

7. Transfer the pan to the top rack of the oven and broil for 2 to 3 minutes, until the skin is crispy. Garnish with parsley and serve with lime wedges, if desired.

8. Store leftovers in an airtight container in the refrigerator for up to 3 days.

NUTRITION INFO:
calories **842** | fat **71g** | protein **48g** | total carbs **3g** | dietary fiber **1g** | net carbs **2g**

BUFFALO CHICKEN SALAD WRAPS

YIELD: **2 wraps (1 per serving)**

PREP TIME: **15 minutes**

Shingling the lettuce leaves for this fun lunch takes a little time, but it's well worth it! You make it once and enjoy it twice.

¼ cup avocado oil mayonnaise

¼ cup Buffalo Wing Sauce (page 108)

1 tablespoon prepared yellow mustard

8 ounces shredded rotisserie chicken, dark meat only (about 2 cups) (see Note)

5 large iceberg lettuce leaves

3 ounces tomato slices (about ½ medium tomato)

1½ ounces sliced red onions (about ½ small onion)

2 slices cheddar cheese (about 1 ounce) (optional)

1. In a medium bowl, whisk together the mayonnaise, Buffalo sauce, and mustard. Add the chicken and stir until evenly coated. Set aside.

2. Place the lettuce leaves on a large piece of parchment paper. Arrange the leaves, slightly overlapping, so that they form an approximately 8 by 9-inch rectangle with a longer side facing you.

3. Spread the chicken down the center of the lettuce. Top with the tomato, onions, and cheese, if using.

4. Using the parchment paper as a guide, and starting with the side closest to you, roll into a tight log, tucking in the ends. Cut the wrap in half to make 2 servings. To make it easier to hold and enjoy, wrap the parchment around both ends.

5. Store leftovers in an airtight container in the refrigerator for up to 3 days.

Note

To save a step, I like to use rotisserie chicken for this recipe. The dark meat from one rotisserie chicken should yield the amount needed here; if you come up short, you can augment the dark meat with a little of the breast meat. If cooking the chicken yourself, you'll need 10 ounces of raw boneless, skinless chicken thighs.

NUTRITION INFO:
calories **412** | fat **41g** | protein **12g** | total carbs **6g** | dietary fiber **3g** | net carbs **3g**

BUFFALO WINGS

option

YIELD: **2 servings (12 ounces per serving)**

PREP TIME: **5 minutes**

COOK TIME: **50 minutes**

Who doesn't love a good crispy chicken wing? If you're not a fan of Buffalo sauce, and/or if you need this recipe to be dairy-free, you can certainly enjoy these wings without it.

2 pounds chicken wings

1 teaspoon fine sea salt

1 teaspoon ground black pepper

1 teaspoon onion powder

1 tablespoon baking powder

½ cup Buffalo Wing Sauce (page 108), warmed if desired

Chopped fresh parsley, for garnish (optional)

1. Preheat the oven to 425°F. Line a rimmed baking sheet with parchment paper.

2. Pat the chicken wings dry with paper towels and place the wings on the prepared baking sheet.

3. Mix together the salt, pepper, onion powder, and baking powder and sprinkle the mixture over both sides of the wings.

4. Bake for 25 minutes, then flip the wings over and bake for another 25 minutes. If you'd like them crispier, broil for 2 to 3 minutes.

5. Place the wings in a bowl and toss with the Buffalo sauce. Garnish with parsley, if desired, and serve immediately.

6. Store leftovers in an airtight container in the refrigerator for up to 4 days.

NUTRITION INFO:
calories **556** | fat **39g** | protein **45g** | total carbs **4g** | dietary fiber **1g** | net carbs **3g**

BUFFALO WING SAUCE

YIELD: 1½ cups (2 tablespoons per serving)

PREP TIME: 5 minutes

1 cup Frank's RedHot Original hot sauce

½ cup (1 stick) salted butter, melted

2 tablespoons white vinegar

½ teaspoon garlic powder

¼ teaspoon cayenne pepper, or more to taste

This sauce is so good and so quick to make! You'll enjoy it with my Buffalo Chicken Salad Wraps (page 104) and Buffalo Wings (page 106).

1. Whisk together all the ingredients. Taste and add more cayenne if desired.

2. Store in an airtight container in the refrigerator for up to 1 month. Rewarm in the microwave for about 1 minute, then whisk vigorously.

NUTRITION INFO:
calories **69** | fat **8g** | protein **1g** | total carbs **1g** | dietary fiber **1g** | net carbs **0g**

CABBAGE ROLL SKILLET

YIELD: **4 servings (12 ounces per serving)**

PREP TIME: **10 minutes**

COOK TIME: **20 minutes**

If you read my blog, Sugar-Free Mom, then you may be familiar with my popular Slow Cooker Unstuffed Low Carb Cabbage Roll Soup recipe. Here, I've taken the same idea of a deconstructed cabbage roll and turned it into a quick skillet meal that's just as hearty and satisfying. To get this quantity of shredded cabbage, you'll need a 1½-pound head; or, to save time, you can use a 16-ounce bag of coleslaw mix.

1 tablespoon avocado oil, for the pan

5 ounces chopped yellow onions (about 1 large onion)

2 cloves garlic, minced

1 pound ground beef

½ teaspoon dried parsley

½ teaspoon fine sea salt

¼ teaspoon ground black pepper

18 ounces shredded green cabbage (from 1 medium head, about 1½ pounds)

1½ cups low-carb marinara sauce, store-bought or homemade (page 172)

2 tablespoons apple cider vinegar

1 (8-ounce) package shirataki rice, rinsed, drained, and dried

FOR GARNISH (OPTIONAL)

A few cherry tomatoes

Chopped fresh parsley

1. Heat the oil in a large skillet over medium-high heat. Add the onions and garlic and cook until the onions are translucent, about 3 minutes.

2. Add the ground beef to the skillet and cook until browned, about 5 minutes, stirring with a wooden spoon to crumble it. Sprinkle the parsley, salt, and pepper over the beef and stir to combine.

3. Add the cabbage, marinara sauce, and vinegar to the skillet. Stir to combine. Cover, reduce the heat to medium-low, and cook, stirring occasionally, until the cabbage is tender, 8 to 10 minutes.

4. Uncover, add the rice, and stir to combine. Serve immediately, garnished with cherry tomatoes and chopped parsley, if desired.

5. Store leftovers in an airtight container in the refrigerator for up to 3 days.

For the meal plan

Enjoy one serving immediately. Freeze the remaining three servings for later, after you've completed the plan; they will keep in the freezer for up to 1 month.

NUTRITION INFO:
calories **428** | fat **32g** | protein **22g** | total carbs **14g** | dietary fiber **4g** | net carbs **10g**

CAULIFLOWER RICE

YIELD: **4 servings (4 ounces per serving)**

PREP TIME: **5 minutes**

COOK TIME: **8 minutes**

This simple side dish is a great accompaniment to just about any entrée.

2 tablespoons extra-virgin olive oil, for the pan

1 pound fresh (not frozen) riced cauliflower (about 4 cups)

¼ cup chopped fresh parsley

1 clove garlic, minced

½ teaspoon fine sea salt

¼ teaspoon ground black pepper

Lime or lemon wedges, for serving (optional)

1. Heat the oil in a large skillet over medium heat. Add the riced cauliflower and sauté for 2 to 3 minutes, until lightly browned. Cover and steam for 5 minutes, or until tender. Remove the pan from the heat.

2. Stir in the parsley, garlic, salt, and pepper. Serve immediately with lime or lemon wedges, if desired.

3. Store leftovers in an airtight container in the refrigerator for up to 5 days or in the freezer for up to 2 months.

For the meal plan

If following the keto track, freeze three servings for after you've completed the plan; if following the low-carb track, refrigerate one serving for Day 5 and freeze the remaining two servings for later in the plan. Store individual servings in airtight containers in the freezer; this will make it easier to pull out and defrost a serving whenever you need one.

NUTRITION INFO:
calories **95** | fat **7g** | protein **2g** | total carbs **7g** | dietary fiber **2g** | net carbs **5g**

CHEDDAR AND BACON-STUFFED BURGERS

YIELD: **4 burgers (1 per serving)**

PREP TIME: **15 minutes**

COOK TIME: **variable (depends on cooking method and preferred doneness)**

In this recipe, I give you two tried-and-true cooking options for making delicious stuffed burgers. The air fryer method takes a bit longer than grilling, but both methods are foolproof! Although I use a burger press to make the patties perfectly round, you can certainly make them without one. During the detox, you will enjoy these burgers on Cloud Bread Rolls (page 126). Feel free to use any fixings you like; just remember to factor in the additional nutrition information.

1¼ pounds ground beef

½ teaspoon fine sea salt

½ teaspoon dried onion flakes or dried minced onion

¼ teaspoon garlic powder

¼ teaspoon mustard powder

¼ teaspoon paprika

¼ teaspoon ground black pepper

½ cup shredded cheddar cheese

4 pieces Easy Bacon (page 144), roughly chopped

1. Put the ground beef and all the seasonings in a large bowl and mix with your hands until combined. Divide into four 5-ounce portions and shape into balls.

2. To stuff the burgers, take a ball and separate it into two uneven pieces: one 3-ounce piece and one 2-ounce piece. Use the larger piece to form the bottom patty, pressing it into a 4-inch circle. Make a well in the center of the bottom patty, then place 2 tablespoons of the cheese in the well. Top with one-quarter of the bacon. Flatten the remaining 2-ounce piece of ground beef until it's large enough to cover the stuffed bottom patty. Place atop the bottom patty and seal the edges together. Repeat this process for the remaining burgers.

3. **To grill the burgers,** preheat a gas or charcoal grill to 450°F to 500°F, or until hot enough that you can hold your hand above the grates for only about 1 second. Place the stuffed burgers on the grill grate over direct heat and cook to your desired doneness, following the cook time and temperature guidance opposite. Serve immediately.

To air-fry the burgers, preheat an air fryer to 375°F. Place the stuffed burgers in the air fryer basket. Air-fry for 8 minutes. Flip the burgers over and air-fry for an additional 6 minutes. The burgers should be medium done; check the temperature in the center of a burger with a meat thermometer to determine doneness, using the temperature guidance opposite. Serve immediately.

4. Store leftovers in an airtight container in the refrigerator for up to 3 days or in the freezer for up to 2 months. To reheat, warm a burger in a small skillet over medium heat for about 5 minutes, flipping over once, or air-fry at 350°F for 3 to 4 minutes.

NUTRITION INFO:
calories **513** | fat **42g** | protein **31g** | total carbs **1g** | dietary fiber **1g** | net carbs **0g**

You'll be eating one burger for dinner on Day 3. Store two in the refrigerator to enjoy as leftovers, and freeze one for after you've completed the plan.

medium burgers:	6 to 7 minutes total (for grilling); internal temp. of 145°F
well-done burgers:	8 to 9 minutes total (for grilling); internal temp. of 160°F

CHICKEN CAULIFLOWER FRIED RICE

YIELD: **4 servings (12 ounces per serving)**

PREP TIME: **20 minutes**

COOK TIME: **20 minutes**

When you're craving Chinese food, this easy fried rice recipe really hits the spot! It comes together even quicker if you use store-bought rotisserie chicken. Leftovers can easily be frozen and enjoyed after the detox.

4 tablespoons avocado oil, divided

4 large eggs, beaten

1 pound fresh (not frozen) riced cauliflower (about 4 cups)

⅓ cup chopped scallions, plus more sliced on the bias for garnish

¼ cup diced carrots

1 tablespoon grated fresh ginger

3 cloves garlic, minced

⅓ cup coconut aminos

12 ounces boneless, skinless chicken breasts, cooked and diced (about 2½ cups)

1. Heat a large skillet over medium-high heat. Pour in 1 tablespoon of the oil.

2. Add the eggs to the hot skillet and scramble until done to your liking, then remove and set aside.

3. Heat 2 more tablespoons of the oil in the skillet, then add the riced cauliflower, scallions, carrots, ginger, and garlic. Cook, stirring constantly, until the vegetables are tender, about 5 minutes.

4. Combine the remaining tablespoon of oil with the coconut aminos and stir the mixture into the skillet. Add the chicken and toss. Cook for 1 to 2 minutes to heat the chicken through.

5. Return the eggs to the pan and stir to combine. Enjoy immediately, garnished with sliced scallions.

6. Store leftovers in an airtight container in the refrigerator for up to 3 days or in the freezer for up to 1 month.

NUTRITION INFO:
calories **358** | fat **21g** | protein **27g** | total carbs **12g** | dietary fiber **3g** | net carbs **9g**

CHICKEN CHILI STUFFED PEPPERS

YIELD: 4 servings
PREP TIME: 15 minutes
COOK TIME: 45 minutes

A delicious meal stuffed into a perfectly portioned package! For the meal plan, you'll be enjoying just one of these peppers, on Day 27; however, they freeze beautifully, making them a great meal prep option to be enjoyed later as an easy lunch or dinner.

4 medium bell peppers (about 5 ounces each, any color)

1 tablespoon extra-virgin olive oil

¼ teaspoon fine sea salt

FOR THE FILLING

1 tablespoon extra-virgin olive oil

1 pound ground chicken

2 tablespoons salted butter or avocado oil

3 ounces diced yellow onions (about 1 medium onion)

1 clove garlic, minced

6 ounces Palmini rice, drained and rinsed

1 (4-ounce) can chopped mild green chiles, drained

1 cup low-carb marinara sauce, store-bought or homemade (page 172), plus more for topping if desired

½ teaspoon ground cumin

½ teaspoon ground dried oregano

½ teaspoon fine sea salt

¼ teaspoon ground black pepper

1 cup shredded cheddar cheese, divided (optional)

1 tablespoon chopped fresh parsley, for garnish (optional)

1. Preheat the oven to 375°F.

2. Cut off the tops of the peppers and remove the seeds and membranes; set the tops aside. Rub the peppers inside and out with the oil, then sprinkle the insides with the salt. Place the peppers, cut side down, on a rimmed baking sheet. Bake until tender, 15 to 20 minutes.

3. Meanwhile, make the filling: Cut around the stems of the reserved pepper tops to remove them; dice the tops. Set aside.

4. Heat the oil in a large skillet over medium heat. Add the ground chicken and cook, stirring often to crumble it, until nicely browned, about 8 minutes. Remove from the pan and set aside.

5. Add the butter to the skillet, still over medium heat. Add the diced pepper tops, onions, and garlic and sauté until the vegetables are soft and translucent, about 5 minutes.

6. Stir in the rice, green chiles, marinara sauce, cumin, oregano, salt, and pepper. Cook until the rice is tender but still has some bite, 6 to 8 minutes. Stir in the cooked chicken and ½ cup of the cheese, if using.

7. Nestle the cooked peppers, cut side up, in a medium baking dish. Evenly spoon the filling into the peppers. If desired, spread a spoonful of marinara sauce over the filling in each pepper. Cover and bake until heated through, about 20 minutes. If using cheese, uncover, top with the remaining ½ cup of cheese, and bake until the cheese is melted, about 5 minutes more. Garnish with the parsley, if desired, and serve immediately.

8. Store leftovers in an airtight container in the refrigerator for up to 2 days, or wrap in parchment paper and then aluminum foil, seal in a plastic bag, and freeze for up to 3 months. Defrost frozen peppers in the refrigerator overnight, then reheat on a rimmed baking sheet in a preheated 350°F oven for 20 to 30 minutes.

NUTRITION INFO:
calories **382** | fat **26g** | protein **23g** | total carbs **16g** | dietary fiber **5g** | net carbs **11g**

CHICKEN KIEV MEATBALLS

YIELD: 12 meatballs (3 per serving)

PREP TIME: 20 minutes

COOK TIME: 18 minutes

A nice change from your typical meatballs. For the meal plan, you'll be eating just one serving; however, these meatballs freeze beautifully, making them a great meal prep option to enjoy as an easy lunch or dinner after you complete the detox. To accompany these meatballs, you'll be making use of leftover mashed cauliflower; once you've completed the plan, you might try them with my Egg Noodles (page 150) or low-carb rice, such as shirataki or cauliflower (see pages 210 and 112).

FOR THE MEATBALLS

1½ pounds boneless, skinless chicken breasts

1 large egg, beaten

¼ cup chopped fresh parsley

¼ cup ground flaxseed

FOR THE FILLING

2 ounces full-fat cream cheese, softened

½ cup shredded pepper Jack or Monterey Jack cheese

1 clove garlic, minced

¼ teaspoon dried dill weed

¼ teaspoon smoked paprika

⅛ teaspoon fine sea salt

¼ cup chopped fresh parsley

FOR THE COATING

1 cup pork rind crumbs (see Note, opposite)

2 tablespoons avocado oil or coconut oil, for the pan

1. Preheat the oven to 350°F. Line a rimmed baking sheet with parchment paper.

2. Prepare the meatballs: Clean the chicken of any tendons or fat. Place in a food processor and pulse until chopped. Add the egg, parsley, and ground flaxseed and process to combine. Transfer to a bowl.

3. Form the mixture into 12 meatballs about 3 inches in diameter. Place the meatballs on the prepared baking sheet and set aside.

4. Make the filling: Using a stand mixer fitted with the paddle attachment, or a mixing bowl and an electric hand mixer, blend the filling ingredients on high speed until combined. Use a small cookie scoop to make 12 balls.

5. Holding a meatball in your hand, insert a cheese ball into the center of the meatball. Wrap around as much as possible to enclose the cheese in the meatball. Repeat with the remaining meatballs and filling.

6. Roll each stuffed meatball in the pork rind crumbs.

7. Heat the oil in a large skillet over medium-high heat. Fry the coated meatballs in the hot oil until browned all around, about 3 minutes.

8. Transfer the meatballs to the prepared baking sheet and bake for 15 minutes, or until the chicken is no longer pink inside.

9. Store leftovers in an airtight container in the refrigerator for up to 3 days or in the freezer for up to 1 month.

NUTRITION INFO:
calories **575** | fat **36g** | protein **44g** | total carbs **4g** | dietary fiber **2g** | net carbs **2g**

Note ————————————————

When finely ground, pork rinds are a useful low-carb swap for breadcrumbs or panko. To save time, I buy preground pork rind crumbs (aka pork panko); see page 288 for my preferred brands. If you wish, you can make pork rind crumbs at home by pulsing pork rinds in a food processor until they become fine crumbs.

CHICKEN MUSHROOM SKILLET

YIELD: **2 servings (6 ounces per serving)**

PREP TIME: **10 minutes**

COOK TIME: **20 minutes**

This recipe is a winner! It's very popular on my website because it's a comforting classic that is quick to get onto the table.

1 tablespoon salted butter, divided

1 tablespoon extra-virgin olive oil, divided

8 ounces chicken tenderloins

1 teaspoon fine sea salt

½ teaspoon ground black pepper

4 ounces cremini mushrooms, thickly sliced

2 tablespoons chopped fresh parsley, plus more for garnish if desired

1 clove garlic, crushed to a paste

¼ cup chicken bone broth

¼ cup heavy cream

2 tablespoons sour cream

1. Heat ½ tablespoon of the butter and ½ tablespoon of the oil in a medium heavy skillet over medium-high heat.

2. Season the chicken with the salt and pepper and sear in batches until browned on all sides and no longer pink in the center, about 10 minutes total. Remove from the pan and set aside.

3. Add the remaining butter and oil to the skillet and cook the mushrooms until browned, about 5 minutes.

4. Add the parsley, garlic, and broth; use a wooden spoon to deglaze the pan, scraping all the good stuff from the bottom.

5. Add the heavy cream and sour cream and simmer until the sauce starts to thicken. Do not allow it to boil, or the cream could break.

6. Return the chicken to the pan and toss it in the sauce. Simmer for 5 minutes, until the chicken is nicely coated. Garnish with more parsley before serving, if desired.

7. Store leftovers in an airtight container in the refrigerator for up to 3 days or in the freezer for up to 1 month.

NUTRITION INFO:
calories **400** | fat **29g** | protein **27g** | total carbs **5g** | dietary fiber **1g** | net carbs **4g**

CHIMICHURRI

YIELD: **about 1 cup**
(2 tablespoons per serving)
PREP TIME: **10 minutes**

My husband calls chimichurri a party in your mouth. It's a classic on steak (see page 192) but can also be enjoyed on chicken or even used as a marinade.

1½ ounces finely chopped shallots (about 1 large shallot)

1 Fresno chili pepper, finely chopped

5 cloves garlic, thinly sliced or minced

¼ cup red wine vinegar

1 teaspoon fine sea salt

½ cup chopped fresh parsley

¼ cup chopped fresh cilantro

½ teaspoon ground black pepper

½ teaspoon ground dried oregano

½ cup extra-virgin olive oil

1. Combine the shallots, chili pepper, garlic, vinegar, and salt in a small bowl. Let sit for about 5 minutes to allow the flavors to release into the vinegar.

2. Stir in the parsley, cilantro, black pepper, and oregano, then, while whisking continuously, slowly pour in the oil.

3. Store leftover chimichurri in an airtight container in the refrigerator for up to 1 month or in a silicone ice cube tray in the freezer for up to 3 months.

NUTRITION INFO:
calories **128** | fat **14g** | protein **1g** | total carbs **1g** | dietary fiber **1g** | net carbs **0g**

CLOUD BREAD ROLLS

YIELD: **8 rolls (1 per serving)**

PREP TIME: **15 minutes**

COOK TIME: **30 minutes**

You can turn these rolls into a loaf and you will get 12 slices. Check my website, www.sugarfreemom.com, for tips and tricks for making a Cloud Bread Loaf. For this detox, however, it's a lot easier to make rolls.

6 large eggs, separated

½ teaspoon cream of tartar

½ cup avocado oil mayonnaise

1 cup unflavored egg white protein powder

¼ cup liquid allulose

½ teaspoon baking powder

¼ teaspoon fine sea salt

Sesame seeds, for topping (optional)

SPECIAL EQUIPMENT:

Silicone hamburger bun pan with 8 or more cavities (optional)

For the meal plan ——

Refrigerate one roll for Day 4 and freeze the remainder for later in the plan and afterward.

1. Place a rack in the middle position in the oven. Preheat the oven to 300°F. Line a rimmed baking sheet with parchment paper, or have on hand a silicone hamburger bun pan (the latter will help the rolls hold their shape better).

2. Put the egg whites in a stand mixer fitted with the whisk attachment. Add the cream of tartar and whip until stiff peaks form, 10 to 15 minutes. Set aside.

3. Put the egg yolks in a blender with the remaining ingredients and blend until well combined.

4. Spoon the yolk mixture, a little at a time, into the egg whites and mix on low speed until it's all incorporated.

5. If using a baking sheet, use a silicone spatula to form the batter into 8 equal-size mounds and place them on the prepared baking sheet. With the spatula, do your best to shape the mounds into circles about 4 inches in diameter. If using a silicone bun pan, fill 8 cavities with batter to reach the edges; do not flatten the batter. Top the rolls with sesame seeds, if desired.

6. Bake on the middle rack for 25 to 30 minutes, or until a toothpick inserted in the center of a roll comes out clean. Turn off the oven but do not open the door; leave the rolls in the oven for 10 minutes more.

7. Remove from the oven and allow the rolls to cool completely on the baking sheet or in the hamburger bun pan. Once cool, remove them from the pan.

8. Store the rolls in a resealable plastic bag with parchment paper layered between them so they don't stick together. They will keep for up to 1 week in the refrigerator or up to 3 months in the freezer.

NUTRITION INFO:
calories **197** | fat **15g** | protein **14g** | total carbs **1g** | dietary fiber **1g** | net carbs **0g**

COBB RANCH SALAD

YIELD: **1 serving**

PREP TIME: **12 minutes**

This hearty salad full of protein and healthy fat will keep you satiated for hours.

2 ounces romaine lettuce, chopped (about 1 cup)

2 pieces Easy Bacon (page 144)

2½ ounces shredded rotisserie chicken, white or dark meat (about ⅓ cup) (see Note)

2 ounces diced Hass avocado (about ¼ avocado)

2 ounces sliced tomato (about ⅓ medium tomato)

2 Easy-Peel Hard-Boiled Eggs (page 146), peeled and halved

¼ cup crumbled blue cheese (optional)

FOR THE RANCH SEASONING

(Makes ½ heaping cup)

¼ cup dried parsley

2 tablespoons dried minced garlic

2 tablespoons onion powder

1 tablespoon dried dill weed

1 teaspoon ground black pepper

FOR THE RANCH DRESSING

1½ teaspoons Ranch Seasoning (from above)

1½ tablespoons avocado oil mayonnaise

1 tablespoon water

⅛ teaspoon fine sea salt

1. Arrange the lettuce on a serving plate. Top with the bacon, chicken, avocado, tomato, hard-boiled egg halves, and blue cheese, if using.

2. Put the ranch seasoning ingredients in a small lidded jar. Cover and shake to combine.

3. Make the dressing: Mix 1½ teaspoons of the ranch seasoning with the mayonnaise, water, and salt.

4. To serve, drizzle the dressing over the salad and enjoy immediately. Store leftover ranch seasoning in the pantry for up to 6 months.

 Note

To save a step, I like to use rotisserie chicken for this recipe. If cooking the chicken yourself, you'll need 3½ ounces of raw boneless, skinless chicken.

NUTRITION INFO:
calories **629** | fat **52g** | protein **35g** | total carbs **12g** | dietary fiber **6g** | net carbs **6g**

CORNED BEEF HASH SKILLET WITH EGGS

option

YIELD: 4 servings (7 ounces per serving)

PREP TIME: 15 minutes

COOK TIME: 3½ hours

Breakfast for dinner is always a nice change. You'll be enjoying this "brinner" twice during the meal plan; I suggest you freeze the remaining two servings of hash for a lazy weekend breakfast later. Keep this recipe up your sleeve for after the plan; it's a great option for entertaining, when you want to cook up a larger skillet all at once for friends or family, as shown.

1 pound corned beef brisket, ready-to-cook (see Notes)

8 ounces daikon radish, peeled and cut into ¼-inch dice (about 2 cups)

¼ cup (½ stick) salted butter or avocado oil

3 ounces diced yellow onions (about 1 medium)

¼ cup chopped scallions

¼ cup chopped fresh parsley, plus more for garnish if desired

¼ cup chicken bone broth

4 large eggs (see Notes)

Salt and pepper

1. Fill a large pot with cold water, then add the corned beef. Bring to a boil, then lower the heat and simmer gently for 3 hours, or until the meat is fork-tender. In the last 30 minutes of cooking, drop in the radish to cook until tender. Once the corned beef is done, remove it from the pot and cut it into ½-inch cubes; once the radish is done, drain it and set it aside.

2. Preheat the oven to 400°F.

3. Melt the butter in a large skillet over medium-high heat. Add the onions and sauté for 5 minutes, or until softened, then add the corned beef and cook until it starts to brown, about 3 minutes.

4. Add the radish and brown for 5 to 6 minutes. Stir in the scallions, parsley, and broth.

5. Scoop one-quarter of the hash into a 3½- to 4-inch oven-safe skillet, mini cocotte, or 5-ounce ramekin. Use a large spoon to make a well in the center of the hash. Crack an egg into the well.

6. Place the skillet in the oven and bake until the egg white is set and the yolk is runny, 8 to 12 minutes. Season with salt and pepper to taste and garnish with parsley, if desired.

7. Refrigerate one-quarter of the remaining hash (it will keep in an airtight container for up to 3 days) and freeze the rest; frozen hash will keep for up to 2 months. Repeat Step 6 with the refrigerated portion of hash and another egg on Day 13 of the meal plan.

Notes

Don't have time to cook a corned beef? You can buy a precooked corned beef or cook up some ground chorizo or Italian sausage instead.

You will need just half of the hash and two eggs for the meal plan. Freeze the remaining hash for after the plan. You could also portion out each serving in its own container or resealable plastic bag to make thawing a single serving easier. Remember to have two more eggs on hand to enjoy along with the leftover hash.

NUTRITION INFO:
calories **423** | fat **33g** | protein **24g** | total carbs **6g** | dietary fiber **2g** | net carbs **4g**

CREAMY CILANTRO LIME SLAW

YIELD: **2 servings (3 ounces per serving)**

PREP TIME: **20 minutes, plus at least 1 hour to chill**

This quick-and-easy side is so versatile that it goes with pretty much any entrée. If you're following the keto track, you'll be eating just one serving; if you don't have someone to offer the leftover serving to, I suggest you cut this recipe in half to avoid food waste. To save time, you can use preshredded coleslaw mix; you'll need half of a 12-ounce bag.

3 ounces shredded green cabbage (about 1 cup)

3 ounces shredded red cabbage (about 1 cup)

¼ cup avocado oil mayonnaise

1 tablespoon white wine vinegar

¼ teaspoon grated lime zest

1 tablespoon fresh lime juice

⅛ teaspoon fine sea salt

⅛ teaspoon ground black pepper

2 tablespoons chopped fresh cilantro

1. Put the green and red cabbage in a medium bowl and set aside.

2. Make the dressing: In a small bowl, whisk together the mayonnaise, vinegar, lime zest, lime juice, salt, and pepper. Stir in the cilantro.

3. Pour the dressing over the cabbage and toss until well combined. Taste and adjust the seasonings, if desired.

4. Refrigerate the slaw for at least 1 hour or up to 24 hours before serving. Serve chilled.

5. Store leftovers in an airtight container in the refrigerator for up to 3 days.

NUTRITION INFO:
calories **236** | fat **24g** | protein **1g** | total carbs **8g** | dietary fiber **3g** | net carbs **5g**

CRISPY BROCCOLI

YIELD: **2 servings (4 ounces per serving)**

PREP TIME: **5 minutes**

COOK TIME: **15 or 40 minutes** (depending on cooking method)

8 ounces broccoli florets (1 medium head broccoli)

1 tablespoon extra-virgin olive oil

¼ teaspoon onion powder

¼ teaspoon fine sea salt

¼ teaspoon ground black pepper

Whether you decide to use the oven or an air fryer, either method will produce deliciously crispy broccoli florets! After you've completed the meal plan, I suggest you serve them with my Spicy Mayo (page 222) as a dipping sauce. It's a winning combo!

Oven Directions:

1. Preheat the oven to 400°F.

2. Put the broccoli florets in a bowl and toss with the oil. Lay the florets on a rimmed baking sheet. Sprinkle with the seasonings and toss again. Spread the florets back out, making sure they are not touching.

3. Bake until crispy and browned, 30 to 40 minutes. Enjoy hot.

4. Store leftovers in an airtight container in the refrigerator for up to 3 days. Reheat in a preheated 350°F oven for 10 minutes.

Air Fryer Directions:

1. Preheat an air fryer to 400°F.

2. Put the broccoli florets in a bowl and toss with the oil. Sprinkle with the seasonings and toss again. Spread the florets in a single layer in the air fryer basket. Depending on the size of your air fryer, you may need to cook them in two batches to avoid crowding them.

3. Air-fry until crispy and browned, 10 to 15 minutes. Enjoy hot.

4. Store leftovers in an airtight container in the refrigerator for up to 3 days. Reheat in the air fryer at 350°F for 5 minutes.

NUTRITION INFO:
calories **102** | fat **7g** | protein **3g** | total carbs **8g** | dietary fiber **3g** | net carbs **5g**

CRUSTLESS HAM AND CHEESE QUICHES

YIELD: **2 servings**

PREP TIME: **15 minutes**

COOK TIME: **30 minutes**

2 ounces cooked ham

2 large eggs

⅓ cup heavy cream

½ cup shredded mozzarella cheese

⅛ teaspoon fine sea salt

Generous pinch of ground black pepper

Chopped fresh parsley, for garnish (optional)

SPECIAL EQUIPMENT:

2 (5-ounce) quiche dishes or (7-ounce) ramekins

These small quiches are creamy and delicious and perfectly portioned. You'll be completely satisfied with this meal for breakfast or lunch.

1. Preheat the oven to 350°F. Grease two 5-ounce quiche dishes or 7-ounce ramekins with butter. Place the dishes on a small rimmed baking sheet.

2. Chop the ham and place 1 ounce in each dish.

3. In a medium bowl, whisk together the eggs, heavy cream, cheese, salt, and pepper. Pour half of the egg mixture into each dish.

4. Bake for 30 minutes, or until the centers are set but still slightly jiggly. Serve garnished with parsley, if desired.

5. Store leftovers covered in the refrigerator for up to 3 days. Reheat in a preheated 350°F oven for 10 minutes or microwave for 1 minute.

NUTRITION INFO:
calories **336** | fat **26g** | protein **19g** | total carbs **2g** | dietary fiber **1g** | net carbs **1g**

CRUSTLESS SKILLET SUPREME PIZZA

YIELD: **2 servings**

PREP TIME: **10 minutes**

COOK TIME: **15 minutes**

If you're craving pizza, this recipe hits the spot. The best part of any pizza is the toppings anyway!

6 ounces ground pork

½ teaspoon ground dried oregano

½ teaspoon dried parsley

¼ teaspoon fine sea salt

¼ teaspoon ground black pepper

2½ ounces chopped green bell pepper (about ½ large pepper)

3 ounces chopped yellow onions (about 1 medium)

2 ounces cooked ham, diced

1 cup low-carb marinara sauce, store-bought or homemade (page 172)

1 cup shredded mozzarella cheese

1 ounce sliced pepperoni

2 pieces Easy Bacon (page 144), diced

¼ cup grated Parmesan or shredded cheddar cheese (optional)

Chopped fresh parsley, for garnish (optional)

1. Heat a medium cast-iron skillet over medium-high heat. Cook the ground pork until nicely browned, about 5 minutes, stirring to crumble it as it cooks. Stir in the oregano, dried parsley, salt, and pepper.

2. Lower the heat to medium, push the cooked pork to one side of the skillet, and add the bell pepper and onions. Cook until softened, about 5 minutes. Stir together with the pork.

3. Stir in the ham, marinara sauce, and mozzarella cheese until well combined.

4. Sprinkle the pepperoni and bacon over the top, then turn off the heat. Sprinkle with the grated Parmesan and garnish with fresh parsley, if desired.

5. Divide the pizza into 2 servings.

6. Store leftovers in an airtight container in the refrigerator for up to 3 days.

NUTRITION INFO:
calories **730** | fat **57g** | protein **43g** | total carbs **13g** | dietary fiber **3g** | net carbs **10g**

DAIRY-FREE MINI WAFFLES

YIELD: **4 mini waffles (2 per serving)**

PREP TIME: **2 minutes**

COOK TIME: **12 minutes**

These dairy-free mini waffles are my take on the famous "chaffles" made with cheese and egg. I wanted a version just as tasty and savory, but without the cheese, so my daughter could enjoy these as a sandwich or for breakfast. They make a fantastic breakfast sandwich (see page 242), as you'll find out on Day 4 of the meal plan!

1 tablespoon avocado oil mayonnaise

1½ tablespoons coconut flour

1 tablespoon unflavored gelatin powder

Pinch of fine sea salt

3 large eggs

TOPPINGS (OPTIONAL)

Butter

Sugar-free maple syrup, store-bought or homemade (page 232)

Fresh berries of choice

SPECIAL EQUIPMENT:

Mini waffle maker

1. Preheat a mini waffle maker according to the manufacturer's instructions.

2. Whisk together the mayonnaise, coconut flour, gelatin, and salt to make a very thick batter with a pastelike texture. Smooth out all the lumps as best you can, then whisk in one egg at a time. Alternatively, you can put all the ingredients in a blender and blend until smooth.

3. Grease the hot waffle maker with avocado oil cooking spray and pour one-quarter of the batter into the center. Close the lid and follow the manufacturer's instructions to cook the waffle until golden brown, typically 2 to 3 minutes. Repeat with the remaining batter, regreasing the waffle maker before each waffle, to make a total of 4 waffles.

4. Enjoy with toppings, if desired, or toast for a sandwich.

5. Store leftovers in an airtight container in the refrigerator for up to 5 days or in the freezer for up to 1 month.

NUTRITION INFO:
calories **192** | fat **14g** | protein **13g** | total carbs **4g** | dietary fiber **2g** | net carbs **2g**

DEVILED EGGS

YIELD: **1 serving**
PREP TIME: **5 minutes**

Deviled eggs for breakfast? Yes! These deliciously creamy eggs are a great start to the day, but of course you can also serve them as an appetizer or snack.

2 Easy-Peel Hard-Boiled Eggs (page 146), peeled

2 tablespoons avocado oil mayonnaise

1 tablespoon chopped fresh parsley, plus more for garnish if desired

1 teaspoon prepared yellow mustard

¼ teaspoon paprika, plus more for garnish if desired

⅛ teaspoon celery salt

Salt and pepper to taste

1. Slice the eggs in half lengthwise and scoop the yolks into a small bowl; set the whites on a plate.

2. Add the remaining ingredients to the yolks. Using a fork, mash the yolks as you stir everything together. Taste and adjust the salt and pepper as needed.

3. Scoop the yolk mixture into the egg whites. Sprinkle with more paprika and/or chopped parsley, if desired. Enjoy immediately.

4. The eggs can be made ahead and stored in an airtight container in the refrigerator for up to 3 days.

NUTRITION INFO:
calories **182** | fat **13g** | protein **13g** | total carbs **2g** | dietary fiber **1g** | net carbs **1g**

EASY BACON

YIELD: variable (two ½-ounce cooked slices per serving)

PREP TIME: 1 minute

COOK TIME: 8 to 20 minutes per batch (depending on cooking method and preferred doneness)

Learning how to make bacon perfectly in the oven and air fryer is a game changer! I use this method often to cook a week's worth of bacon, ready to be crumbled on salads or reheated and enjoyed alongside an egg for breakfast. I've given the number of slices as a range to give you the option to cook all the bacon you'll need for the entire 30 days of the plan, cook the amount needed every 5 days, or split the difference and cook a large batch at the start of the plan and another large batch on Day 15. Of course, you can also cook one slice here, two slices there. But I suggest you take advantage of meal prepping and cook, at a minimum, what you'll need for 5 days at a time. Note that a 1-pound package of thick-cut bacon contains an average of 8 to 12 slices; it depends on the exact thickness of the cut.

9 to 24/25 slices thick-cut uncured bacon (see meal prep chart, opposite)

Oven Directions:

1. Place an oven rack in the bottom position. Preheat the oven to 400°F.

2. Lay the bacon slices on a rimmed baking sheet, with none overlapping.

3. Place the pan on the lower rack of the oven. Bake for 15 minutes for soft, chewy bacon or 20 minutes for crispy bacon.

4. Drain the slices on a paper towel–lined plate.

Air Fryer Directions:

1. Preheat an air fryer to 350°F.

2. Cut the bacon in half crosswise if needed to fit. Place the bacon in a single layer in the air fryer basket; cook in batches if needed.

3. Air-fry for 8 to 9 minutes for chewy bacon or 12 to 14 minutes for crispy bacon. If cooking in multiple batches, remove the fat from the drip pan between batches.

Store the bacon in the refrigerator for up to 5 days or in the freezer for up to 1 month. I prefer to reheat cooked bacon in my air fryer at 350°F for 1 to 2 minutes, but you can also reheat slices in a skillet over medium-high heat.

NUTRITION INFO:
calories **296** | fat **28g** | protein **9g** | total carbs **1g** | dietary fiber **0g** | net carbs **1g**

Notes

If you want to cook a large batch of bacon, the oven method is more efficient since most air fryer baskets cannot accommodate more than three or four slices. In fact, you can bake two pans of bacon at once, placing one pan on the bottom rack and the second on the rack just above. Note that the top pan of bacon may require a couple extra minutes of baking time to become crispy.

When shopping, look for bacon with no sugar added; avoid brands that are cured with sugar. One of my favorites is Pederson's Farms No Sugar Added Hickory Smoked Uncured Bacon.

EASY BACON MEAL PREPPING

Cook day in meal plan	Total slices cooked per 5-day increment	Total slices cooked if making 2 large batches	Total slices cooked for entire meal plan
DAY 3	9	15 (freeze 6 slices for later)	24 or 25* (freeze 15 or 16** slices for later)
DAY 9	6		
DAY 15	5 (omit 1 slice if low-carb)	9 (freeze 4 or 5** slices for later)	
DAY 24	4 or 5*		

*Cook 25 or 5 slices if following the low-carb track.
**Freeze 16 or 5 slices for later if following the low-carb track.

EASY-PEEL HARD-BOILED EGGS

YIELD: **4 eggs (2 per serving)**

PREP TIME: **1 minute**

COOK TIME: **6 to 10 minutes** (depending on method)

I will never boil eggs in a pot on the stove again now that I have perfected this Instant Pot method. The steam created in the process permeates the shells, making them easier to remove. This, along with plunging the eggs into an ice bath immediately after cooking, is the most important trick in peeling eggs without destroying the whites. No worries if you don't have an Instant Pot; I've also included stovetop directions.

4 large eggs

SPECIAL EQUIPMENT:

6-quart Instant Pot (optional)

Instant Pot Directions:

1. Put the insert rack in the Instant Pot. Fill the pot with water to just below the rack. Place the eggs on the rack and close the lid. Make sure the valve is set for sealing. Press Manual and set the timer for 6 minutes with low pressure.

2. Once the timer beeps, press Cancel and wait 1 minute. After 1 minute, use a long wooden spoon to move the valve to venting for quick release.

3. Once the pressure is down and the pin has dropped, carefully remove the lid. Be careful of the escaping steam. Remove the eggs with tongs and place in a bowl of ice water.

Stovetop Directions:

Place the eggs in a medium saucepan and fill with enough water to cover the eggs. Bring to a boil over medium heat and continue to cook at a low boil for 10 minutes. Remove the eggs with tongs and place in a bowl of ice water.

Once cool enough to handle, peel the eggs. Enjoy immediately or store in an airtight container in the refrigerator for up to 5 days.

For the meal plan

I suggest you make one batch of hard-boiled eggs on Day 6, one batch on Day 14, one batch on Day 23, and a half batch on Day 29 for the Cobb Ranch Salad (page 128).

NUTRITION INFO:
calories **143** | fat **10g** | protein **13g** | total carbs **1g** | dietary fiber **0g** | net carbs **1g**

EGG FOO YOUNG

YIELD: 2 servings (4 ounces per serving)

PREP TIME: 5 minutes

COOK TIME: 25 minutes

This is a fun lunch or dinner that makes you feel like you just ordered takeout!

FOR THE SAUCE

1 cup water

2 tablespoons coconut aminos

1 teaspoon extra-virgin olive oil

Pinch of ground white pepper

½ teaspoon glucomannan or xanthan gum

FOR THE OMELETS

4 large eggs

4 ounces ground chicken or turkey

2 cups bean sprouts

4 scallions, sliced (about ½ cup), plus more for garnish if desired

½ teaspoon fine sea salt

½ teaspoon ground white pepper

2 tablespoons avocado oil, for the pan

1 clove garlic, minced

Sesame seeds, for garnish (optional)

1. Make the sauce: Place the water, coconut aminos, olive oil, and pepper in a small saucepan. Bring to a simmer over medium heat, then sprinkle in the glucomannan. Continue to simmer, stirring constantly, until the sauce thickens to a thin syrupy consistency, 3 to 4 minutes. Remove the pan from the heat and set aside.

2. Make the omelets: Whisk the eggs in a medium bowl. Add the chicken and break apart into crumbles; you may need to use your hands. Add the sprouts, scallions, salt, and pepper and stir to combine.

3. Heat the avocado oil in a large skillet over medium-high heat. Add the garlic and sauté for just a minute, until fragrant.

4. Ladle ¼ cup of the egg mixture into the pan and use a wooden spoon or silicone spatula to pull the edges inward to form, as best you can, a round shape. Cook until the underside is lightly golden brown, about 2 minutes, then flip and cook the other side for 2 to 3 minutes, until the omelet is lightly golden on both sides and the chicken is no longer pink. Repeat with the remaining egg mixture to make a total of 4 omelets.

5. Serve 2 omelets on a plate with half of the sauce drizzled over them. Sprinkle with sesame seeds and scallions, if desired.

6. Store leftover sauce and omelets in separate airtight containers in the refrigerator for up to 3 days. Reheat the omelets in a small skillet over medium heat for about 5 minutes, flipping over once. Reheat the sauce in a small saucepan for 2 to 3 minutes, until warmed through.

NUTRITION INFO:
calories **417** | fat **29g** | protein **25g** | total carbs **14g** | dietary fiber **3g** | net carbs **11g**

EGG NOODLES

YIELD: **3 servings (3 ounces per serving)**

PREP TIME: **5 minutes**

COOK TIME: **30 minutes**

These easy, tasty egg noodles are dairy-free, gluten-free, and nut-free. You can also make them with egg whites rather than whole eggs. During the plan, the noodles are finished simply with a drizzle of olive oil and fresh herbs. After the plan, you can try them with my Roasted Garlic Cream Sauce (page 244).

6 teaspoons avocado oil or salted butter, for the pan

6 large eggs

1/3 cup chicken bone broth

1 teaspoon glucomannan or xanthan gum

1/2 teaspoon fine sea salt

1/4 teaspoon ground black pepper

FOR SERVING

1 tablespoon avocado oil or salted butter

1 tablespoon extra-virgin olive oil

1 tablespoon chopped fresh parsley or basil

1. Heat 1 teaspoon of the oil in a 6-inch skillet over medium heat. Put the eggs, broth, glucomannan, salt, and pepper in a blender and blend on high speed just until combined and free of lumps.

2. Pour 1/4 cup of the batter into the skillet and quickly swirl the pan until the batter reaches the edges. (Monitor the heat, lifting the pan off the heating element while swirling to allow the batter to spread; if the pan gets too hot, the batter will set up before it reaches the edges.) Allow the crepe to cook until the edges release easily, 2 to 3 minutes, then flip over carefully. Cook for another 2 to 3 minutes, until lightly browned.

3. Carefully remove the crepe to a sheet of parchment paper. Repeat the process to make a total of 6 crepes, regreasing the skillet with another teaspoon of oil after each crepe and pulsing the batter in the blender for 10 seconds before pouring. Stack the crepes on the parchment paper.

4. Using a pizza cutter or knife, slice the crepes into 1/4-inch strips to create "noodles."

5. Just before serving, heat 1 tablespoon of avocado oil in a skillet over medium-low heat. Add the noodles and cover for a few minutes to warm through. To serve, toss with the olive oil and parsley.

6. Store in an airtight container in the refrigerator for up to 3 days or in the freezer for up to 2 months. Thaw frozen noodles overnight before reheating. Once thawed, reheat in a dry skillet over medium heat until warmed through.

Note

You may use any type of skillet you like here. Nonstick skillets are popular for egg recipes such as this one; however, due to the chemicals used to create the nonstick surface in that type of skillet, I prefer stainless steel. To create a nonstick surface in a stainless-steel skillet, preheat the skillet before adding fat or oil. (Never preheat a nonstick skillet when dry.)

For the meal plan

Store one serving in the freezer to enjoy later in the plan if following the low-carb track, or after the plan if following the keto track. Store the rest in the refrigerator.

NUTRITION INFO:
calories **152** | fat **10g** | protein **14g** | total carbs **2g** | dietary fiber **1g** | net carbs **1g**

EGG SALAD

YIELD: **1 serving**

PREP TIME: **5 minutes**

This creamy egg salad is a weekly staple in my home. We most often enjoy it on lettuce or as a sandwich filling in a Cloud Bread Roll (page 126). When not following the meal plan, feel free to add another egg for even more protein!

2 Easy-Peel Hard-Boiled Eggs (page 146), peeled

2 tablespoons avocado oil mayonnaise

1 tablespoon dill relish (optional)

1 tablespoon finely diced red onions

1 teaspoon fresh lime juice

1 teaspoon Dijon or prepared yellow mustard

Salt and pepper to taste

Chop the eggs and place in a small bowl with the remaining ingredients. Stir to combine. The salad can be made ahead and stored in an airtight container in the refrigerator for up to 3 days.

NUTRITION INFO:
calories **372** | fat **36g** | protein **13g** | total carbs **3g** | dietary fiber **1g** | net carbs **2g**

EGGS BENEDICT

YIELD: 1 serving

PREP TIME: 7 minutes

COOK TIME: 10 minutes

A fancy upgrade from your typical egg breakfast with a luscious hollandaise sauce on top! Typically, hollandaise is made using lemon juice, but I prefer the bolder flavor of lime juice. If you prefer a subtler, more neutral-tasting sauce, use lemon juice; if you want something with an extra bite, go with lime. If making this dish to enjoy with another person, feel free to double the recipe.

FOR THE HOLLANDAISE SAUCE

3 tablespoons salted butter

1 large egg yolk

1 teaspoon fresh lime or lemon juice

1½ teaspoons heavy cream

Dash of cayenne pepper

Pinch of fine sea salt

Pinch of ground black pepper

1 teaspoon salted butter

½ Cloud Bread Roll (page 126), bottom or top

1 slice Canadian bacon

1½ teaspoons white vinegar

1 large egg

Chopped fresh parsley, for garnish (optional)

1. Make the hollandaise: In a small saucepan, melt the butter over low heat.

2. In a small bowl, whisk the egg yolk.

3. Add the lime juice, heavy cream, cayenne, salt, and pepper to the butter in the pan. Stir to combine.

4. Pour a spoonful of the melted butter mixture into the bowl with the yolk. Stir to slowly temper the egg and repeat until most of the butter mixture is no longer in the pan. This will prevent the yolk from curdling.

5. Once incorporated, pour the yolk mixture into the saucepan and continue to cook over low heat, stirring constantly, until the sauce starts to thicken. Once it coats the back of a spoon, remove the pan from the heat. Cover and set at the back of the stove to keep warm.

6. Prepare the rest of the ingredients: Melt the teaspoon of butter in a small skillet over medium heat. Toast the roll in the butter, then remove to a serving plate.

7. In the same skillet, cook the Canadian bacon for about 1 minute on each side, until browned around the edges. Place the slice on the toasted roll.

8. In a medium pot, bring 3 inches of water to a boil. Reduce the heat to maintain a gentle simmer, with small bubbles on the surface. Add the vinegar.

9. Crack the egg into a small bowl. Using a long-handled spoon, stir the water to form a whirlpool. Gently lower the egg into the center of the whirlpool. As carefully and quickly as you can, use the spoon to fold the white over the yolk as it spins. Continue to

NUTRITION INFO:
calories **683** | fat **41g** | protein **32g** | total carbs **3g** | dietary fiber **2g** | net carbs **1g**

stir around the edge of the pan to keep the whirlpool going. For a very runny yolk, cook the egg for 2 minutes; for a more solid yolk, cook for 4 to 5 minutes more. Remove the egg with a slotted spoon and place on the bacon.

10. Spoon the hollandaise sauce over the egg and garnish with parsley, if desired. Best served fresh.

FISH TACO BOWL

YIELD: **1 serving**

PREP TIME: **15 minutes**

COOK TIME: **8 minutes**

This fish taco bowl is a quick recipe yet is packed full of flavor and spice! The fish gets some heat from homemade taco seasoning, and the zesty and creamy chipotle lime dressing, from chipotle powder. The dressing is equally delicious on burgers or coleslaw. If you'd like to experiment with other uses, you can always double the dressing ingredients; the leftovers will keep for a couple of weeks in the refrigerator. If you're not a fan of spice, simply omit the chipotle powder.

FOR THE CREAMY CHIPOTLE LIME DRESSING

2½ tablespoons avocado oil mayonnaise

Grated zest of ½ lime

1½ teaspoons fresh lime juice

1 tablespoon apple cider vinegar

1 clove garlic, minced

¼ teaspoon chipotle powder

¼ teaspoon fine sea salt

FOR THE BOWL

1 (8-ounce) wild-caught skinless cod fillet

¼ teaspoon fine sea salt

1½ teaspoons Taco Seasoning (page 234)

1 tablespoon avocado oil, for the pan

2 ounces shredded green cabbage (about ⅔ cup)

1 ounce halved cherry tomatoes or diced tomatoes (about 2 cherry tomatoes or ¼ small tomato)

⅛ avocado (about 1 ounce), sliced

1 ounce sliced red onions (about ½ small onion)

1 scallion, sliced

½ lime, cut into wedges, for serving

Chopped fresh cilantro or parsley, for garnish (optional)

1. Make the dressing: Place all the dressing ingredients in a small bowl and whisk together. Taste and adjust the salt and chipotle powder as needed.

2. Season both sides of the cod fillet with the salt and allow to sit for 5 minutes. Pat dry with a paper towel. Rub half of the taco seasoning on one side of the fillet, then flip over and rub the remaining seasoning on the other side.

3. Heat the oil in a medium skillet over medium-high heat. Once hot, place the cod in the skillet and cook for 3 to 4 minutes on each side, or until the fish is no longer translucent and flakes easily with a fork.

4. Arrange the cabbage, tomatoes, avocado, red onions, and scallion in a serving bowl. Top with the fish and drizzle with the dressing. Serve with lime wedges and, if desired, garnish with cilantro. Best served fresh.

NUTRITION INFO:
calories **549** | fat **36g** | protein **44g** | total carbs **16g** | dietary fiber **6g** | net carbs **10g**

FRENCH ONION MEATBALLS

YIELD: **4 servings (6 ounces per serving)**

PREP TIME: **20 minutes**

COOK TIME: **35 minutes**

These tasty meatballs have all the flavors of French onion soup packed in a perfect size. This is comfort food all the way!

FOR THE MEATBALLS

1 pound ground pork

½ cup shredded mozzarella cheese

⅓ cup pork rind crumbs

1 tablespoon chopped fresh parsley, plus more for garnish

1 large egg

1 teaspoon minced garlic

1 teaspoon onion powder

¼ teaspoon fine sea salt

⅛ teaspoon ground black pepper

FOR THE SAUCE

¼ cup (½ stick) salted butter

10 ounces yellow onions (about 2 large onions)

2 cups beef bone broth

1 teaspoon minced garlic

¼ teaspoon fine sea salt

CHEESE TOPPING (OPTIONAL)

½ cup shredded mozzarella cheese

1. Preheat the oven to 425°F. Line a rimmed baking sheet with parchment paper.

2. Place all the meatball ingredients in a large bowl and mix thoroughly.

3. Using a large cookie scoop, form the meat mixture into 20 golf ball–size balls and place on the prepared pan.

4. Bake for 30 minutes, until browned.

5. While the meatballs cook, make the sauce: Melt the butter in a large deep-sided skillet over medium heat. Thinly slice the onions and cook in the butter until softened, 6 to 8 minutes.

6. Stir in the broth, garlic, and salt. Simmer until the sauce is reduced and thickened, about 5 minutes.

7. Nestle the meatballs in the sauce. If adding the cheese topping, top the meatballs with the cheese, remove the pan from the heat, cover with a lid, and let sit until the cheese is melted, about 5 minutes. Garnish with parsley and enjoy.

8. Store leftovers in an airtight container in the refrigerator for up to 5 days or in the freezer for up to 2 months.

For the meal plan

Store one serving in the refrigerator for Day 13 of the plan; stash the remaining two servings in the freezer to enjoy after you've completed the plan.

NUTRITION INFO:
calories **553** | fat **44g** | protein **31g** | total carbs **8g** | dietary fiber **1g** | net carbs **7g**

GARLIC BUTTER MUSHROOMS

YIELD: 4 servings (3 ounces per serving)

PREP TIME: 10 minutes

COOK TIME: 12 minutes

Another simple but delicious side dish to pair with any entrée.

12 ounces small cremini or button mushrooms

¼ cup (½ stick) salted butter

2 tablespoons extra-virgin olive oil

1½ ounces chopped shallots (about 1 large shallot)

2 tablespoons beef bone broth

4 cloves garlic, minced

2 tablespoons chopped fresh parsley

¼ teaspoon ground dried thyme

½ teaspoon fine sea salt

¼ teaspoon ground black pepper

1. Clean the mushrooms with a damp paper towel to remove any dirt. Cut about ⅛ inch off the stems. Set the mushrooms aside.

2. Heat the butter and oil in a large skillet over medium-high heat. Add the shallots and cook until softened, 3 to 4 minutes.

3. Add the mushrooms to the skillet and cook until golden brown, about 5 minutes.

4. Pour in the broth and cook for 1 to 2 minutes, or until the mushrooms have softened and the broth has reduced.

5. Stir in the garlic, parsley, and thyme and cook for another 1 to 2 minutes, until fragrant.

6. Season with the salt and pepper, then taste and adjust the seasoning if needed. Serve warm.

7. Store leftovers in an airtight container in the refrigerator for up to 5 days or in the freezer for up to 1 month.

For the meal plan

If following the keto track, stash two servings in the freezer to enjoy after completing the plan; if following the low-carb track, freeze one serving. Store the remaining portion in the refrigerator for later in the plan.

NUTRITION INFO:
calories **209** | fat **19g** | protein **4g** | total carbs **10g** | dietary fiber **2g** | net carbs **8g**

GARLIC BUTTER STEAK BITES

YIELD: **2 servings (7 ounces per serving)**

PREP TIME: **10 minutes**

COOK TIME: **8 minutes**

An easy recipe for garlic butter steak bites that are tender, juicy, and ready in under 20 minutes!

1 clove garlic, minced

2¼ tablespoons salted butter, softened

1 pound boneless sirloin steak

½ teaspoon fine sea salt

¼ teaspoon ground black pepper

1½ tablespoons chopped fresh parsley

1. Mix together the garlic and softened butter in a small bowl.

2. Trim the excess fat off the steak and cut the meat into 1½-inch cubes. Season with the salt and pepper.

3. Heat half of the garlic butter in a large cast-iron or nonstick skillet over medium-high heat. Add half of the steak cubes in a single layer, increase the heat to high, and cook without disturbing until browned on the bottom, about 2 minutes. Resist the urge to turn; turn only once browned.

4. Turn the steak and continue cooking until all sides are browned, about another 2 minutes. The steak should be medium done at this point; increase the cooking time if you prefer more well-done meat. Remove the steak from the pan and set aside on a plate.

5. Repeat with the remaining garlic butter and steak.

6. After cooking the second batch, return all the steak bites to the pan along with any accumulated juices. Toss with the parsley and serve.

7. Store leftovers in an airtight container in the refrigerator for up to 2 days.

NUTRITION INFO:
calories **423** | fat **23g** | protein **50g** | total carbs **1g** | dietary fiber **1g** | net carbs **0g**

GERMAN "POTATO" SALAD

YIELD: **2 servings (4 ounces per serving)**

PREP TIME: **10 minutes**

COOK TIME: **15 minutes**

This dish has all the flavors of a traditional potato salad, but don't be fooled; the flavor of radish does come through.

6 ounces daikon radish, peeled and ends trimmed

1/2 teaspoon fine sea salt

2 slices thick-cut bacon

1 1/2 ounces diced yellow onions (about 3/4 small onion)

2 tablespoons white vinegar

1 clove garlic, minced

1/4 teaspoon ground black pepper

1 tablespoon chopped fresh parsley

FOR SERVING (OPTIONAL)

1 tablespoon extra-virgin olive oil

Coarse sea salt

1. Cut the radish into 1/2-inch chunks and place in a medium pot. Cover with water and bring to a boil over medium-high heat. Once boiling, add the salt. Reduce the heat to a simmer and cook for 10 to 15 minutes, until the radish is fork-tender.

2. Once done, drain the radish and return it to the pot, with the burner turned off. This will help the excess water evaporate.

3. While the radish is simmering, chop the bacon into bite-size pieces and place in a large skillet over medium-high heat. Add the onions and cook until the bacon is crisp and the onions are softened, about 5 minutes.

4. Add the vinegar to the skillet and cook for 1 to 2 minutes more, scraping the bits of bacon from the bottom of the pan. Add the garlic and pepper and cook for about 30 seconds.

5. Add the drained radish to the skillet along with the parsley and stir to combine. Serve warm with a drizzle of olive oil and a sprinkle of coarse salt, if desired.

6. Store leftovers in an airtight container in the refrigerator for up to 3 days.

NUTRITION INFO:
calories **295** | fat **23g** | protein **9g** | total carbs **13g** | dietary fiber **4g** | net carbs **9g**

GRILLED ROMAINE SALAD

YIELD: **2 servings (4 ounces per serving)**

PREP TIME: **5 minutes**

COOK TIME: **5 minutes**

After the detox, you can enjoy this warm grilled salad with any protein you like. Reheat it or enjoy it cold the next day.

1 tablespoon extra-virgin olive oil

1 large or 2 small heads romaine lettuce (about 9 ounces), halved lengthwise

¼ teaspoon fine sea salt

⅛ teaspoon ground black pepper

⅛ teaspoon garlic powder

⅛ teaspoon onion powder

1 tablespoon shredded Parmesan cheese

1¾ ounces cherry tomatoes (2 to 3 tomatoes), halved

1 tablespoon balsamic vinegar

Red pepper flakes (optional)

1. Preheat a grill to between 450°F and 500°F, until it's hot enough that you can hold your hand above the grates for only about 1 second.

2. Drizzle the oil evenly over the cut sides of the romaine halves, then whisk together the salt and spices in a small bowl and sprinkle the seasoning over the cut sides.

3. Grill the romaine until wilted, about 5 minutes.

4. Remove the romaine from the grill and sprinkle on the cheese, tomatoes, balsamic vinegar, and red pepper flakes, if using. Serve immediately.

NUTRITION INFO:
calories **139** | fat **9g** | protein **5g** | total carbs **13g** | dietary fiber **7g** | net carbs **6g**

HOMEMADE KETCHUP

YIELD: 3¾ or 4¾ cups, depending on preparation method (¼ cup per serving)

PREP TIME: 5 minutes

COOK TIME: 20 minutes (for stovetop method)

This recipe makes a whole lot of ketchup, and you'll need just ¾ cup during the meal plan. So feel free to halve the ingredients if your family just doesn't use that much ketchup. However, you'll have plenty of time to use up a full batch, as this ketchup keeps for up to six months. I've given you two methods: blender and stovetop. I often use the blender method because it's quicker, but the stovetop method really marries all the flavors, giving the ketchup an unbeatable depth.

1 (28-ounce) can tomato puree

1 (6-ounce) can tomato paste

¼ cup apple cider vinegar

¼ cup red wine vinegar

2 tablespoons yacón syrup, or ¼ cup Swerve confectioners'-style sweetener

2 cloves garlic, minced

1 tablespoon extra-virgin olive oil

1 tablespoon dried minced onion

1 teaspoon fine sea salt

½ teaspoon dried oregano leaves

¼ teaspoon ground cloves

Stovetop Directions:

To make on the stovetop, place all the ingredients in a 5-quart enameled Dutch oven or other heavy nonreactive pot and stir to combine. Bring to a boil, then lower the heat and simmer until the ketchup is thickened and reduced by about half, 15 to 20 minutes. Use an immersion blender to blend the ketchup for a smoother texture. Taste and adjust the spices and sweetener, if desired. Allow to cool before storing. *Makes 3¾ cups.*

Blender Directions:

Place all the ingredients in a blender and pulse until the ketchup has the desired consistency. Taste and adjust the spices and sweetener, if desired. *Makes 4¾ cups.*

To store the ketchup, transfer it to a glass jar. It will keep in the refrigerator for up to 6 months.

NUTRITION INFO:
calories **15** | fat **0g** | protein **0g** | total carbs **2g** | dietary fiber **0g** | net carbs **2g**

JAMBALAYA

YIELD: **2** servings (12 ounces per serving)

PREP TIME: **10** minutes

COOK TIME: **35** minutes

This recipe takes a little more time than others in this book, but the flavors of this classic dish can't be beat. My grandmother would make jambalaya often, but of course with white rice. If you're following the low-carb track, feel free to swap out the shirataki rice for cauliflower rice or Palmini rice.

1½ tablespoons avocado oil

1 tablespoon coconut flour

1½ ounces diced yellow onions (about ¾ small onion)

1¼ ounces diced green bell peppers (about ½ small pepper)

2 tablespoons chopped scallions

2 tablespoons sliced celery

1½ teaspoons minced garlic

4 ounces shirataki rice, drained and rinsed

4 ounces cooked ham, diced

8 ounces canned diced tomatoes

1 tablespoon paprika

1½ teaspoons ground cumin

¼ teaspoon cayenne pepper

¼ teaspoon ground dried oregano

¼ teaspoon ground dried thyme

¼ teaspoon fine sea salt

½ cup chicken bone broth

8 ounces jumbo shrimp, peeled and deveined

1 teaspoon glucomannan or xanthan gum (optional, to thicken)

Chopped scallions, for garnish (optional)

Chopped fresh parsley, for garnish (optional)

1. Heat the oil in a 10-inch sauté pan or braiser over medium heat. Add the coconut flour and cook, stirring constantly, for 1 to 2 minutes.

2. Add the onions, bell peppers, scallions, celery, and garlic. Cook until the vegetables have begun to soften, about 5 minutes.

3. Add the rice, ham, tomatoes, paprika, cumin, cayenne, oregano, thyme, salt, and broth. Stir to combine and bring to a boil. Reduce the heat to medium-low and simmer, uncovered, until the vegetables are fork-tender, 10 to 15 minutes.

4. Add the shrimp and cook until the shrimp have turned pink and the liquid has reduced by half, about 10 minutes. If you'd like it thicker, sprinkle in the glucomannan and cook, stirring constantly, until thickened, about 5 minutes.

5. Garnish with chopped scallions and/or parsley, if desired, and serve.

6. The jambalaya can be made ahead and stored in an airtight container in the refrigerator for up to 2 days. Reheat leftovers in a medium skillet over medium heat until heated through, 6 to 8 minutes.

For the meal plan

Freeze the leftover portion for up to a month to enjoy after you've completed the plan.

NUTRITION INFO:
calories **352** | fat **18g** | protein **30g** | total carbs **19g** | dietary fiber **6g** | net carbs **12g**

LOW-CARB MARINARA SAUCE

YIELD: **8 cups** (½ **cup per serving**)

PREP TIME: **5 minutes**

COOK TIME: **35 minutes**

This is an authentic Italian marinara sauce, but it comes together in just over 30 minutes. You'll never go back to jarred sauce again!

2 (28-ounce) cans tomato puree

1 cup water

2 tablespoons extra-virgin olive oil

2 cloves garlic, minced

2 teaspoons dried basil

2 teaspoons dried parsley

2 teaspoons fine sea salt

1 teaspoon ground black pepper

1 teaspoon fennel seeds

FOR GARNISH (OPTIONAL)

Red pepper flakes

Chopped fresh basil

Chopped fresh flat-leaf parsley

1. Place all the ingredients in an enameled Dutch oven or other large nonreactive pot with a lid over medium-high heat. Stir to combine well and bring to a boil.

2. Reduce the heat to medium-low, cover, and simmer for 30 minutes. Taste and add more salt and pepper, if desired.

3. Use to sauce pizzas, pasta, meatballs, and so forth, garnished with red pepper flakes, fresh basil, and/or parsley, if desired.

4. Store in an airtight container in the refrigerator for up to 5 days or in the freezer for up to 3 months.

NUTRITION INFO:
calories **33** | fat **1g** | protein **0g** | total carbs **4g** | dietary fiber **1g** | net carbs **3g**

MASHED ROASTED CAULIFLOWER

YIELD: **8 servings (3 ounces per serving)**

PREP TIME: **10 minutes**

COOK TIME: **30 minutes**

This mash goes wonderfully with my French Onion Meatballs (page 158) and Garlic Butter Steak Bites (page 162). But there's no need to stop there. This is the keto side dish that goes with everything! Roasting the cauliflower imparts a lot of flavor, but if you're short on time, you can use thawed frozen cauliflower florets and skip the roasting step. If you do, simply steam the florets until hot and add the olive oil and seasonings to the food processor in Step 4.

2 pounds cauliflower florets (from about 1 large head cauliflower)

2 tablespoons extra-virgin olive oil

½ teaspoon garlic powder

½ teaspoon fine sea salt

¼ teaspoon ground black pepper

¼ cup (½ stick) salted butter, sliced and softened

1. Preheat the oven to 400°F.

2. Arrange the cauliflower florets on a rimmed baking sheet. Drizzle the oil over the cauliflower and stir until well coated. Sprinkle the garlic powder, salt, and pepper over the cauliflower.

3. Roast for 30 minutes, or until tender.

4. Transfer the roasted cauliflower to a food processor, add the butter, and process until the mixture has a smooth mashed potato–like texture. Enjoy immediately.

5. Store leftovers in an airtight container in the refrigerator for up to 5 days or in the freezer for up to 1 month.

For the meal plan

Freeze two servings for Days 5 and 6, one serving for Day 12, and another serving for Day 28. Depending on whether you're following the keto or the low-carb track, you will have either one or two additional leftover servings to stash in the freezer to enjoy after the detox.

NUTRITION INFO:
calories **110** | fat **8g** | protein **2g** | total carbs **5g** | dietary fiber **2g** | net carbs **3g**

MOMMA'S ITALIAN DRESSING

YIELD: 1½ cups (2 tablespoons per serving)

PREP TIME: 5 minutes

My mom has been making this delicious dressing for as long as I can remember. Because she just tosses in a little of this and a little of that, getting precise measurements to bottle it wasn't easy, but I did it! Once you try this version, you will never want another Italian dressing again.

1 cup extra-virgin olive oil

½ cup red wine vinegar

2 cloves garlic, grated

1 tablespoon chopped fresh parsley, or 1 teaspoon dried parsley

1 teaspoon garlic powder

1 teaspoon onion powder

½ teaspoon fine sea salt

¼ teaspoon ground black pepper

1. Put all the ingredients in a large mason jar, secure the lid, and shake vigorously. Alternatively, whisk the ingredients vigorously in a bowl.

2. Taste and adjust the seasoning if needed. If you want more tang, add another tablespoon of vinegar; less tang, add another tablespoon of oil.

3. Store in the refrigerator for up to 2 weeks.

NUTRITION INFO:
calories **163** | fat **18g** | protein **1g** | total carbs **1g** | dietary fiber **1g** | net carbs **0g**

MONTE CRISTO WAFFLE SANDWICHES

YIELD: 2 sandwiches (1 per serving)

PREP TIME: 15 minutes

COOK TIME: 8 minutes

This sandwich has it all: savory, sweet, salty, creamy, crunchy. Each bite is an explosion of flavor in your mouth!

2 tablespoons avocado oil mayonnaise

2 tablespoons Dijon mustard

2 slices Gruyère cheese (about 1 ounce)

8 raspberries

1 batch Dairy-Free Mini Waffles (page 140)

6 slices deli ham (about 5 ounces)

1 tablespoon salted butter, for the pan

FOR THE BATTER

2 large eggs

2 tablespoons heavy cream

Pinch of fine sea salt

1/4 teaspoon vanilla extract

1 tablespoon Swerve granular sweetener (optional)

1. Whisk together the mayonnaise and mustard in a small bowl.

2. Cut each slice of Gruyère in half to make a total of 4 slices.

3. Put the raspberries in a separate small bowl and smash with the back of a fork.

4. To assemble the sandwiches, lay 2 waffles on a piece of parchment paper. Spread 1 tablespoon of the mayo-mustard mixture on each waffle. Top each with a slice of cheese and 3 slices of ham. Divide the smashed raspberries evenly between the sandwiches and spread on top of the stacked ham slices. Spread 1 tablespoon of the mayo-mustard mixture on the raspberries. Lay another slice of cheese on top. Spread the remaining tablespoon of mayo-mustard mixture on the other 2 waffles and press the sandwiches together as best you can. You could place another piece of parchment on top of each sandwich and set a heavy cast-iron skillet on it to weight it down.

5. Whisk together the batter ingredients in a shallow bowl. Melt the butter in a large skillet over medium-high heat. Dip the sandwiches, one at a time, in the batter, carefully turning to coat both sides. Cook the sandwiches in the skillet for 3 to 4 minutes per side, until golden brown. Enjoy immediately.

6. To store the leftover sandwich, wrap it in parchment, then seal tightly with aluminum foil; it will keep in the refrigerator for up to 4 days. To reheat it, melt a tablespoon of butter in a small skillet over medium-high heat, then add the sandwich and cook for 1 to 2 minutes on each side.

NUTRITION INFO:
calories **561** | fat **45g** | protein **37g** | total carbs **7g** | dietary fiber **3g** | net carbs **4g**

OPEN-FACE TUNA CHAFFLES

option

YIELD: **1 serving**
PREP TIME: **10 minutes**
COOK TIME: **5 minutes**

This is another quick and easy but satisfying meal. For a dairy-free version, substitute two Dairy-Free Mini Waffles (page 140) or a 2-Minute English Muffin (page 240) for the chaffles and omit the cheese topping.

FOR THE CHAFFLES

1 large egg

1 teaspoon coconut flour

½ cup shredded mozzarella cheese

1 batch Tuna Salad (page 238)

¼ cup shredded cheddar or Swiss cheese (optional)

Sliced dill pickles, for serving (optional)

Chopped fresh parsley, for garnish (optional)

SPECIAL EQUIPMENT:

Mini waffle maker

1. Preheat a mini waffle maker.

2. Make the chaffles: In a small bowl, mix together the egg, coconut flour, and mozzarella cheese until combined.

3. Grease the preheated waffle maker with avocado oil cooking spray, then pour half of the batter into the center. Close the lid and follow the manufacturer's instructions to cook the chaffle until golden brown, typically 2 to 3 minutes. Repeat with the remaining batter to make a second chaffle.

4. Spread half of the tuna salad over each chaffle. If desired, top with the cheddar cheese and place in a toaster oven or broil to melt the cheese. Garnish with pickles and/or fresh parsley, if desired, and enjoy immediately.

NUTRITION INFO:
calories **696** | fat **52g** | protein **54g** | total carbs **9g** | dietary fiber **3g** | net carbs **6g**

PALMINI RICE

YIELD: **2 servings (4 ounces per serving)**

PREP TIME: **5 minutes**

COOK TIME: **5 minutes**

Palmini rice is a new-to-the-market product. It is made from cultivated hearts of palm that are harvested in a sustainable way. It makes a wonderful low-carb substitute for rice. The Palmini brand also sells hearts of palm noodles, which make a great low-carb pasta replacement; and even mashed hearts of palm, for replacing mashed potatoes. These products are most easily found online.

1 (12-ounce) package Palmini rice

2 tablespoons extra-virgin olive oil

1 teaspoon minced garlic

Salt and pepper

Chopped fresh parsley, for garnish (optional)

1. Drain and rinse the Palmini rice in a fine-mesh sieve.

2. Place the rice in the center of a clean kitchen towel. Pull the corners of the towel toward the center, cinch together, and twist to squeeze as much liquid from the rice as possible.

3. Heat the oil in a small skillet over medium-high heat. Add the garlic and sauté until fragrant. Add the rice and cook for about 5 minutes, until golden brown.

4. Season with salt and pepper to taste and serve, garnished with fresh parsley, if desired.

5. Store leftovers in an airtight container in the refrigerator for up to 5 days.

NUTRITION INFO:
calories **146** | fat **14g** | protein **1g** | total carbs **4g** | dietary fiber **2g** | net carbs **2g**

PAN-SEARED LEMON BUTTER SALMON

YIELD: 2 servings (6 ounces per serving)

PREP TIME: 10 minutes

COOK TIME: 10 minutes

1 (1-pound) skin-on salmon fillet, cut into 4 equal pieces

1 teaspoon fine sea salt, divided

2 tablespoons extra-virgin olive oil, for the pan

2 tablespoons fresh lemon juice, divided

1/4 teaspoon ground black pepper

2 tablespoons salted butter

4 cloves garlic, minced

2 tablespoons chopped fresh parsley, for garnish

Lemon slices, for garnish

The keys to a perfect sear and a "melt-in-your-mouth" salmon are to preheat your pan until hot and to allow the salmon to sear, undisturbed, for 6 to 8 minutes. After trying this simple preparation method, you'll never want salmon another way.

1. Place the salmon on the counter and allow to come to room temperature, 15 to 20 minutes.

2. Preheat a large cast-iron or ceramic skillet over medium-high heat. If you have an electric stovetop, this should take about 5 minutes; a gas stovetop, 3 to 4 minutes.

3. Pat the salmon pieces dry with paper towels. Sprinkle 1/2 teaspoon of the salt over the skin and rub it in with your hands.

4. Heat the oil in the hot pan until shimmering but not smoking. Place the salmon pieces, skin side down, in the skillet. Sear undisturbed until the skin is crispy and the internal temperature in the thickest part of the fish is between 125°F (for medium done) and 140°F (for well-done), 6 to 8 minutes. While the skin is searing, drizzle 1 tablespoon of the lemon juice over the flesh. Sprinkle with the remaining 1/2 teaspoon of salt and the pepper.

5. Once the desired internal temperature is reached, flip the fillets over to sear on the flesh side, 1 to 2 minutes. Reduce the heat to medium-low. Add the butter, garlic, and remaining tablespoon of lemon juice to the pan. Cook for 30 seconds. Turn off the heat, flip the fillets back over, skin side down, and spoon the pan juices over the top.

6. Garnish with the fresh parsley and lemon slices. Serve immediately.

Note

It's best to season salmon just before cooking. If you salt it too soon, the salt can pull moisture out of the fish prior to cooking.

NUTRITION INFO:
calories **461** | fat **27g** | protein **46g** | total carbs **8g** | dietary fiber **2g** | net carbs **6g**

PHILLY CHEESESTEAK STIR-FRY

YIELD: **2 servings (8 ounces per serving)**

PREP TIME: **10 minutes**

COOK TIME: **15 minutes**

This stir-fry is ready in under 30 minutes and is delicious with or without the cheese.

8 ounces boneless sirloin steak or flank steak, thinly sliced

½ teaspoon fine sea salt

⅛ teaspoon ground black pepper

1 tablespoon avocado oil, for the pan

1½ teaspoons apple cider vinegar

1½ teaspoons coconut aminos

1½ ounces sliced yellow onions (about ¾ small onion)

1¼ ounces sliced green bell pepper (about ½ small pepper)

1¼ ounces sliced red bell pepper (about ½ small pepper)

1¼ ounces sliced cremini mushrooms (about ½ cup)

2 cloves garlic, minced

½ cup shredded mozzarella cheese (optional)

1. Put the steak slices in a bowl and season with the salt and pepper.

2. Heat the oil in a large skillet over medium-high heat. Add the steak and cook for 2 to 3 minutes on each side, until browned. Remove from the pan and set aside.

3. Pour the vinegar and coconut aminos into the skillet. Stir to release the browned bits from the bottom of the pan. Add the onions, bell peppers, mushrooms, and garlic and cook until tender, 5 to 6 minutes.

4. Return the steak and any accumulated juices to the skillet and stir to combine with the vegetables. If using the cheese, sprinkle it over the contents of the skillet, cover, and cook over low heat until the cheese is melted, about 5 minutes.

5. Store leftovers in an airtight container in the refrigerator for up to 3 days or in the freezer for up to 1 month.

NUTRITION INFO:
calories **341** | fat **19g** | protein **33g** | total carbs **9g** | dietary fiber **2g** | net carbs **7g**

PIZZA CHAFFLES

YIELD: **2 servings**

PREP TIME: **10 minutes**

COOK TIME: **12 minutes**

Here's a quick and easy recipe to enjoy all the flavors of pizza in a low-carb way!

FOR THE CHAFFLE CRUST

1 large egg

1 teaspoon coconut flour

½ cup shredded mozzarella cheese

¼ teaspoon ground dried oregano

¼ teaspoon dried parsley

⅛ teaspoon garlic powder

TOPPINGS

2 tablespoons low-carb marinara sauce, store-bought or homemade (page 172)

½ cup shredded mozzarella cheese

6 slices pepperoni, cut into quarters

Chopped fresh parsley, for garnish (optional)

1. Preheat a mini waffle maker according to the manufacturer's instructions.

2. Preheat the oven to 400°F. Line a small rimmed baking sheet with parchment paper.

3. In a small bowl, whisk together the crust ingredients until combined.

4. Grease the preheated waffle maker with olive oil cooking spray, then pour half of the batter into the center. Close the lid and follow the manufacturer's instructions to cook the chaffle until golden brown, typically 2 to 3 minutes. Repeat with the remaining batter to make a second chaffle.

5. Spread 1 tablespoon of the marinara sauce on each chaffle, then top each with ¼ cup of the mozzarella. Place half of the pepperoni on top of each chaffle.

6. Place the chaffles on the prepared baking sheet and bake until the cheese melts, about 5 minutes. Garnish with parsley, if desired. Best served fresh. However, they can be made ahead, wrapped in foil, and stored in the refrigerator for up to 5 days. To reheat, place on a small baking sheet and bake in a preheated 350°F oven for 5 minutes.

SPECIAL EQUIPMENT:

Mini waffle maker

NUTRITION INFO:
calories **482** | fat **35g** | protein **33g** | total carbs **7g** | dietary fiber **2g** | net carbs **5g**

PROTEIN PANCAKES

YIELD: 6 pancakes (2 per serving)

PREP TIME: 5 minutes

COOK TIME: 8 minutes

These quick blender pancakes are full of protein and can be enjoyed all week long.

4 large eggs

4 ounces full-fat cream cheese, softened

1 teaspoon vanilla extract

2 scoops unflavored whey protein powder

¼ cup Swerve granular sweetener

½ teaspoon baking powder

Pinch of fine sea salt

¼ cup water

4 tablespoons avocado oil, divided, for the pan

FOR SERVING (OPTIONAL)

Fresh berries

Sugar-free maple syrup, store-bought or homemade (page 232)

1. Place the eggs, cream cheese, vanilla extract, protein powder, sweetener, baking powder, salt, and water in a blender and blend until smooth.

2. Heat 2 tablespoons of the oil in a large skillet over medium-low heat. To test the temperature, stick the end of a wooden spoon handle into the oil; if tiny bubbles form around the wood, the oil is ready.

3. Drop ⅓ cup of the batter into the skillet. Repeat twice more to make a total of 3 pancakes. Cover and cook for 2 to 3 minutes, then check the pancakes. Once you see the edges are browning and bubbles are forming in the center, flip the pancakes and cook for about 1 minute more. Remove from the pan and add the remaining 2 tablespoons of oil. Repeat with the rest of the batter.

4. Enjoy the pancakes with fresh berries and/or sugar-free maple syrup, if desired.

5. Store leftovers in an airtight container in the refrigerator for up to 1 week. To reheat, melt 1 tablespoon of butter in a small skillet over medium heat, add a pancake, and cook for 1 to 2 minutes on each side.

For the meal plan ———————————

Freeze one serving of pancakes for Day 21.

NUTRITION INFO:
calories **247** | fat **19g** | protein **17g** | total carbs **1g** | dietary fiber **1g** | net carbs **0g**

REVERSE-SEARED RIB EYE WITH CHIMICHURRI

YIELD: **2 servings**

PREP TIME: **10 minutes**

COOK TIME: **25 to 45 minutes,** depending on preferred doneness

The most common way to cook steak is to begin by searing it. Here, you'll be using the reverse-sear technique, a consistently foolproof method that results in perfectly cooked meat (no more overcooked steak!). Note that in the meal plan, on Day 18, you'll be consuming just one of these steaks; I find it just as easy to cook two at once, providing an extra serving for later. If you prefer, simply halve the ingredients.

2 (8-ounce) boneless rib-eye steaks, 1½ inches thick

1 teaspoon fine sea salt

1 teaspoon ground black pepper

2 tablespoons extra-virgin olive oil, for the pan

3 tablespoons salted butter

2 cloves garlic, thinly sliced

1 sprig fresh rosemary

1 sprig fresh thyme

4 tablespoons Chimichurri (page 124), for serving

Internal Temperature Targets

rare:	105°F, 20–25 minutes
medium-rare:	115°F, 25–30 minutes
medium:	125°F, 30–35 minutes
medium-well:	135°F, 35–40 minutes

1. Remove the steaks from the refrigerator 30 minutes prior to cooking.

2. Preheat the oven to 250°F. Place a wire rack on a rimmed baking sheet.

3. Using paper towels, pat the steaks dry. Season both sides with the salt and pepper. Place on the wire rack. Bake until the desired internal temperature is reached (see the chart below for guidance). Remove the steaks from the oven and cover loosely with aluminum foil to keep warm while you preheat the pan for searing.

4. Preheat a large cast-iron skillet over medium-high heat. When the skillet is hot, pour in the oil and heat until shimmering. Place the steaks in the pan and sear, without moving, for about 1 minute. Flip the steaks and reduce the heat to medium. Add the butter, garlic, rosemary, and thyme to the opposite side of the skillet. Once the butter has melted, tilt the pan toward the butter mixture and spoon it over the steaks for 1 to 2 minutes. Using tongs, sear the fat cap to crisp it up, about 1 minute.

5. Slice and serve immediately (no need to rest), spooning the pan juices and 2 tablespoons of the chimichurri over each slice.

6. Store leftover steak in an airtight container in the refrigerator for up to 3 days or in the freezer for up to 1 month. To reheat frozen steak, defrost in the refrigerator overnight, then preheat a skillet over medium-high heat with some oil or fat and give the steak a quick sear to heat it up. You can also use an air fryer at 400°F for 3 to 5 minutes.

NUTRITION INFO (MINUS EXCESS COOKING FAT):
calories **607** | fat **46g** | protein **47g** | total carbs **3g** | dietary fiber **2g** | net carbs **1g**

For the meal plan ———————————————————————

Freeze the leftover steak to enjoy after you've completed the plan.

Note ———————————————————————————————

You won't end up consuming all the fat in which the steak is seared.

ROASTED BALSAMIC VEGETABLES

YIELD: 4 servings (4 ounces per serving)

PREP TIME: 15 minutes

COOK TIME: 30 minutes

A super easy side dish that you can enjoy with a variety of proteins.

5 ounces cauliflower florets (about 1 cup)

4 ounces sliced zucchini (about 1 cup)

3 ounces broccoli florets (about 1 cup)

2 ounces sliced bell peppers (any color or a mix; about ½ large pepper)

2 ounces sliced yellow onions (about 1 small onion)

2 tablespoons extra-virgin olive oil

1 tablespoon balsamic vinegar

5 cloves garlic, unpeeled (outer papery skin removed)

½ teaspoon onion powder

½ teaspoon fine sea salt

¼ teaspoon ground black pepper

Chopped fresh basil, for garnish (optional)

1. Place an oven rack in the bottom position. Preheat the oven to 400°F.

2. Put the vegetables in a large bowl. Whisk together the oil and vinegar and pour over the vegetables. Stir to coat well.

3. Arrange the vegetables and garlic cloves on a rimmed baking sheet. Sprinkle with the onion powder, salt, and pepper.

4. Place the pan on the lower rack of the oven and roast for 30 minutes, or until the vegetables are fork-tender and browned. Serve garnished with fresh basil, if desired.

5. Store leftovers in an airtight container in the refrigerator for up to 3 days or in the freezer for up to 1 month. To reheat, microwave for 1 minute or rewarm in a small skillet over medium heat.

For the meal plan

Enjoy on Days 10 and 13; freeze the remaining two servings to eat after you've completed the plan.

NUTRITION INFO:
calories **103** | fat **7g** | protein **2g** | total carbs **9g** | dietary fiber **2g** | net carbs **7g**

RUTABAGA FRIES

   option

YIELD: 4 servings (4 ounces per serving)

PREP TIME: 15 minutes

COOK TIME: 40 minutes

1 small rutabaga (about 1 pound), peeled and stem and root ends trimmed

2 tablespoons avocado oil

2 teaspoons paprika

1 teaspoon garlic powder

½ teaspoon fine sea salt

½ teaspoon ground black pepper

Rutabaga is a great substitute for potato fries. It has almost the same texture as a white potato but with less carbs and calories, making it a nice option for the low-carb track.

1. If using an air fryer, skip ahead to Step 2. If using the oven, preheat the oven to 425°F and line a rimmed baking sheet with parchment paper.

2. Cut the rutabaga in half, through the ends, then cut each half evenly into sticks about ¼ inch thick.

3. Place the sticks in a large bowl and toss with the oil. Sprinkle with the seasonings and toss again to evenly coat.

4. To cook the fries in the oven, lay them in a single layer on the prepared baking sheet. Bake for 25 minutes, then flip over and bake for another 10 to 15 minutes, until crisp-tender.

5. To cook the fries in an air fryer, preheat the air fryer to 400°F. Place an even layer of fries in the air fryer basket; do not overlap. You will need to cook them in 2 or 3 batches, depending on the size of your basket. Air-fry for 12 minutes. Flip over and air-fry for 5 to 8 minutes more, until crisp and tender. Remove and continue with the remaining fries.

6. Store leftovers in an airtight container in the refrigerator for up to 1 week or in the freezer for up to 2 months. Thaw frozen fries prior to reheating. To reheat leftover fries, place in a preheated 400°F oven for 10 minutes or in an air fryer for 5 minutes.

For the meal plan

Freeze one serving of fries to enjoy after you've completed the plan; refrigerate the remainder for later in the week.

NUTRITION INFO:
calories **115** | fat **3g** | protein **2g** | total carbs **11g** | dietary fiber **2g** | net carbs **9g**

SAUSAGE EGG CUPS

YIELD: **6 egg cups (3 per serving)**
PREP TIME: **10 minutes**
COOK TIME: **20 minutes**

Another fine option for changing up your egg routine.

8 ounces ground pork

½ teaspoon ground nutmeg

½ teaspoon dried parsley

¼ teaspoon fine sea salt

⅛ teaspoon ground black pepper

½ cup chopped fresh spinach

6 small or medium eggs

1 tablespoon chopped fresh parsley, for garnish

1. Preheat the oven to 350°F. Place a standard-size 12-cup muffin pan on a rimmed baking sheet.

2. Put the pork, nutmeg, parsley, salt, and pepper in a bowl and mix until the seasonings are thoroughly combined with the meat. Evenly divide the pork mixture among 6 of the muffin cups, then press it into the bottoms and up the sides of the cups to create vessels for the spinach and eggs.

3. Divide the spinach evenly among the cups. Carefully crack an egg into each cup.

4. Bake for 18 to 20 minutes, or until the egg whites are set. Serve garnished with the parsley.

5. Store leftovers in an airtight container in the refrigerator for up to 3 days or in the freezer for up to 1 month. To reheat, place egg cups in a casserole dish with a lid. Cover and bake in a preheated 350°F oven for 5 to 8 minutes.

NUTRITION INFO:
calories **463** | fat **35g** | protein **34g** | total carbs **1g** | dietary fiber **1g** | net carbs **0g**

SAUSAGE ZUCCHINI SKILLET

YIELD: **4 servings (3 ounces per serving)**

PREP TIME: **10 minutes**

COOK TIME: **18 minutes**

The scrumptious flavor of Italian sausage combined with the spices in this dish creates an amazing, flavorful meal, all in one pan. My kids actually eat the zucchini without complaint!

1½ teaspoons avocado oil, for the pan

1 pound ground Italian sausage or links with casings removed

10 ounces diced zucchini (about 1 large zucchini)

3 ounces diced yellow onions (about 1 medium onion)

1½ teaspoons minced garlic

½ teaspoon ground dried oregano

¼ teaspoon dried parsley

¼ teaspoon ground dried rosemary

¼ teaspoon fine sea salt

¼ teaspoon ground black pepper

Red pepper flakes, to taste (optional)

½ cup shredded mozzarella cheese (optional)

¼ cup chopped fresh parsley, for garnish

1. Heat the oil in a large skillet over medium-high heat, then add the sausage. Cook until browned, about 5 minutes, stirring to crumble the meat as it cooks. Remove to a covered dish to keep warm.

2. Add the zucchini, onions, and garlic to the skillet and season with the dried herbs, salt, pepper, and red pepper flakes, if using. Cook until the onions are translucent and the zucchini is fork-tender, 6 to 8 minutes. Taste and adjust the salt and pepper if needed.

3. Return the sausage to the skillet and toss with the vegetables. If using the cheese, sprinkle it over the sausage mixture, stir to combine, and cook over low heat until the cheese is melted.

4. Top with the fresh parsley and serve.

5. Store leftovers in an airtight container in the refrigerator for up to 3 days or in the freezer for up to 1 month.

For the meal plan ———————————————

Freeze two servings to enjoy after you've completed the plan.

NUTRITION INFO:
calories **463** | fat **40g** | protein **20g** | total carbs **5g** | dietary fiber **1g** | net carbs **4g**

SAUTÉED SUMMER SQUASH

option

YIELD: 4 servings (4 ounces per serving)

PREP TIME: 5 minutes

COOK TIME: 15 minutes

This simple recipe can really go with any protein you like.

2 tablespoons extra-virgin olive oil, for the pan

2 ounces sliced yellow onions (about 1 small onion)

8 ounces yellow squash (about 1 large squash), sliced

8 ounces zucchini (about 1 large zucchini), sliced

1 tablespoon salted butter or avocado oil

½ teaspoon ground dried thyme

½ teaspoon fine sea salt

¼ teaspoon ground black pepper

¼ cup grated Parmesan cheese (optional)

Chopped fresh parsley, for garnish (optional)

1. Heat the oil in a large skillet over medium-high heat. Add the onions and cook until translucent and softened, about 5 minutes. Add the yellow squash and zucchini and sauté until lightly browned and softened, 5 to 8 minutes.

2. Add the butter, thyme, salt, and pepper; stir to combine.

3. Serve sprinkled with the Parmesan cheese and/or fresh parsley, if desired.

4. Store leftovers in an airtight container in the refrigerator for up to 5 days or in the freezer for up to 1 month.

For the meal plan ——————————

If you're on the low-carb track, you'll use all four servings of this side dish during the plan; if on the keto track, you'll need just two servings. Freeze the leftovers to enjoy after you've completed the detox, or, to avoid leftovers, simply cut the recipe in half.

NUTRITION INFO:
calories **114** | fat **10g** | protein **2g** | total carbs **6g** | dietary fiber **2g** | net carbs **4g**

SCOTCH EGGS

YIELD: 4 Scotch eggs (2 per serving)

PREP TIME: 15 minutes

COOK TIME: 40 minutes

4 large eggs

8 ounces ground pork

1 teaspoon Dijon mustard, plus more for serving if desired

2 tablespoons chopped fresh parsley

½ teaspoon dried parsley

¼ teaspoon ground nutmeg

¼ teaspoon fine sea salt

⅛ teaspoon ground black pepper

½ cup pork rind crumbs

Eggs wrapped in pork with a crusty outer layer make for a tasty meal with added protein. I enjoy these with some Dijon mustard as a dipping sauce.

1. Bring a large saucepan of water to a boil. Add the eggs and cook for 5 to 7 minutes for soft yolks or 8 to 10 minutes for firm, hard-cooked yolks.

2. Immediately transfer the eggs to a bowl of ice water. Once cool enough to handle, carefully peel the eggs and set aside.

3. Preheat the oven to 350°F. Grease a rimmed baking sheet.

4. Put the pork, mustard, fresh and dried parsley, nutmeg, salt, and pepper in a bowl and mix well. Form into 4 equal-size balls and flatten each ball into an oval-shaped patty.

5. Place an egg in each sausage patty and wrap the sausage around the egg as best you can. Pinch the sausage closed.

6. Roll each sausage-wrapped egg in the pork rind crumbs and place on the prepared baking sheet.

7. Bake for 25 to 30 minutes, until the sausage is fully cooked.

8. Store leftovers in an airtight container in the refrigerator for up to 3 days or in the freezer for up to 1 month. To reheat, place Scotch eggs on a rimmed baking sheet and bake in a preheated 350°F oven for 5 minutes.

NUTRITION INFO:
calories **506** | fat **37g** | protein **39g** | total carbs **1g** | dietary fiber **1g** | net carbs **0g**

SHEET PAN CHICKEN FAJITAS

YIELD: **4 servings (6 ounces per serving)**

PREP TIME: **15 minutes**

COOK TIME: **30 minutes**

Another simple recipe that is full of flavor and easy to make for a quick meal on a busy weeknight!

12 ounces bell peppers (mix of colors; about 3 small peppers), sliced

2 ounces chopped yellow onions (about 1 small onion)

1 pound boneless, skinless chicken breasts, chopped into bite-size chunks

2 tablespoons avocado oil

1 teaspoon fine sea salt

1 teaspoon ground cumin

½ teaspoon ground black pepper

½ teaspoon chili powder

½ teaspoon garlic powder

Juice of ½ lime (optional)

TOPPINGS (OPTIONAL)

Salsa

Sour cream

Shredded Mexican cheese blend

Sliced avocado

Chopped fresh cilantro

Lime wedges

1. Preheat the oven to 400°F.

2. Spread the bell peppers, onions, and chicken on a rimmed baking sheet.

3. Drizzle the oil over the veggies and chicken and toss.

4. In a small bowl, whisk together the salt and spices. Sprinkle the mixture over the veggies and chicken and toss to coat. Spread out the veggies and chicken into a single layer.

5. Bake for 25 to 30 minutes, until the peppers are tender and the chicken is cooked through.

6. Squeeze the lime juice over the veggies and chicken, if desired. Serve with the toppings of your choice.

7. Store leftovers in an airtight container in the refrigerator for up to 3 days or in the freezer for up to 1 month. To reheat, microwave for 1 minute or warm in a small skillet over medium heat.

For the meal plan

Refrigerate one serving for Day 5; freeze the remaining two servings to enjoy after you've completed the plan.

NUTRITION INFO:
calories **246** | fat **12g** | protein **26g** | total carbs **6g** | dietary fiber **2g** | net carbs **4g**

SHEET PAN SHRIMP WITH CRISPY PEPPERONI

YIELD: 2 servings (6 ounces per serving)

PREP TIME: 10 minutes

COOK TIME: 20 minutes

Sheet pan meals save you time because the oven does the work for you. Once the ingredients are prepped, you can relax, and your meal will be ready in less than 20 minutes! This is a great recipe to double after you've completed the meal plan and are looking for a satisfying family-size meal, as shown.

4 ounces cherry tomatoes (10 or 11 tomatoes)

½ small red onion (about 1½ ounces), cut into wedges

1 tablespoon plus 1½ teaspoons extra-virgin olive oil, divided

1½ teaspoons salted butter, melted, or avocado oil

2 cloves garlic, unpeeled (outer papery skin removed)

3 sprigs fresh thyme

½ teaspoon fine sea salt, divided

¼ teaspoon ground black pepper, divided

8 ounces large shrimp, peeled and deveined

½ teaspoon smoked paprika

6 slices pepperoni

1. Preheat the oven to 350°F.

2. Place the tomatoes and onion on a rimmed baking sheet and carefully toss with 1½ teaspoons of the oil, the melted butter, garlic cloves, thyme sprigs, ¼ teaspoon of the salt, and ⅛ teaspoon of the pepper. Roast for 10 minutes, or until the tomatoes and onion are soft.

3. Meanwhile, butterfly the shrimp: Place a shrimp on a cutting board. Holding a paring knife parallel to the cutting board, insert the tip of the knife about three-quarters of the way into the shrimp near the head and cut nearly all the way down the center of the shrimp's back to the tail. (Do not cut through the shrimp.) Using your hands, open the shrimp until it lies flat. Repeat with the rest of the shrimp.

4. Put the butterflied shrimp in a bowl and toss with the paprika, remaining ¼ teaspoon of salt, and remaining ⅛ teaspoon of pepper. Add the shrimp and pepperoni to the baking sheet and toss to combine. Bake for 3 minutes more, or until the shrimp are slightly pink.

5. Drain the pan juices into a tall cup or jar that's wide enough to fit an immersion blender; if you don't have an immersion blender, drain the juices into a countertop blender. Remove 1 clove of garlic and 2 tomatoes from the pan and set aside. Return the pan to the oven for about 5 minutes to crisp up the pepperoni and finish cooking the shrimp; they are done when they are no longer translucent and have become opaque in the thickest part (be careful not to overcook them).

6. Meanwhile, make the sauce: Peel the reserved garlic clove and blend it with the pan juices and reserved tomatoes using an immersion blender (or countertop blender), then pour the mixture into a small saucepan. Simmer for about 5 minutes to concentrate and thicken the sauce.

NUTRITION INFO:
calories **285** | fat **4g** | protein **26g** | total carbs **5g** | dietary fiber **1g** | net carbs **4g**

7. To serve, drizzle the shrimp mixture with the sauce and the remaining tablespoon of oil and sprinkle with pepper.

8. Store leftovers in an airtight container in the refrigerator for up to 3 days. To reheat, melt a tablespoon of butter in a small skillet over medium-high heat. Add the leftovers and cook, stirring constantly, for 3 to 5 minutes, until heated through.

SHIRATAKI RICE

option

YIELD: 2 servings (3 ounces per serving)

PREP TIME: 5 minutes

COOK TIME: 3 to 5 minutes

You may not be in love with shirataki rice straight up, but it makes a great accompaniment to flavorful meals, like my Sheet Pan Shrimp with Crispy Pepperoni (page 208). It also works well as an ingredient in a savory recipe like my Jambalaya (page 170) or Spicy Smoked Salmon Wrap (page 224). Compared to white rice, which has 32 grams of carbs per 4 ounces, shirataki rice is a much better choice!

1 (8-ounce) package shirataki rice

Salt and pepper

1 tablespoon salted butter or extra-virgin olive oil (optional)

Chopped fresh parsley, for garnish (optional)

1. Rinse and drain the rice in a fine-mesh sieve.

2. Place the rice in the middle of a clean kitchen towel. Pull the ends of the towel toward the center, cinch together, and twist to squeeze as much liquid from the rice as possible.

3. Put the rice in a microwave-safe bowl or in a small skillet. Microwave for 3 minutes or cook over medium heat for about 5 minutes, until any remaining liquid has been absorbed.

4. Season with salt and pepper to taste and top with the butter and/or some chopped parsley, if desired.

5. Store leftovers in an airtight container in the refrigerator for up to 1 week. To reheat, put the rice in a small skillet over medium-high heat and cook, stirring continually, for 3 to 4 minutes, until heated through.

NUTRITION INFO:
calories **13** | fat **1g** | protein **1g** | total carbs **4g** | dietary fiber **4g** | net carbs **0g**

SHRIMP LINGUINE IN GARLIC BUTTER SAUCE

YIELD: **2 servings (8 ounces per serving)**

PREP TIME: **10 minutes**

COOK TIME: **8 minutes**

Made with a lemony garlic butter sauce, this simple shrimp dish is delicious and one of the quickest meals to prepare in the entire meal plan.

4 tablespoons salted butter, divided

4 cloves garlic, minced

½ teaspoon ground dried oregano

Pinch of red pepper flakes (optional)

1½ pounds large shrimp, peeled and deveined

2 tablespoons extra-virgin olive oil

2 tablespoons fresh lemon juice

1 tablespoon chopped fresh parsley

8 ounces shirataki linguine, rinsed and drained, or other low-carb noodles of choice (see Note)

Salt and pepper

1. Heat 2 tablespoons of the butter in a large skillet over medium-high heat. Add half of the garlic and sauté for 1 minute. Add the oregano and red pepper flakes, if using, and stir for 1 to 2 minutes, until fragrant.

2. Add the shrimp and cook until no longer pink, 2 to 3 minutes. Remove from the pan and set aside.

3. Heat the remaining 2 tablespoons of butter and the oil in the skillet. Add the lemon juice, parsley, and linguine and stir to coat. Return the shrimp to the pan and toss everything together. Season with salt and pepper to taste and serve.

Note

Good low-carb noodle options here are Palmini noodles, zucchini noodles (see page 244), or my Egg Noodles (page 150).

NUTRITION INFO:
calories **601** | fat **40g** | protein **48g** | total carbs **7g** | dietary fiber **1g** | net carbs **6g**

SIMPLE SKILLET CHILI

YIELD: **4 servings (8 ounces per serving)**

PREP TIME: **10 minutes**

COOK TIME: **40 minutes**

This recipe has all the favors of a slow-cooked chili, but it's made in under an hour for those busy nights!

3 tablespoons avocado oil

3¾ ounces diced yellow onions (1 medium-large onion)

3 cloves garlic, minced

2½ ounces diced green bell pepper (about ½ large pepper)

2½ ounces diced red bell pepper (about 1 small pepper)

1 small jalapeño pepper, sliced

2 tablespoons chili powder

2 teaspoons ground cumin

2 teaspoons paprika

½ teaspoon cayenne pepper

½ teaspoon fine sea salt

1 tablespoon unsweetened cocoa powder

1 pound ground beef

1 cup mild salsa

1 cup beef bone broth

TOPPINGS (OPTIONAL)

Shredded cheddar cheese

Sour cream

Diced red onions

Chopped fresh cilantro

Sliced cherry tomatoes

Sliced jalapeños

1. Heat the oil in a large skillet over medium-high heat. Add the onions, garlic, bell peppers, and jalapeño. Cook until the vegetables have softened, 5 to 7 minutes.

2. Sprinkle the spices, salt, and cocoa powder over the contents of the skillet and stir well. Cook for about a minute, then add the beef. Cook, stirring to crumble the meat as it cooks, until browned, 6 to 8 minutes.

3. Stir in the salsa and broth. Cover and simmer for 20 to 25 minutes, until the mixture thickens and the broth is absorbed.

4. Serve immediately with the toppings of your choice.

5. Store leftovers in an airtight container in the refrigerator for up to 5 days or in the freezer for up to 2 months.

For the meal plan

Store one serving in the refrigerator for Day 24 and freeze the rest to enjoy after you've completed the plan; you'll freeze two servings if following the keto track or one serving if following the low-carb track.

NUTRITION INFO:
calories **457** | fat **35g** | protein **24g** | total carbs **13g** | dietary fiber **5g** | net carbs **8g**

SMOKED SALMON OMELET ROLL-UPS

YIELD: **2 roll-ups (1 per serving)**
PREP TIME: **10 minutes**
COOK TIME: **10 minutes**

A tasty little change from the typical egg breakfast. If you're not a fan of smoked salmon, you could swap it for deli ham or turkey.

4 large eggs, separated

2 tablespoons heavy cream or coconut milk (optional)

¼ heaping teaspoon fine sea salt

¼ teaspoon ground black pepper

2 teaspoons salted butter or avocado oil, divided, for the pan

Chopped fresh parsley, for garnish (optional)

FOR THE FILLING

2 tablespoons full-fat cream cheese, softened

⅔ Hass avocado, sliced

3½ ounces smoked salmon

1. In a bowl, using a fork or balloon whisk, whisk the egg yolks, heavy cream (if using), salt, and pepper until combined.

2. Put the egg whites in a clean mixing bowl and whisk using an electric hand mixer until stiff peaks form. With a silicone spatula, gently fold the whites into the yolks.

3. Melt 1 teaspoon of the butter in a 10-inch skillet over medium heat. Add half of the egg mixture and cook until golden brown on the bottom, just over 2 minutes. Flip and cook for another 2 to 3 minutes, until golden brown on both sides.

4. Remove the omelet from the pan and allow to cool slightly and settle, which will make it easier to roll. Repeat with the remaining butter and egg mixture to make a second omelet.

5. Spread 1 tablespoon of cream cheese on each omelet, then divide the avocado and smoked salmon evenly between the omelets, placing them in the center. Roll up and slice in half. (You may slice the roll-ups into rounds if you prefer, like sushi.) Garnish with parsley, if desired.

6. Best eaten fresh, but can be stored in the refrigerator for up to 2 days. For optimal flavor and texture, remove the leftover portion from the fridge 15 to 20 minutes before eating.

NUTRITION INFO:
calories **402** | fat **31g** | protein **24g** | total carbs **7g** | dietary fiber **4g** | net carbs **3g**

SMOKY GRILLED PORK CHOPS

YIELD: **2 servings**

PREP TIME: **5 minutes**

COOK TIME: **20 minutes**

Pork, "the other white meat"! My boys love the smoky spices used in this recipe, and grilling the chops makes them so moist. I often make a large batch, as shown in the photo, but for the meal plan, you'll be preparing just two chops.

2 (6-ounce) bone-in pork loin chops or center-cut pork rib chops (about 1½ inches thick)

2 tablespoons extra-virgin olive oil

1½ teaspoons fine sea salt

2 teaspoons garlic powder

2 teaspoons smoked paprika

½ teaspoon ground black pepper

1. Preheat a grill to between 400°F and 500°F with two cooking zones: one for direct heat and the other for indirect heat.

2. Rub both sides of the pork chops with the oil.

3. In a small bowl, stir together the salt and spices.

4. Sprinkle both sides of the chops with the spice mixture, then rub the spices into the meat.

5. Grill the pork chops over direct heat for 2 to 3 minutes on each side.

6. Remove the chops to the indirect heat zone of the grill to finish cooking. Close the lid and cook for 12 to 15 minutes more, until the internal temperature of the chops reaches 145°F.

7. Rest the chops for 5 to 10 minutes before serving.

8. Store leftovers in an airtight container in the refrigerator for up to 3 days. To reheat, melt a tablespoon of oil in a medium skillet over medium-high heat. Add a pork chop and cook for 1 to 2 minutes per side, until heated through.

NUTRITION INFO:
calories **404** | fat **26g** | protein **37g** | total carbs **3g** | dietary fiber **1g** | net carbs **2g**

SOFT SCRAMBLED EGGS

YIELD: 1 serving

PREP TIME: 1 minute

COOK TIME: 4 minutes

If you've been a hater of scrambled eggs, it may be that you've eaten them dry and overcooked. Once you make soft scrambled eggs, you will never want to eat them any other way!

1 tablespoon salted butter

2 large eggs

2 tablespoons water

1 tablespoon heavy cream

Salt and pepper

Chopped fresh parsley, for garnish (optional)

1. Heat the butter in a small skillet over medium-low heat.

2. Whisk the eggs with the water.

3. When the butter is just barely bubbling, add the eggs.

4. Swipe a silicone spatula around the edge of the pan, gently folding the eggs to form curds, 2 to 3 minutes. Be sure to move the pan on and off the heat if it looks like the eggs are cooking too quickly. You may need to lower the heat.

5. When the eggs are barely set and still glossy looking, pour in the heavy cream. Turn off the heat and continue to fold and stir until the cream is absorbed. Season to taste with salt and pepper and garnish with parsley, if desired. Best served fresh.

NUTRITION INFO:
calories **294** | fat **26g** | protein **13g** | total carbs **1g** | dietary fiber **0g** | net carbs **1g**

SPICY MAYO

YIELD: ½ heaping cup
(2 tablespoons per serving)

PREP TIME: 3 minutes

½ cup avocado oil mayonnaise

1 tablespoon Sriracha sauce, or more to taste

1½ teaspoons lime juice

½ teaspoon minced garlic

⅛ teaspoon fine sea salt

This flavorful mayonnaise gives you a little bit of heat and a whole lot of satisfaction with each creamy bite! You'll use it for the Spicy Smoked Salmon Wrap (page 224), but this recipe makes more than you'll need for one wrap. The leftover sauce goes nicely with my Crispy Broccoli (page 134).

Whisk together the ingredients in a small bowl. Taste and add more Sriracha and/or salt, if desired. Store in an airtight container in the refrigerator for up to 1 month.

NUTRITION INFO:
calories **201** | fat **24g** | protein **1g** | total carbs **1g** | dietary fiber **1g** | net carbs **0g**

SPICY SMOKED SALMON WRAP

YIELD: 1 serving

PREP TIME: 8 minutes

These wraps are a little messy but oh, so good! If you're following the low-carb track, you can replace the shirataki rice with cauliflower or Palmini rice. If you don't like smoked salmon, you can substitute canned tuna or sushi-grade salmon.

FOR THE FILLING

4 ounces smoked salmon, chopped

2 ounces shirataki rice, rinsed, drained, and squeezed of excess liquid in a towel

2 ounces diced Hass avocado (about ¼ avocado)

1 scallion, thinly sliced

1 tablespoon chopped fresh parsley

1 tablespoon fresh lime juice

2 tablespoons Spicy Mayo (page 222)

¼ teaspoon fine sea salt

⅛ teaspoon ground black pepper

2 large butter lettuce leaves, for serving

1. Mix together all the filling ingredients in a small bowl. Taste and adjust the salt and pepper as needed.

2. To assemble the wrap, cut off the hard stem end of each lettuce leaf. Lay the leaves facing each other with the stem ends in the middle, overlapping slightly, as if forming a pair of wings. Place the filling in the center and roll up. Cut in half to serve, if desired. Best served fresh.

NUTRITION INFO:
calories **425** | fat **34g** | protein **23g** | total carbs **8g** | dietary fiber **4g** | net carbs **4g**

SPRING ROLL CHICKEN SALAD WITH CREAMY ASIAN DRESSING

option

YIELD: **2 servings (8 ounces per serving)**

PREP TIME: **15 minutes**

This salad is like a deconstructed spring roll, with the yummy filling made easily using store-bought rotisserie chicken. After you've completed the meal plan, I suggest you double the dressing recipe to make ½ cup (or quadruple it to make 1 cup) to have on hand for green salads; it will keep for up to two weeks in the refrigerator.

FOR THE DRESSING

1 tablespoon plus 1 teaspoon avocado oil

1½ teaspoons coconut aminos

1 tablespoon apple cider vinegar

½ teaspoon minced garlic

1 tablespoon plus 1 teaspoon sunflower seed butter, tahini, or nut butter of choice

¼ to ½ teaspoon Swerve confectioners'-style sweetener (optional)

Salt to taste

6 ounces coleslaw mix or shredded green cabbage (about 2 cups)

8 ounces shredded rotisserie chicken breast (about 2 cups) (see Note)

½ cup half-moon cucumber slices

2½ ounces cherry tomatoes (about 6 tomatoes)

2 tablespoons sliced scallions, plus more for garnish if desired

1. Make the dressing: Whisk together all the ingredients in a small bowl until smooth. Taste and adjust the salt and/or sweetness if needed.

2. Evenly divide the coleslaw mix, chicken, cucumber slices, tomatoes, and scallions between 2 serving bowls.

3. Pour 2 tablespoons of dressing over each salad. If desired, serve with lime wedges, a sprinkle of sesame seeds, chopped peanuts, and/or additional scallions.

4. Store leftovers in an airtight container in the refrigerator for up to 3 days.

Note

To save a cooking step, I like to use rotisserie chicken for this recipe. The breast meat from one rotisserie chicken will yield the amount needed here. If cooking the chicken yourself, you'll need 10 ounces of raw boneless, skinless chicken breasts.

NUTRITION INFO:
calories **260** | fat **10g** | protein **31g** | total carbs **10g** | dietary fiber **3g** | net carbs **7g**

Lime wedges

Sesame seeds

Chopped peanuts

For the meal plan

Divide the ingredients between a serving bowl and a storage container and refrigerate the second portion for Day 11.

STUFFED CHICKEN THIGHS

YIELD: **2 servings (7½ ounces per serving)**

PREP TIME: **10 minutes**

COOK TIME: **30 minutes**

This high-protein meal will keep you full and satisfied for hours.

1¼ pounds boneless, skinless chicken thighs (4 or 5 small thighs)

½ teaspoon fine sea salt, divided

4 ounces ground pork

⅓ cup chopped fresh parsley, plus more for garnish

1 tablespoon minced garlic

1 tablespoon dried minced onion

¼ teaspoon ground black pepper

½ cup shredded mozzarella cheese

4 or 5 slices thick-cut bacon (depending on number of thighs)

1. Preheat the oven to 400°F. Line a rimmed baking sheet with parchment paper.

2. Lay the chicken thighs flat, facedown, on a cutting board. Open the thighs with your fingers by unfolding any portions of folded-over meat to make the thighs as thin and even in thickness as possible. Sprinkle ¼ teaspoon of the salt over the thighs. Set aside.

3. In a large bowl, mix together the pork, parsley, garlic, dried minced onion, remaining ¼ teaspoon of salt, pepper, and cheese until well combined. Divide the pork mixture into 4 or 5 equal portions, depending on the number of thighs you have.

4. Working with one portion of the pork mixture and one chicken thigh at a time, shape the pork mixture into a log with a length equal to the width of the thigh. Place the log in the center of the thigh. Fold the ends of the thigh toward the center of the log, overlapping them slightly, and place seam side down on the prepared baking sheet. Repeat with the remaining pork mixture and thighs.

5. Wrap each chicken thigh with a piece of bacon, tucking the ends under the bottom of the thigh.

6. Bake for 30 minutes, or until the internal temperature registers 165°F. If you want the bacon a bit crispier, broil for 1 to 2 minutes.

7. Garnish with parsley and enjoy immediately.

8. Store leftovers in an airtight container in the refrigerator for up to 3 days. To reheat, bake in a preheated 350°F oven for about 10 minutes.

NUTRITION INFO:
calories **667** | fat **37g** | protein **78g** | total carbs **5g** | dietary fiber **1g** | net carbs **4g**

SUGAR-FREE BBQ SAUCE

YIELD: 2 cups (2 tablespoons per serving)

PREP TIME: 3 minutes

This super fast and delicious BBQ sauce (no cooking needed!) is sure to become a staple in your sugar-free kitchen. During the detox, you'll use it to make the Bacon Bourbon Burgers (page 98) on Day 28. You'll need only 1 cup of this sauce for the burgers, so feel free to halve this recipe if you like, but I suggest you make the full batch. I'm sure you won't have trouble thinking of ways to use it up.

1½ cups sugar-free ketchup, store-bought or homemade (page 168)

¼ cup apple cider vinegar

1 tablespoon yacón syrup or sugar-free maple syrup, store-bought or homemade (page 232)

1 teaspoon maple extract

¼ cup packed Swerve brown sugar sweetener

2 tablespoons smoked paprika

Pinch of fine sea salt

Place all the ingredients in a blender and blend until smooth. Taste and add more sweetener and/or salt if needed. Store in an airtight container in the refrigerator for up to 1 month.

NUTRITION INFO:
calories **14** | fat **0g** | protein **0g** | total carbs **3g** | dietary fiber **0g** | net carbs **3g**

SUGAR-FREE MAPLE SYRUP

YIELD: 1¼ cups (2 tablespoons per serving)

PREP TIME: 5 minutes, plus 30 minutes to cool

COOK TIME: 12 minutes

You can certainly buy sugar-free maple syrup, but it can be costly. Making it at home ensures that you can choose your sweetener as well as how sweet you like the syrup to be. It's best to use a brown sugar substitute if you want that authentic maple syrup flavor. If you don't have yacón syrup, you can use molasses instead; it will not change the carb count.

1 tablespoon salted butter, ghee, or coconut oil

1½ cups water

1 tablespoon yacón syrup or molasses

½ cup packed Swerve brown sugar sweetener

½ teaspoon ground cinnamon

¼ scant teaspoon fine sea salt

½ teaspoon glucomannan or xanthan gum

2 teaspoons maple extract

1 teaspoon vanilla extract

1. Melt the butter, ghee, or coconut oil in a small saucepan over medium-high heat. If using butter, continue to heat until it is browned, about 3 minutes longer.

2. Add the water, yacón syrup, sweetener, cinnamon, and salt. Whisk together and bring to a boil, then reduce the heat to a simmer.

3. Sprinkle in the glucomannan a little at a time while whisking. Continue simmering for about 10 minutes, or until the syrup thickens.

4. Remove from the heat and stir in the extracts. Allow the syrup to cool for 30 minutes; it will thicken as it cools. Serve warm.

5. Store in an airtight container in the refrigerator for up to 2 months. Just before serving, reheat the refrigerated syrup in a small saucepan over medium-low heat, stirring constantly, until warmed through, about 5 minutes.

NUTRITION INFO:
calories **15** | fat **1g** | protein **0g** | total carbs **1g** | dietary fiber **0g** | net carbs **1g**

TACO SEASONING

YIELD: about 1½ cups
(1 tablespoon per serving)
PREP TIME: 2 minutes

I use this homemade seasoning blend for my Fish Taco Bowl (page 156) and Taco Soup (page 236). It's also perfect for simple tacos, or you can use it anytime you cook some ground beef. It's even great on chicken! Use ¼ cup per pound of meat, or more to your taste.

¼ cup plus 2 tablespoons chili powder

¼ cup plus 1 tablespoon ground cumin

3 tablespoons dried oregano leaves

3 tablespoons onion powder

3 tablespoons smoked paprika

3 tablespoons fine sea salt

2 tablespoons garlic powder

Place all the ingredients in a small bowl and whisk to combine. Store in an airtight container in the pantry for up to 1 year.

NUTRITION INFO:
calories **9** | fat **0g** | protein **0g** | total carbs **2g** | dietary fiber **0g** | net carbs **2g**

TACO SOUP

YIELD: **4 servings**

PREP TIME: **15 minutes**

COOK TIME: **20 minutes**

This easy keto taco soup is a quick meal that can be made in under 40 minutes. It's perfect for a cool day when you need some comfort in a bowl!

1 tablespoon extra-virgin olive oil, for the pan

2½ ounces diced yellow onions (about ½ large onion)

2 cloves garlic, minced

1 pound ground beef

2 tablespoons Taco Seasoning (page 234)

2 ounces diced green bell pepper (about ½ medium pepper)

2 ounces diced red bell pepper (about ½ medium pepper)

8 ounces canned diced tomatoes

2 tablespoons tomato paste

2 cups beef bone broth

½ teaspoon fine sea salt

½ teaspoon ground black pepper

TOPPINGS (OPTIONAL)

Chopped avocado

Chopped fresh cilantro

Shredded cheddar cheese

Sliced jalapeño pepper

Sour cream

1. Heat the oil in a Dutch oven or soup pot over medium heat. Add the onions and cook until softened, about 2 minutes. Add the garlic and sauté for another 30 seconds, or until fragrant.

2. Add the beef and cook, breaking it up with a wooden spoon, until browned, 4 to 5 minutes. If desired, drain and discard the fat.

3. Stir in the taco seasoning and bell peppers and sauté for 1 minute.

4. Add the diced tomatoes, tomato paste, broth, salt, and pepper and stir to combine. Reduce the heat to a simmer and cook for 15 to 20 minutes, until thickened. Taste and adjust the seasoning if needed.

5. Serve with the toppings of your choice.

6. Store in an airtight container in the refrigerator for up to 3 days or in the freezer for up to 3 months. Thaw frozen soup the night before reheating. To reheat, place some soup in a small pot and bring to a simmer to heat through.

For the meal plan

Refrigerate one serving for Day 9; freeze the remaining two servings to enjoy after you've completed the plan.

NUTRITION INFO:
calories **365** | fat **27g** | protein **22g** | total carbs **8g** | dietary fiber **2g** | net carbs **6g**

TUNA SALAD

YIELD: 1 serving

PREP TIME: 10 minutes

A simple recipe that's packed with flavor! If you don't have Dijon, simply swap in yellow mustard. If you're out of dill relish, chop up some dill pickles instead. Even if you're not a fan of tuna, I encourage you to try this recipe. It may just change your mind about tuna fish! You could also swap out the canned tuna for canned salmon, sardines, or even chicken if you prefer.

1 (5-ounce) can tuna (packed in water), drained

3 tablespoons avocado oil mayonnaise

1 tablespoon Dijon mustard

1 tablespoon finely diced red onions

1 tablespoon chopped fresh parsley (optional)

1½ teaspoons dill relish

¼ teaspoon fine sea salt

Ground black pepper to taste

1 to 2 teaspoons fresh lemon juice (optional)

2 romaine lettuce leaves, whole or chopped, or 1 Cloud Bread Roll (page 126), for serving

2 tablespoons unsweetened Italian dressing, store-bought or homemade (page 176), for serving (optional)

1. Put the tuna in a medium bowl and break apart using a fork until there are no chunks.

2. Add the remaining ingredients and stir well to combine. Taste and adjust the seasoning if needed.

3. If following the keto track, scoop the tuna salad into the lettuce leaves to serve as boats, or serve it on a bed of chopped lettuce tossed with the Italian dressing; if following the low-carb track, serve as a sandwich on a Cloud Bread Roll.

4. The tuna salad can be made ahead and stored in an airtight container in the refrigerator for up to 3 days.

Note

Looking for a good store-bought Italian dressing? See the Shopping Guide on page 288.

NUTRITION INFO (TUNA SALAD ONLY):

calories **554** | fat **42g** | protein **42g** | total carbs **6g** | dietary fiber **2g** | net carbs **4g**

2-MINUTE ENGLISH MUFFINS

YIELD: 2 muffins (1 per serving)
PREP TIME: 5 minutes
COOK TIME: 2 minutes

I created this recipe for my website several years ago, and it became popular for good reason. These English muffins have real nooks and crannies, just like traditional ones made with wheat flour. If you want lots of nooks and crannies, don't overmix the batter—the less you work it, the more "holes" you will get. You want to just combine the wet and dry ingredients.

For flatter muffins that are about the size of traditional ones, it's best to use 5-ounce quiche dishes, about 4¼ inches in diameter and 1 inch tall; 4-ounce quiche dishes will work, too, for slightly smaller muffins. Seven-ounce ramekins will work fine as well—the muffins just won't be as wide.

2 tablespoons unsweetened almond butter

1 tablespoon salted butter or coconut oil

2 tablespoons blanched almond flour

½ teaspoon baking powder

⅛ teaspoon fine sea salt

1 tablespoon unsweetened almond milk

1 large egg, beaten

Butter, for serving (optional)

SPECIAL EQUIPMENT:

2 (5- or 4-ounce) quiche dishes or 2 (7-ounce) ramekins

1. Grease two 5- or 4-ounce quiche dishes or 7-ounce ramekins with olive oil or coconut oil spray.

2. Put the almond butter and butter in a small microwave-safe bowl. Microwave for 30 seconds, or until melted, then stir until smooth. Set aside to cool.

3. In another small bowl, whisk together the almond flour, baking powder, and salt.

4. Pour the almond milk and beaten egg into the dry ingredients and stir until just combined, then stir in the almond butter mixture. Do not overmix.

5. Pour the batter evenly into the prepared quiche dishes or ramekins. Microwave one at a time for 1 minute. Check the center with a toothpick; if it comes out clean, the muffin is done. If not, continue to microwave in 30-second intervals until the center is cooked. (If you use shallow quiche dishes, the muffins will likely be done in 1 minute.)

6. Allow to cool for a few minutes, then remove the muffins from the dishes and slice in half horizontally. Toast, if desired, and enjoy with some butter.

7. The muffins can be made ahead and stored untoasted in an airtight container in the refrigerator for up to 5 days. Toast when ready to enjoy.

NUTRITION INFO:
calories **222** | fat **20g** | protein **7g** | total carbs **5g** | dietary fiber **2g** | net carbs **3g**

Note ————————————————————————————

To make these muffins nut-free, swap out the almond butter for sunflower seed butter (I suggest you steer clear of peanut butter—its flavor is too strong here), and replace the almond milk with another nondairy milk, such as coconut milk, or heavy cream or even water. The almond flour can be replaced with sunflower seed flour.

WAFFLE BREAKFAST SANDWICH

YIELD: 1 serving
PREP TIME: 5 minutes
COOK TIME: 5 minutes

Super simple, low in carbs, and high in protein, this hearty breakfast sandwich will easily carry you through to lunch while you are detoxing. It makes a great lunch as well! (Something to look forward to once you've completed the meal plan…)

2 Dairy-Free Mini Waffles (page 140)

2 slices deli ham (about 1 ounce)

1 tablespoon salted butter, for the pan

1 large egg

2 slices cheddar cheese (about 1 ounce)

1. Toast the waffles. Lay the ham on one of the waffles. Set aside.

2. Heat the butter in a small skillet over medium heat. Crack the egg into the pan and fry to your liking. Turn off the heat. Top the fried egg with the cheese and cover the pan to melt the cheese.

3. Lay the fried egg on top of the ham. Top with the second waffle to form a sandwich and enjoy. Best served fresh.

NUTRITION INFO:
calories **547** | fat **44g** | protein **33g** | total carbs **5g** | dietary fiber **2g** | net carbs **3g**

ZUCCHINI NOODLES WITH ROASTED GARLIC CREAM SAUCE

YIELD: 2 servings (6 ounces per serving)

PREP TIME: 15 minutes

COOK TIME: 40 minutes

Zucchini noodles are an easy and tasty way to enjoy "pasta" but with a whole lot less carbs! For the meal plan, I've paired them with a garlicky cream sauce; after the plan, when you're looking for a change, try serving them with marinara sauce and my French Onion Meatballs (page 158).

FOR THE SAUCE

1 small bulb garlic

1½ teaspoons extra-virgin olive oil

3 tablespoons salted butter

1 cup heavy cream

¼ cup grated Parmesan cheese

¼ teaspoon ground black pepper, or to taste

¼ teaspoon glucomannan or xanthan gum (optional)

FOR THE NOODLES

6 ounces zucchini (about 1 medium zucchini), ends trimmed

1 tablespoon extra-virgin olive oil, for the pan

¼ teaspoon fine sea salt

Red pepper flakes (optional)

Chopped fresh parsley (optional)

1. Preheat the oven to 350°F.

2. Roast the garlic for the sauce: Slice off just enough of the top of the garlic bulb to expose the tips of the cloves inside. Place a small square of aluminum foil—large enough to wrap around the bulb—on the counter. Set an equal-size piece of parchment paper on top of the foil, then place the garlic bulb on the parchment. Drizzle the oil over the exposed cloves. Wrap the foil around the bulb, making a tented packet. Roast for 20 to 25 minutes, until the garilc is fragrant and browned. Carefully open the packet and set aside to cool.

3. Remove the garlic cloves by squeezing the unopened end of the bulb; the cloves should slide right out. Mash the cloves with a fork to a pastelike texture.

4. Prepare the sauce: Melt the butter in a medium skillet over medium-low heat, then add the roasted garlic and heavy cream. Bring to a low simmer, stirring occasionally.

5. Whisk in the Parmesan and black pepper and continue to stir until thickened, 5 to 8 minutes. If it's not quite thick enough for your liking, sprinkle the glucomannan over the sauce while stirring and simmer for a few more minutes to thicken further. Cover the pan and set the sauce aside while you make the noodles.

6. Prepare the noodles: Following the manufacturer's instructions for your spiral slicer, cut the zucchini into noodles; discard the core with the seeds. Alternatively, cut the zucchini into noodles using a serrated vegetable peeler: hold the zucchini at an angle and, applying light pressure, peel down the sides. Continue to peel each side of the zucchini until you get to the center with the seeds. Discard the center.

NUTRITION INFO:
calories **235** I fat **20g** I protein **6g** I total carbs **7g** I dietary fiber **3g** I net carbs **4g**

Note

If you don't have time to roast the garlic for the sauce, omit the 1½ teaspoons olive oil and replace the bulb of garlic with 1 tablespoon minced garlic. Jump ahead to Step 4, but cook the garlic in the melted butter until fragrant before pouring in the cream. Continue with the recipe as written.

7. Heat the oil in a large skillet over medium heat. Add the zucchini noodles and sauté, using tongs to constantly toss them with the oil, until al dente, 3 to 4 minutes. Sprinkle with the salt.

8. To serve, top the noodles with the cream sauce and, if desired, red pepper flakes and parsley. Enjoy!

9. Store leftovers in an airtight container in the refrigerator for up to 3 days. Reheat in a skillet over medium-high heat.

DETOX DESSERTS & BEVERAGES

If, when I made the commitment to remove white sugar and processed carbs from my life, anyone had told me that I could never again have dessert, I would have given up. To me, that would have been like living as a prisoner; it simply would not have been sustainable. My solution? To start creating sugar-free, low-carb dessert recipes that would satisfy my sweet tooth without spiking my blood sugar or causing cravings.

There is always a decision to be made when it comes to what is realistic as you learn to navigate life without sugar. If enjoying sugar-free, low-carb desserts helps you avoid sugar and processed carbs, then keeping them on the menu is a wise decision for you. If eating a sugar-free dessert triggers out-of-control cravings, causing you to eat more than one serving at a time, then you need to abstain from the desserts in this chapter, at least for a while. You can always revisit this decision later. Remember, it's one day at a time: all you need to think about is making choices each day that move you toward your health goals.

Moderation is key to consuming sweets. To progress from sugar addiction to sugar freedom, I highly suggest you enjoy the very delicious desserts I'm sharing here no more than three times per week (and not three days in a row!), or save desserts for weekends. This will train your brain not to expect a sweet treat each day. Delayed gratification is a wonderful tool!

Berry Fluff / 248

Brownie in a Mug / 250

Keto Chocolate Lava Cakes for Two / 252

Keto Dalgona Coffee / 254

Deep Dish Chocolate Chip Cookie / 256

Egg Custard / 258

Keto Electrolyte Drink—Three Ways / 260

No-Churn Vanilla Ice Cream / 262

Panna Cotta / 264

Raspberry Clafoutis / 266

Scrambled Egg Chocolate Pudding / 268

Sugar-Free Whipped Cream / 270

Tiramisu for Two / 272

BERRY FLUFF

YIELD: **3 servings**

PREP TIME: **10 minutes**

This super quick and tasty dessert provides three servings for you to enjoy during a busy week.

4 ounces full-fat cream cheese, softened

½ cup heavy cream

⅓ cup confectioners'-style sweetener (Better Than Sugar or Swerve) (see Note)

½ teaspoon vanilla extract

Pinch of fine sea salt

½ cup halved strawberries or whole blackberries, blueberries, or raspberries

3 strawberries, or 6 blackberries, blueberries, or raspberries, for garnish (optional)

1. Put the cream cheese, heavy cream, sweetener, vanilla extract, and salt in a blender and blend until smooth and fluffy. Taste and add more sweetener if needed.

2. Divide the berries among three 8-ounce serving glasses.

3. Spoon the fluff over the berries in each glass. Garnish with additional berries, if desired.

4. Store in an airtight container in the refrigerator for up to 5 days.

Note ————

When I call for confectioners'-style sweetener, aka powdered sugar, in my sugar-free desserts, I provide two options: Better Than Sugar and Swerve. If you are accustomed to very sweet desserts and this lifestyle is brand-new to you, I suggest using Better Than Sugar, at least to start; it is as sweet as sugar and will provide a sweetness level comparable to what you've been used to. I find Swerve confectioners'-style sweetener to be less sweet-tasting than Better Than Sugar; you may find Swerve doesn't provide as much sweetness as you like in a dessert. Ultimately, either sweetener will work just fine in these recipes; the choice comes down to your preference.

NUTRITION INFO:

calories **272** | fat **26g** | protein **2g** | total carbs **4g** | dietary fiber **1g** | net carbs **3g**

BROWNIE IN A MUG

YIELD: **2 servings**

PREP TIME: **5 minutes**

COOK TIME: **1 minute**

A quick and easy brownie that makes just two servings—perfect for portion control during the detox or when bringing desserts back into your life later on. To make this recipe nut-free, simply replace the almond flour with sunflower seed flour.

1 large egg, beaten

2 tablespoons heavy cream

1 tablespoon salted butter, softened, plus more for greasing

1 teaspoon vanilla extract

¼ cup blanched almond flour

2 tablespoons Swerve granular sweetener

2 tablespoons unsweetened cocoa powder

2 teaspoons instant espresso powder

¼ teaspoon baking powder

Pinch of fine sea salt

1 tablespoon sugar-free chocolate chips (optional)

1. Grease two 8-ounce coffee mugs, ramekins, or microwave-safe bowls with butter.

2. In a small bowl, stir together the egg, heavy cream, butter, and vanilla extract until combined. In a medium bowl, whisk together the dry ingredients, including the chocolate chips, if using. Stir the wet mixture into the dry until combined.

3. Divide the batter evenly between the prepared mugs.

4. Microwave one brownie at a time in 30-second intervals until the center is no longer wet and a toothpick inserted in the center comes out clean. (Mine was done after 1 minute of cooking on high power.)

5. Store covered in the refrigerator for up to 1 week. Reheat in the microwave for 30 seconds or enjoy chilled from the fridge.

 Notes

If using a coffee mug versus a ramekin or bowl, the texture of the brownie will be a little lighter, more like a muffin; if you prefer a denser texture, like a classic brownie, use a ramekin or bowl.

You can also bake these brownies in the oven. Be sure to use an ovenproof mug, ramekin, or bowl and bake at 350°F for 16 to 18 minutes, or until a toothpick comes out clean when inserted in the center.

NUTRITION INFO:
calories **235** | fat **20g** | protein **6g** | total carbs **7g** | dietary fiber **3g** | net carbs **4g**

KETO CHOCOLATE LAVA CAKES FOR TWO

option

YIELD: 2 servings

PREP TIME: 5 minutes

COOK TIME: 15 minutes

Decadent chocolate cake with a gooey, oozing center—it's a good thing this recipe makes only two servings! This cake is best served fresh, so if you're making it just for yourself, simply cut the recipe in half. To make this recipe nut-free, replace the almond flour with sunflower seed flour.

2 large eggs

1 teaspoon vanilla extract

2 ounces sugar-free chocolate chips

¼ cup (½ stick) salted butter, plus more for greasing

1 teaspoon instant coffee granules

2 tablespoons confectioners'-style sweetener (Better Than Sugar or Swerve)

1 tablespoon blanched almond flour

FOR SERVING (OPTIONAL)

Sugar-Free Whipped Cream (page 270)

Fresh berries

1. Preheat the oven to 350°F. Generously grease two 8-ounce ramekins or ovenproof bowls with butter.

2. Using a stand mixer (or a medium mixing bowl and an electric hand mixer), beat the eggs and vanilla extract until thick and creamy.

3. Put the chocolate chips, butter, and coffee granules in a microwave-safe bowl and heat in 30-second bursts, stirring between increments, until melted and smooth.

4. Slowly pour the melted chocolate mixture into the egg mixture, beating on low speed until combined.

5. Fold in the sweetener and almond flour until well incorporated.

6. Evenly pour the batter into the prepared ramekins and bake until the tops are set but still jiggle when gently shaken, 10 to 15 minutes. (The exact cooking time will depend on the shape and size of your ramekins; deeper ones will take more time to bake, while shallower ones will take less time.) Set aside for 5 minutes to cool slightly.

7. Serve directly from the ramekins or bowls or turn onto serving plates. Top with whipped cream and berries, if desired, and enjoy immediately.

NUTRITION INFO:

calories **394** | fat **38g** | protein **9g** | total carbs **6g** | dietary fiber **1g** | net carbs **5g**

KETO DALGONA COFFEE

YIELD: **1 serving**

PREP TIME: **3 minutes**

COOK TIME: **3 minutes (for hot version)**

1½ teaspoons instant coffee granules

1½ tablespoons confectioners'-style sweetener (Better Than Sugar or Swerve)

⅛ teaspoon ground cinnamon (optional)

¼ teaspoon caramel extract or vanilla extract

Pinch of fine sea salt

1 tablespoon hot water

FOR SERVING

1 cup water, unsweetened almond milk, or other milk of choice

Ice (if serving iced)

With just three main ingredients—coffee, low-carb sweetener, and hot water—and the aid of an electric mixer, you've got a fantastic keto whipped coffee beverage that can be enjoyed iced or hot!

1. Put all the ingredients, except the hot water, in a stand mixer fitted with the whisk attachment (or use a medium mixing bowl and an electric hand mixer). Mix on high speed until combined.

2. Add the tablespoon of hot water and continue to mix on high speed for 1 minute. Scrape down the sides of the bowl, then beat on high for 2 to 3 minutes more, until the mixture has lightened in color and has a texture similar to whipped cream.

3. If serving the coffee hot, heat 1 cup of water or milk and pour it into a 12-ounce mug; if serving the coffee iced, pour the water or milk into an ice-filled 12-ounce glass. Spoon the whipped coffee mixture into the mug or glass. If the coffee is iced, stir well to incorporate the whipped coffee into the water/milk.

NUTRITION INFO (USING WATER, NOT MILK):
calories **10** | fat **1g** | protein **1g** | total carbs **2g** | dietary fiber **1g** | net carbs **1g**

DEEP DISH CHOCOLATE CHIP COOKIE

YIELD: 1 serving

PREP TIME: 5 minutes

COOK TIME: 45 seconds to 15 minutes (depending on method)

No need to get derailed on this 30-day sugar detox when you are able to make this quick, delicious dessert in 20 minutes tops, and even more quickly if using the microwave! For a bit more indulgence, top it with a scoop of my No-Churn Vanilla Ice Cream (page 262) or Sugar-Free Whipped Cream (page 270) and a drizzle of melted sugar-free chocolate chips. To make this recipe nut-free, simply use sunflower seed butter and replace the almond flour with sunflower seed flour.

1 tablespoon salted butter or coconut oil

1 tablespoon unsweetened peanut butter or nut butter of choice

2 tablespoons blanched almond flour

⅛ teaspoon fine sea salt

½ teaspoon vanilla- or chocolate-flavored liquid stevia

¼ teaspoon vanilla extract

1 large egg yolk

1 tablespoon sugar-free chocolate chips

1. If using the oven, preheat the oven to 350°F.

2. Grease an 8-ounce ramekin or mug with avocado oil cooking spray.

3. Put the butter and peanut butter in the prepared ramekin. Heat in the microwave for 30 seconds, or until the butter is melted. Stir until well combined.

4. Mix in the almond flour, salt, stevia, and vanilla extract until well combined.

5. Whisk in the egg yolk, then stir in most of the chocolate chips, reserving 3 or 4 chips for the top of the cookie. Sprinkle the reserved chocolate chips on top.

6. If using the oven, place the ramekin on a small rimmed baking sheet and bake until the center of the cookie is set, 12 to 15 minutes.

If using the microwave, microwave the ramekin for 30 seconds. Wait 30 seconds. When ready, the cookie will be set in the center and a toothpick inserted will come out clean. If it still looks wet in the center, continue microwaving in 15-second intervals until set. (My cookie was done after 45 seconds of cooking on high power.) It's best to undercook the cookie in the microwave; overcooking will produce a dry cookie.

NUTRITION INFO:
calories **391** | fat **36g** | protein **11g** | total carbs **9g** | dietary fiber **2g** | net carbs **7g**

EGG CUSTARD

option

YIELD: **5 servings**

PREP TIME: **5 minutes**

COOK TIME: **30 minutes**

A creamy custard dessert with just 1 gram of total carbohydrate! To make this recipe nut-free, simply replace the almond milk with another nondairy milk of your choice or even heavy cream.

FOR THE CUSTARD

4 large eggs

1½ cups heavy cream

½ cup unsweetened almond milk

½ teaspoon vanilla-flavored liquid stevia

1 teaspoon vanilla extract

⅓ cup confectioners'-style sweetener (Better Than Sugar or Swerve)

Pinch of fine sea salt

FOR SERVING (OPTIONAL)

Fresh berries and/or Sugar-Free Whipped Cream (page 270)

1. Preheat the oven to 350°F. Set five 8-ounce ramekins in a 9 by 13-inch baking dish.

2. Put all the custard ingredients in a blender and blend until smooth. Pour the mixture evenly into the ramekins.

3. Place the baking dish in the oven. Carefully pour hot water into the baking dish until it reaches halfway up the sides of the ramekins.

4. Bake for 30 minutes, or until the tops are lightly golden brown but the custard is still a bit jiggly. (If you have a gas oven, you may need to bake the custards for 40 minutes.) Remove from the oven and allow to cool and set up for about 10 minutes.

5. Enjoy warm or chilled, topped with berries and/or whipped cream, if desired.

6. Store covered in the refrigerator for up to 1 week. Enjoy leftovers chilled.

NUTRITION INFO:
calories **222** | fat **20g** | protein **5g** | total carbs **1g** | dietary fiber **0g** | net carbs **1g**

KETO ELECTROLYTE DRINK— THREE WAYS

YIELD: *four 8-ounce servings*
PREP TIME: **5 minutes**

These electrolyte drinks are a fantastic way to get vitamins and minerals, and it costs a lot less to make them at home than to buy them at a store. You can control the sweetness using your favorite sugar-free sweetener. Any sweetener will work here, but to enhance the flavor, try a flavored stevia. My favorite for these drinks is SweetLeaf Water Drops in the lemon-lime flavor. These drinks can be enjoyed cold, but using hot herbal, black, or green tea is a wonderful option when the weather gets cold and you need a warm pick-me-up!

LEMON GINGER

½ teaspoon grated fresh ginger

¼ teaspoon fine sea salt

¼ cup fresh lemon juice

4 cups cold water, coconut water, or sparkling water or hot tea (any type)

Lemon slices or wedges, for garnish (optional)

LIME MINT

1 teaspoon fresh mint leaves

¼ teaspoon fine sea salt

¼ cup fresh lime juice

4 cups cold water, coconut water, or sparkling water or hot tea (any type)

Lime slices or wedges, for garnish (optional)

ORANGE BASIL

1 teaspoon fresh basil leaves

¼ teaspoon fine sea salt

¼ cup fresh orange juice

4 cups cold water, coconut water, or sparkling water or hot tea (any type)

Orange slices or wedges, for garnish (optional)

OPTIONAL (FOR ALL FLAVORS)

1 teaspoon calcium magnesium powder

½ teaspoon liquid stevia or stevia-based sweetener

1. If making the lemon ginger flavor, put all the ingredients in a 32-ounce mason jar, including the optional ingredients, if using, and stir well.

If making the lime mint or orange basil flavor, put the herb, salt, and juice in a heavy-bottomed 8-ounce glass container (a liquid measuring cup is ideal). Using a muddler or the back of a wooden spoon, muddle the herb to release its flavor. Strain the mixture through a fine-mesh sieve into a 32-ounce mason jar. Add the water and the optional ingredients, if using, and stir well.

2. Garnish each serving with a citrus slice or wedge, if desired, and enjoy. Store covered in the refrigerator for up to 3 days. Stir before serving.

NUTRITION INFO (LEMON GINGER AND LIME MINT FLAVORS):
calories **4** | fat **1g** | protein **1g** | total carbs **1g** | dietary fiber **0g** | net carbs **1g**

NUTRITION INFO (ORANGE BASIL FLAVOR):
calories **4** | fat **1g** | protein **1g** | total carbs **2g** | dietary fiber **0g** | net carbs **1g**

NO-CHURN VANILLA ICE CREAM

YIELD: **3 cups** (½ **cup per serving**)

PREP TIME: **15 minutes, plus 4 to 5 hours to freeze**

COOK TIME: **15 minutes**

4 large egg yolks

½ cup confectioners'-style sweetener (Better Than Sugar or Swerve)

2 cups heavy cream

½ cup liquid allulose

2 teaspoons vanilla extract

Pinch of fine sea salt

With this recipe, you can make incredibly creamy sugar-free vanilla ice cream at home without an ice cream maker! This delicious no-churn keto ice cream is soft and scoopable right out of the freezer, and it has just 2 grams of total carbs per serving. For an extra-fancy treat, try topping a scoop of this ice cream with a dollop of Sugar-Free Whipped Cream (page 270) or a drizzle of melted sugar-free chocolate chips—or both!

1. Bring an inch or two of water to a simmer in the bottom of a double boiler over medium-high heat, or create your own double boiler setup using a saucepan or pot over which a heatproof bowl fits snugly, without the bottom of the bowl touching the water.

2. Place the egg yolks and confectioners'-style sweetener in the bowl sitting over the simmering water and whisk together. Continue whisking until the mixture thickens, 5 to 8 minutes.

3. To test the thickness, scrape a wooden spoon across the bottom of the bowl. When you can clearly see the bottom as you scrape, the ice cream mixture is ready. Remove the bowl and set aside.

4. Pour the heavy cream, allulose, vanilla extract, and salt into a stand mixer fitted with the whisk attachment (or use a medium mixing bowl and an electric hand mixer). Beat until stiff peaks form. Taste and add more sweetener if needed.

5. Stir a small spoonful of the whipped cream into the egg mixture to temper the yolks. Repeat 3 more times, stirring after each addition. Turn the mixer to low speed and slowly pour the egg mixture into the whipped cream, mixing until just combined.

6. Pour into a 9 by 5-inch loaf pan and freeze until set, 4 to 5 hours.

7. Store covered in the freezer for up to 2 months.

NUTRITION INFO:
calories **307** | fat **2g** | protein **30g** | total carbs **2g** | dietary fiber **0g** | net carbs **2g**

PANNA COTTA

YIELD: **4 servings**

PREP TIME: **5 minutes, plus
6 hours to set**

COOK TIME: **10 minutes**

1½ cups heavy cream

½ cup unsweetened almond milk

2 teaspoons unflavored gelatin powder

⅓ cup confectioners'-style sweetener (Better Than Sugar or Swerve)

Pinch of fine sea salt

½ teaspoon vanilla extract

FOR SERVING (OPTIONAL)

Fresh berries and/or Sugar-Free Whipped Cream (page 270)

This is the perfect dessert for those who are just done with eggs! To make this recipe nut-free, replace the almond milk with another nondairy milk of your choice or more heavy cream.

1. Grease four 7-ounce ramekins with butter.

2. Pour the heavy cream and almond milk into a medium saucepan. Turn the heat to medium-high and sprinkle the gelatin over the cream mixture. Don't stir; allow the gelatin to bloom while the mixture comes to a simmer, 3 to 5 minutes.

3. Once at a simmer, reduce the heat to low and continually whisk the mixture until the gelatin is completely dissolved.

4. Whisk in the sweetener and salt and continue to simmer for 2 to 3 minutes, just until thickened. Turn off the heat and stir in the vanilla extract. Taste and add more sweetener if needed.

5. Evenly pour the mixture into the ramekins and allow to cool for 15 minutes. Place in the refrigerator until fully set up, about 6 hours or overnight.

6. Serve out of the ramekins or turn onto serving plates. Garnish with berries and/or whipped cream, if desired.

7. Store covered in the refrigerator for up to 1 week.

NUTRITION INFO:
calories **308** | fat **30g** | protein **1g** | total carbs **1g** | dietary fiber **0g** | net carbs **1g**

RASPBERRY CLAFOUTIS

option

YIELD: **4 servings**

PREP TIME: **5 minutes, plus 2 hours to chill (optional)**

COOK TIME: **15 minutes**

An easy dessert made in a blender. It's comforting, creamy, and bursting with fresh berries. If you're feeling fancy, I recommend topping these with a dusting of confectioners'-style sweetener or a dollop of Sugar-Free Whipped Cream. To make this recipe nut-free, simply replace the almond flour with sunflower seed flour.

⅔ cup fresh raspberries

2 large eggs

½ cup plus 1 tablespoon heavy cream

2½ tablespoons salted butter, melted, plus more for greasing

½ cup blanched almond flour

¼ cup confectioners'-style sweetener (Better Than Sugar or Swerve), plus more for dusting if desired

½ teaspoon baking powder

¼ teaspoon xanthan gum or glucomannan

Sugar-Free Whipped Cream (page 270), for topping (optional)

1. Place an oven rack in the middle of the oven and preheat the oven to 375°F. Grease four shallow 8-ounce quiche dishes or ramekins with butter. Place the dishes on a rimmed baking sheet.

2. Put 2 or 3 raspberries in each dish; set the remaining berries aside.

3. Put the rest of the ingredients in a blender and blend until just combined. Evenly pour the batter into the prepared dishes.

4. Place the remaining raspberries on top of the batter, dividing them equally among the dishes.

5. Place the baking sheet on the middle rack of the oven and bake the clafoutis for 15 minutes, or until the centers are just set; they should still be slightly jiggly.

6. Let cool slightly and enjoy warm or, for a firmer, flanlike custard, let cool completely and then refrigerate for about 2 hours before serving.

7. If desired, serve with a dusting of confectioners'-style sweetener or a dollop of whipped cream.

8. Store covered in the refrigerator for up to 1 week.

SPECIAL EQUIPMENT:

4 (8-ounce) quiche dishes or ramekins

NUTRITION INFO:
calories **351** | fat **33g** | protein **7g** | total carbs **6g** | dietary fiber **3g** | net carbs **3g**

SCRAMBLED EGG CHOCOLATE PUDDING

YIELD: **4 servings**

PREP TIME: **5 minutes, plus 1 hour to set**

COOK TIME: **5 minutes**

I know it sounds odd, but you really can't tell that there are scrambled eggs in this pudding. I fooled my daughter for a whole year until I asked her to help me make a video for this popular recipe. She was shocked she'd been eating scrambled eggs all that time! But devising a perfectly disguised pudding was a process of trial and error. My friend Maria Emmerich created this pudding using hard-boiled eggs. My daughter has a good nose, so I had to find a quicker egg method to hide the evidence. Scrambling is faster and produces no smell like when hard-boiling. For an extra-indulgent treat, top the pudding with Sugar-Free Whipped Cream (page 270), some grated sugar-free chocolate, or both!

2 tablespoons salted butter or coconut oil, for the pan

8 large eggs

1 cup unsweetened almond milk or other nondairy milk of choice

½ cup confectioners'-style sweetener (Better Than Sugar or Swerve)

¼ cup unsweetened cocoa powder

½ teaspoon vanilla extract

½ teaspoon ground cinnamon

Pinch of fine sea salt

1. Heat the butter in a large skillet over medium heat.

2. Whisk the eggs, then pour them into the skillet and cook, stirring, until the eggs are hard-scrambled, about 5 minutes; for this recipe, the eggs should be firm and dry, no longer creamy or wet.

3. Put the scrambled eggs in a high-powered blender or food processor with the rest of the ingredients. Blend until completely smooth. Taste and add more sweetener, if desired.

4. Evenly pour the pudding mixture into four 4-ounce serving glasses and refrigerate until set, about 1 hour.

5. Store covered in the refrigerator for up to 4 days.

NUTRITION INFO:
calories **163** | fat **11g** | protein **13g** | total carbs **5g** | dietary fiber **3g** | net carbs **2g**

SUGAR-FREE WHIPPED CREAM

YIELD: 2 cups (¼ cup per serving)

PREP TIME: 5 minutes

Whipped cream is a no-brainer on any dessert, and don't forget iced coffee…but why stop there? I like whipped cream on just about everything. In fact, I even enjoy it on top of a couple tablespoons of peanut butter!

1 cup heavy whipping cream

¼ cup confectioners'-style sweetener (Better Than Sugar or Swerve)

½ teaspoon vanilla extract

¼ teaspoon vanilla-flavored liquid stevia (optional)

Place all the ingredients in a stand mixer fitted with the whisk attachment (or use a medium bowl and an electric hand mixer). Beat on high speed until soft peaks form, 3 to 4 minutes. Store in an airtight container in the refrigerator for up to 2 days.

Note

Placing the whisk attachment (or beaters) and mixing bowl in the freezer for 10 minutes beforehand will make whipping the cream go even quicker!

NUTRITION INFO:
calories **100** | fat **10g** | protein **0g** | total carbs **0g** | dietary fiber **0g** | net carbs **0g**

TIRAMISU FOR TWO

YIELD: **2 servings**

PREP TIME: **15 minutes, plus 30 minutes to chill**

A traditional tiramisu takes quite a long time to make, but this recipe using Cloud Bread Rolls is nice and easy and tastes just like the real thing!

2 Cloud Bread Rolls (page 126)

2 tablespoons unsweetened cocoa powder, divided

FOR THE ESPRESSO SOAK

2 shots espresso, or ¼ cup triple-strength coffee

⅓ cup water

¼ cup confectioners'-style sweetener (Better Than Sugar or Swerve)

2 teaspoons rum extract

FOR THE CREAM FILLING

3 ounces mascarpone or softened full-fat cream cheese

⅓ cup heavy cream

1 teaspoon coffee extract

¼ cup confectioners'-style sweetener (Better Than Sugar or Swerve)

1. Cut the rolls into bite-size cubes. Set aside.

2. In a shallow dish, whisk together the ingredients for the espresso soak. Place half of the bread cubes in the espresso mixture, stirring to coat the pieces on all sides. Set aside to soak while you prepare the cream filling.

3. Make the filling: Put the mascarpone, heavy cream, coffee extract, and sweetener in a stand mixer fitted with the paddle attachment. (Or use a medium mixing bowl and an electric hand mixer.) Beat on medium speed until completely combined and smooth; the mixture will be thick. Taste and add more sweetener if needed.

4. Evenly divide the soaked bread cubes between two 12-ounce serving glasses. Set aside.

5. Place the remaining bread cubes in the espresso mixture; stir to coat the bread on all sides and set aside to soak.

6. Spoon one-quarter of the cream filling over the bread cubes in one serving glass, pressing the cream down to push the bread pieces together in the bottom of the glass. Repeat for the second serving, using another quarter of the filling.

7. Using 1 tablespoon of the cocoa powder, evenly dust the cream in both glasses.

8. Place the remaining soaked bread cubes on top of the cream in the glasses, pressing down to push the bread pieces together.

9. Spoon the remaining cream filling evenly into the two glasses and dust with the remaining tablespoon of cocoa powder. Refrigerate for at least 30 minutes before serving.

10. Store covered in the refrigerator for up to 3 days.

NUTRITION INFO:
calories **506** | fat **42g** | protein **18g** | total carbs **7g** | dietary fiber **2g** | net carbs **5g**

4

KEEPING
the Momentum
GOING

You've completed the 30-Day Sugar Elimination Diet, and now you must decide whether you will bring sugar back into your life. Can you enjoy treats on special occasions without feeling out of control, or would having "just a little" trigger you to overindulge?

ARE YOU A MODERATOR OR AN ABSTAINER?

One controversial topic among people working hard to lose weight is whether it's better to moderate consumption of processed, refined carbs and the packaged products that turn to sugar in our bodies, or to abstain from them entirely.

The advice many nutritionists give is "Eat anything you want in moderation." The idea is that if you perceive a food as being off-limits, you'll only want it more. Therefore, if you embrace the mentality that you can have any food you want and nothing is off the table, you will be less likely to crave and overeat those less-than-optimal foods. It's said that "diet mentality," or swearing off certain foods, only makes you want those foods more.

For people who can successfully moderate sugar and refined carbs, avoiding strict rules and allowing occasional indulgences can help them follow through on their weight-loss goals. Those who have dieted their entire lives may fall into this category of moderators. However, other people fail miserably at moderation. I tried to moderate sugar and refined carbs for years, and no amount of attempting to change my mindset by telling myself, "I will allow any food; I just need to portion it out, and then I will be satisfied," ever worked to control the constant urge I had to eat more and more until I was stuffed and disgusted with myself. I put so much time and thought into how to allow small indulgences of sugary snacks into my life that I was utterly exhausted.

I know I'm not the only one who has a very real inability to moderate sugar and refined carbs. For people like me, overconsuming sugar causes a dopamine response similar to what alcoholics and drug addicts experience when they use alcohol and drugs. In fact, in his article "Are Sugary Foods Addictive?" on NutritionFacts.org, Dr. Michael Greger says PET scans have shown that overeating sugar changes brain activity in ways similar to drug addiction.

I wished for years that I could control my impulses and enjoy sugar and refined carbs on special occasions, just for holidays, or only once a week. *I could not do it.* The struggle was too great, and the holiday or special occasion just rolled into the next day as I dealt with nagging thoughts of having another small portion. And then that day rolled into the next and the next and the next.

My brain's response to sugar and refined carbs felt unlike anything else I have ever experienced. Until I chose abstinence, I truly felt like an addict who needed a fix. Abstaining from my drug—sugar and refined carbs—was easier than trying to moderate my consumption.

So I am an abstainer. Once I decided sugar and refined carbs were no longer an option for me because of the harm they were doing to my body and my mind, my life changed forever. The struggle was over.

Only you can determine whether you are a moderator or an abstainer. If you truly are a moderator, you can leave bites of a delicious dessert on your plate. Can you push the plate away after a few bites and feel satisfied, or do you feel compelled to eat it all even if you are full? Have you tried to eat sugar and refined carbs just once a week? How has that plan worked out for you?

I am not trying to convince you that you are an abstainer. But I do know this: you purchased this book because you want to lessen sugar's role in your life. Now, after completing the detox, you must take a hard look at how you've felt, physically and mentally, for the past month. If eliminating sugar and refined carbs ended that constant battle in your mind, leaving you feeling happy and free rather than obsessed about whether you should indulge in sugar each day, well, my friend, I think you have your answer.

REINTRODUCING CARBS

Through this sugar detox, I hope you've come to realize the value in eating whole, unprocessed foods and understand that this is not a one-size-fits-all approach. Each person has an individual response to carbohydrates, even natural carbs. Your body responds to some types one way and other types a different way. How much you choose to eat can affect your response, too.

Why is it a good idea to reintroduce carbs? It gives you insight into your body and how to keep sugar and carb cravings at bay. Gaining knowledge about various foods helps you understand how to incorporate or avoid those foods and keep your body functioning optimally. For example, say you love bananas, but bananas cause a huge spike in your blood sugar. Maybe, though, you can have one banana each week after a sweaty exercise session because your blood sugar level always drops after strenuous exercise (physical activity helps release glucose from the blood).

Without reintroducing foods to test your reactions, you must rely on subjective measures like how you feel between meals. Of course, you can get enough information from those measures to know that a certain food caused you to feel hungry only an hour after you ate it or brought your cravings back with a vengeance.

If you're like me and you wonder whether you really need to avoid a certain food, this kind of testing is priceless—especially when you discover that you're able to eat some of a particular higher-carb whole food occasionally without it spiking your blood sugar or causing cravings.

After using carb testing to find out what is and is not a good fit for your body, it's best to avoid any problematic foods for at least three months to give your gut plenty of time to heal from any inflammation. Then you can retest those foods to see if you tolerate them better than you did before.

Note ───────────────────────────────

My goal with this sugar detox is to help you reach your goals, and reintroducing carbs is just another tool for finding what works for you. It is completely optional.

Carb Testing

You can use the following process to test the effects that carbs have on your body. You'll need a food scale, a blood glucose monitor (see pages 72 and 73), and your journal for recording the results. You must track what you eat, when you eat it, and how your blood glucose responds to it.

You'll test a specific carbohydrate every morning at breakfast. You'll eat 40 grams (just shy of 1.5 ounces) of that carb and no other food—no coffee with collagen, no creamer, no snack. If you want to drink plain black coffee, tea, or water before eating the food, you may, but keep it the same every morning you test.

Immediately after eating, set a timer for two hours. When the timer goes off, test your blood glucose following the manufacturer's instructions for your meter.

Ideally, your blood glucose at the two-hour mark will be between 90 and 115 mg/dL. If it is within that range, that carbohydrate is a good fit for you, and you can have it when you like, although I still recommend that you limit it to two or three times per week if you are trying to lose weight.

If your blood glucose is higher than 115 mg/dL, retest the same food at breakfast the next day, but eat only 20 grams of it. Again, test your blood glucose after two hours. If the level is still higher than 115 mg/dL, this particular carbohydrate is not a good fit for you. Test a different carbohydrate the next day.

A Word on Grains and Gluten

You need to know some things about grains and gluten before reintroducing these foods into your life after the detox. Barley, corn, millet, oats, rice, sorghum, teff, and wheat are just a few of the common grains that you may be interested in reintroducing or at least testing to see how your blood glucose reacts to them.

GRAINS

Unfortunately, many "whole grain" labels are misleading. Turning grains into flour strips them of most of their nutrients. The bran and germ of the grain are where the nutritional benefits are found. The germ contains magnesium, potassium, and B and E vitamins, and the bran (the outermost layer) is the part that can pass through the intestines undigested. Processing the grain removes both; all that's left is the starch, which has a high glycemic load and no nutrients. Even products marked "whole grain" are highly refined, and if you read the ingredient lists, you may notice that the whole grains are at the end, meaning the products contain a minimal amount.

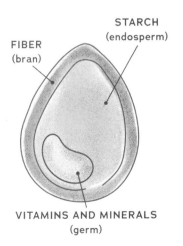

STARCH (endosperm)

FIBER (bran)

VITAMINS AND MINERALS (germ)

Why does this matter? Because refined grains spike insulin, raise blood sugar, and cause you to have cravings and feel hungry shortly after eating them. If you are still dealing with cravings, you seem to be sensitive to certain foods, or you have digestive issues, bloating after eating, diabetes, autoimmune conditions, or reflux, I urge you to avoid grains. If you don't have any of these issues and enjoyed much success during the cleanse, I still recommend eating grains only occasionally. Think of grains as being like alcohol and make them a "sometimes" pleasure.

GLUTEN

Celiac disease is an autoimmune disorder that affects only a small population, but many more people have non-celiac gluten sensitivity (NCGS) and don't realize it. I have the gene that is present in 95 percent of people who suffer from celiac disease, but I do not have the disease itself. I am just highly sensitive to gluten.

NCGS causes an inflammatory response that makes it difficult for the body to digest and process gluten. In fact, there are studies showing that no one can process gluten well, even if they have no symptoms of sensitivity. Gluten can damage your gut lining and possibly lead to leaky gut. When the lining of your gut is damaged, particles from inside your gut can leak into your bloodstream, which leads to inflammation and ultimately disease. For a study published in the *Annals of the New York Academy of Sciences*, researchers found that when a person eats a food containing gluten, their body produces a protein called zonulin, which allows intestinal cells to open up and leads to leaky gut.

Foods labeled "gluten-free" are no better for you than gluten-laden products because manufacturers often replace the gluten with refined potato and rice flours, highly refined and inflammatory vegetable oils, sugar, and artificial ingredients. Refined vegetable oils are high in omega-6 fatty acids, and consuming them will create an imbalance with omega-3 (refer to page 51). Sugar and artificial ingredients will contribute to increased cravings. It's better to eat whole-food pseudograins such as quinoa, hemp seeds, and chia seeds.

KNOWLEDGE IS POWER

I hope this cleanse has opened your eyes to the truth about what you once may have believed was healthy. I too believed for years in the tales we've all been told: whole grains are good for you, lean meats are healthier, eating more often keeps your metabolism going, everything in moderation, and so on. It's all a bunch of crap!

My goal isn't to convince you to stop eating grains or gluten. But I hope I have helped you understand how these types of foods could be causing inflammation in your body and/or spiking your blood sugar. Including them in your diet is ultimately your decision, but the fact remains that grains cause sugar cravings. If you're going to eat them, limit them to once a week or less. Also, consider buying organic to avoid the insecticides that often end up on these crops.

WHAT'S NEXT?

You should be feeling amazing after completing the 30-Day Sugar Elimination Diet. I do hope that this has been a meaningful experience for you and that you've learned a great deal about your body and what works best for diminished cravings and weight-loss success.

You may be wondering how to keep this momentum going. If you're still working toward a weight-loss goal, I encourage you to continue with three meals a day. You may have quite a few leftovers from the meal plan in your freezer that you can pull out over the next few weeks. If you enjoyed a particular breakfast, lunch, or dinner recipe from the plan, keep that meal on repeat and carry on with this way of life.

If you've already reached your goal of removing sugar, eliminating refined carb cravings, and losing all the weight you wanted to, congratulations! You should be very proud of yourself. But I have a word of caution: Sometimes we get lax after being diligent about reaching a goal. We may want to "reward" ourselves with food because we've been so good. This is a trap! I repeat, *this is a trap!* Do not allow yourself to fall into this kind of thinking, because it will bring you right back to where you were before the start of your detox.

The most important part of any program is the plan you make once it's over. You may be the type of person who says, "I've learned what works for my body, and now I will continue to do what works." If you don't need further support, that's awesome. However, you may be the type of person who feels best when you have a buddy or support system because it provides the outward accountability you need to carry on. And that's awesome, too. There is no one path that leads everyone to success.

Only you can decide what will meet your needs. However, if you've completed weight-loss programs in the past only to regain the weight because you reverted to old habits, don't believe for one minute that things will be different this time. You have established that you are a person who requires outward accountability to make this a lifestyle change and not just a diet that you follow a few times a year to lose a few pounds.

My online course with weekly support meetings for members has been the missing link for many people who have struggled to sustain weight loss. Some have been able to continue losing weight even after completing the six-week online course. I am happy to share that readers of this book can participate in this course at a 50 percent discount! Visit https://sugarfreemomtribe.com/book-bonus/ to find the discount code. You will have access to the videos from the online course as well as downloadable PDFs of helpful documents. You will also have access to the Q&A videos for each week as well as bonus weeks that cover protein-sparing modified fasting, plateaus, and carb testing. In the wrap-up week of the online course, you will receive a coupon code for 30 percent off my meal plan membership.

I hope you've been beyond blessed with your purchase of *The 30-Day Sugar Elimination Diet,* and I pray you continue on in good health and happiness with hope for a great future. Most of all, I pray you find freedom from the bondage that sugar once had on your life!

TESTIMONIALS

Since I joined Brenda Bennett, my life has changed. I do not plan on going back to the life of sugar and overeating—EVER! I have learned so much this last year about myself and have been able to get to a point in my life where I am healthy and feel good. Yes, we are all human and will make mistakes, but Brenda has given us the tools to get back on track and keep on going. Having Brenda be available for any questions, concerns, or just a good laugh of positivity has meant so much to me. Her recipes are amazing, and I do not feel deprived. I use them to make meals for my family, and they do not even know that the food doesn't include gluten or sugar! I really appreciate the emotional support from the group because it backs everything up that I have learned.

—Margret Wunsch

I had bariatric gastric bypass surgery on August 22, 2016, and in two years, I lost 171.7 pounds. But then my weight loss stalled. I still wanted to lose 30 pounds. I made my goal with Brenda's information on keto eating, her Stall Buster and Sugar Detox courses, her recipes, and the weekly Zoom meetings. By the time of my yearly weigh-in on August 22, 2021, I had lost my last 33.3 pounds to reach my goal of losing 205 pounds! Brenda's recipes are created even for bariatric life! I don't feel deprived because Brenda's recipes give me the satisfaction of the foods I loved— and sometimes, they're better!

—Sheree Ann Meier

I have struggled with weight my entire life. I was a chubby kid, and I was about 20 pounds overweight as a teen. As an adult, I went through several cycles of losing weight and regaining all that I lost and more. Each time, I shed pounds using a low-carb diet, but I would eventually give in to sugar's sweet siren song. It wasn't until I found Brenda's 6-Week Sugar Detox course that I realized my compulsion for sugar is an addiction just like any other. The good news is that there is a sustainable way of eating that eliminates sugar without giving up sweets forever. While following Brenda's plan, I have lost 40 pounds and kept it off. I've never felt like I was starving myself, and I don't feel deprived. If you feel like you've tried everything else and failed, this is the plan for you!

—Danette Anderson

My decision to join Brenda's sugar detox in January 2021 was twofold. First, I wanted to adopt a new lower-carbohydrate eating lifestyle that would lower my insulin as a type 1.5 diabetic. Second, I wanted to lose the 15 pounds I put on during the COVID-19 pandemic.

I found it empowering to clean out my cupboards of things I would not eat and stock up on healthy alternatives. I was amazed at how empty my refrigerator and cupboards were once I was done purging. Only my meat and veggie crisper had evidence of food.

I lost the 15 pounds pretty quickly, and it's been easy to maintain the weight loss. My diabetic pump readings started stabilizing, with hardly any highs. At my first appointment three months after starting, my endocrinologist called me his model patient as my pump showed that my blood sugars were in the normal range 80 to 85 percent of the time. That was a first for me!

What helped me the most was the support I received from our weekly online Zoom meetings, where Brenda is always teaching us something new, and our group shares our successes and our struggles. It really helps to have each other for accountability.

I highly recommend this program to anyone, but especially to people struggling with any form of diabetes. Keeping my blood sugar stable by eating low carbohydrates (20 grams) a day makes a big difference in managing the highs and lows that can play havoc in our lives.

—Carol Arnzen

I met Brenda through Facebook. After trying her amazing keto and low-carb recipes, I was hooked! Then one day during the pandemic, I came across an invitation to join a five-day sugar detox. I was already following a keto lifestyle, but I wanted more accountability and companionship, so I joined.

The results were amazing. I lost about 5 to 7 pounds in those five days. Little did I know that I would continue to lose weight so happily and with great company!

I started this journey in January 2020, and I am very proud to say that I've lost around 30 pounds and still counting. I am now part of Brenda's alumni group; we get together every week online to discuss different things, all related to everyday or extraordinary situations of living a sugar-free lifestyle.

I could have lost the weight on my own, but doing it with accountability and companionship has been so much better.

—Aura M. de Leon

I have struggled since childhood with sugar cravings, food temptation, portion control, overeating, and inconsistent physical activity. I've tried a variety of weight-loss plans, but nothing stuck. I would lose weight, be happy, and feel great physically and mentally, but then routines would change or temptation would get the best of me. I'd find myself with the weight back on, experiencing daily negative self-talk, and turning to "comfort food" both for stress relief and as a way to reward myself for accomplishments. I needed something to make an impact on my mental relationship with food as well as my physical relationship with food.

The fall of 2020 is when I made up my mind that I needed to make some changes to last. I was fed up with myself that I allowed my weight to roller coaster up and down for so many years, and I wanted to get control. A couple of years before starting the Sugar Detox course, I followed Brenda on social media and made some recipes periodically, but I was inconsistent with a routine. I knew myself well enough to know that I needed guidance and accountability to help me stay on track. I wanted this to be a lifestyle change, not just a temporary diet to shed pounds only to leave the door open for bad habits to take control again. I needed something impactful that would give me the strength I needed to persevere through vacations, holidays, celebrations, and all other events that seemed to be triggers for returning to bad eating habits.

I started Brenda's Sugar Detox course online at the end of September 2020, intending to lose 40 pounds. With her easy-to-make recipes, essential coaching through the challenges, focus on whole foods (not heavily processed or packaged), and, most important, weekly check-ins, I had a successful six weeks (down 15 pounds, 2.8 percent less body fat, and 8.25 total inches in body circumferences). I was thrilled! But a part of me wondered if I could keep this momentum going after the course ended.

I found the key to continued success and the support I needed to turn my new habits into lifestyle changes through Brenda's alumni VIP group. I get supportive interaction through various platforms (live online interactive weekly meetings, recorded meeting replays, social media private group, direct email communication with Brenda), that work with my busy life.

It's been almost a year since I started the 6-week Sugar Detox course and transitioned into the Alumni VIP group. I'm down 42 pounds, 8.4 percent body fat, and 23.25 total inches in body circumference, and I incorporate physical activity and self-care/stress relief into every week. I have found my recipe for lifetime success!

—Angie H.

I have been struggling with my weight for the past 25 years. I am 50, so that's half my life. I had followed the keto lifestyle for about three years, from 2013 to 2017, but I hit a wall that I hadn't been able to break through. And to be honest, I had really given up and gained back what I had lost those few years.

In January 2021, I joined Brenda's 5-Day Sugar Detox Challenge, and the weight began to come off again. Her personalized interaction and the practical tips she shares with her clients are second to none! The camaraderie I have experienced (and still do as a VIP member of her membership group) cannot be compared to attempting to come off of sugar and live a new way of life by myself. The multitude of handouts, self-reflective worksheets, notes, templates, and links are a unique and incredibly helpful resource. Each thing has benefited me incredibly, and I have them printed out so I can refer to them often. It is so helpful to know that Brenda is available and super responsive and that she has created such an amazing, supportive community of those who are committing themselves to the same choices I am making—being sugar free!

—**Dawn Strickland**

Brenda, aka the Sugar-Free Mom, is such a kindhearted, no-nonsense, guiding light. Her program was like getting tough love from a close friend!

Her sugar-free detox program has changed my life. She has put me on a positive wellness journey. It is very important to approach Brenda's sugar-free program less as a "quick fix" and more as the beginning of a journey that will move you closer to many different types of personal goals. I am so happy I decided to jump into this experience, and I have learned skills that will help me continue to lose and maintain my weight in the future! I learned so much about myself and realized that changing your brain is possible. I look forward to being part of the SFM community for life.

—**Susan Commarato**

SHOPPING GUIDE

Living a sugar-free, refined carb–free lifestyle can present some challenges if you aren't prepared. Making every single meal and snack from scratch just isn't possible for many of us. As a busy homeschool mom of three who also runs a business, I get that. Convenience is key to making this lifestyle sustainable. Here, I've provided a list of quality products you can purchase to have on hand in your pantry, fridge, and freezer for when life throws you a curveball!

SAUCES, CONDIMENTS, AND OTHER PANTRY STAPLES

Here are some of my favorite pantry staples. They can easily be used when you just don't have time to make them from scratch.

ALFREDO SAUCE

• Rao's

AVOCADO OIL MAYONNAISE

• Chosen Foods
• Primal Kitchen

BBQ SAUCE

• Primal Kitchen

BONE BROTH

• Epic
• Fond
• Kettle & Fire

CHOCOLATE CHIPS

• Lakanto (sweetened with monk fruit)
• Lily's Sweets (sweetened with stevia)

FLAVORED LIQUID EXTRACTS (unsweetened)

• Frontier Co-Op
• OOOFlavors

HEART OF PALM PASTA AND RICE

• Palmini

KETCHUP

• Primal Kitchen

LOW-CARB SWEETENERS

• Swerve confectioners'-style sweetener
• Swerve granular sweetener

OPTIONAL:

• Better Than Sugar confectioners'-style sweetener
• Swerve brown sugar sweetener
• Vanilla-flavored liquid stevia
• Wholesome allulose liquid sweetener
• Yacón syrup

MAPLE SYRUP

• Lakanto

MARINARA SAUCE

• Primal Kitchen
• Rao's

PORK RINDS AND PORK RIND CRUMBS (aka pork panko)

• Bacon's Heir
• Pork King Good

SALAD DRESSING (CAESAR, ITALIAN)

• Primal Kitchen

SHIRATAKI PASTA AND RICE

• It's Skinny Pasta
• Miracle Noodle

STEAK SAUCE

• Primal Kitchen

SNACKS AND OTHER PREPARED FOODS

Here is a list of the products I turn to when I need help getting a sugar-free, refined carb–free dinner on the table quickly, or when I need a snack or sweet that won't derail my sugar-free lifestyle.

But please remember this: Although packaged foods can be a savior, they can also be a crutch. If you notice that you are having a packaged product at every meal or that you spend most of your day grazing on snacks rather than eating a meal, weight gain is imminent! Be cautious and pull in the reins by getting back to basics.

FREEZER

- Cali'flour Foods Pizza Crusts
- Realgood Foods Bacon-Wrapped Stuffed Chicken

PANTRY

- 4505 Chicharrones (fried pork rinds)
- Carnivore Crisps (meat chips)
- ChocZero Chocolate Bark
- Chomps Jerky
- Defy Foods Cheddar Crackers
- Epic Bars
- Evolved Keto Almond Butter Cups
- Fat Snax Cookies
- Fat Snax Crackers
- Fbomb Nut Butter Packets
- Lily's Milk Chocolate Style Covered Peanuts
- Lily's Peanut Butter Cups
- Nush Foods Keto Snack Cakes
- Paleovalley Beef and Turkey Sticks
- Perfect Keto Bars
- Siete Foods Grain-Free Taco Shells
- Whisps Cheese Crisps

FRIDGE

- Coconut Wraps (NuCo)
- Egglife Egg White Wraps
- Folios Cheese Wraps
- Fox Hill Kitchen "Bagelz" and "Bunz"
- Kiss My Keto Bread
- Nutpods Dairy-Free Creamer
- Trader Joe's Fresh Cauliflower Thins

BOXED MIXES

- Good Dee's Brownie Mix
- Good Dee's Corn free Bread Mix
- Good Dee's Rainbow or Chocolate ("Midnight Moon") Sprinkles
- HighKey Bread & Muffin Mix
- HighKey Pancake & Waffle Mix
- Keto and Co Banana Caramel Muffin Mix
- Swerve Cake Mixes

SWEETENER CONVERSION CHART

SWEETENER TYPES AND MEASUREMENT EQUIVALENTS

Sugar (listed for comparison only)	1/2 teaspoon	1 teaspoon	1 tablespoon	1/4 cup	1/3 cup	1/2 cup	1 cup
Liquid stevia	5 drops	10 drops	1/8 teaspoon	1/2 teaspoon	3/4 teaspoon	1 teaspoon	2 teaspoons
Pure stevia extract			1/32 teaspoon	1/16 teaspoon	1/8 teaspoon	1/4 teaspoon	1/2 teaspoon
Better Than Sugar	1/2 teaspoon	1 teaspoon	1 tablespoon	1/4 cup	1/3 cup	1/2 cup	1 cup
Swerve/ erythritol	1 tablespoon	2 tablespoons	1/4 cup	1/2 cup	3/4 cup	1 cup	1 1/2 cups
Liquid allulose	1 tablespoon	2 tablespoons	1/4 cup	1/2 cup	3/4 cup	1 cup	1 1/2 cups
Liquid monk fruit	5 drops	10 drops	1/8 teaspoon	1/2 teaspoon	3/4 teaspoon	1 teaspoon	2 teaspoons
Granulated allulose	1 tablespoon	2 tablespoons	1/4 cup	1/2 cup	3/4 cup	1 cup	1 1/2 cups
Granulated monk fruit	1/2 teaspoon	1 teaspoon	1 tablespoon	1/4 cup	1/3 cup	1/2 cup	1 cup
Stevia glycerite	2 drops	5 drops	1/16 teaspoon	1/4 teaspoon	1/2 teaspoon	3/4 teaspoon	1 1/4 teaspoons

Note —————
Sweetness level will vary by brand.

THE SCALE WORKSHEET

Remember to weigh every week, only once a week, same day, same time, undressed, and after using the bathroom.

This week I (lost _____, gained _____, or stayed the same _____).

How does this number make me feel? _____

_____

_____

How did I feel before I stepped on the scale and read the number? _____

_____

_____

Looking back at my food journal, what did I do really well this week? _____

_____

_____

Where did I struggle this week? _____

_____

_____

Was there any particular food that triggered me to overeat this week? _____

_____

_____

What do I need to work on or tweak this coming week to reach my goals? _____

_____

_____

_____

RECITE THIS EACH TIME YOU FINISH THIS WORKSHEET:

I may not be where I want to be, but I am honestly working toward achieving my goals for my body, mind, and spirit and getting stronger every day. The scale has no control over me anymore. I am more than enough, and I can do all things I set my mind to do. I will achieve my health goals and continue to be open and honest with myself and others who support me. This is a marathon, not a sprint, and today I am grateful I'm able to run this race at my own pace.

HUNGER OR HABIT?

? Time of day?

Give yourself 1 point if it is between 2pm–6pm

? When did I last eat?

1 point if more than 3 hours ago

? Did I eat protein at my last meal?

1 point if yes

? Was my last meal heavy in carbs?

1 point if no

? Have I had electrolytes today?

1 point if yes

? How do I feel now: nervous, shaky, foggy, angry, and/or depressed, or clear-headed but hungry?

1 point if clear-headed

? Do I want something sweet or savory?

1 point if savory

? Am I delaying a project, chore, or work deadline?

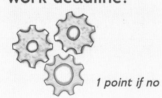

1 point if no

5–8 POINTS:

You may be truly hungry. If you are eating enough food and protein at each meal, you should not be hungry for at least 4–6 hours. If you are hungry enough to eat an egg, then have some type of protein.

0–5 POINTS:

You could be experiencing habit hunger. Reevaluate your last meal. Did you eat enough food, with enough protein? Did you eat too many carbs? If you feel jittery, light-headed, or shaky, place some sea salt on your tongue and wait 15 minutes. If you're still hungry, eat only protein.

WITH GRATITUDE

I owe a multitude of thanks to so many people in my life, but I must begin with sharing my faith in Jesus Christ. Without Him, this book would not even be available. He turned my mess into my message. He turned my trials into my triumph. When I felt like a victim of my circumstances, He turned it around for my victory. When I surrendered my will for His, my struggles became my successes. He turned my greatest weakness into strength, resolve, fortitude, discipline, stamina, grit, determination, and, most of all, perseverance to continue to fight for my sugar freedom. Everything I have today is because of believing in Him and trusting that He would make a way when there seemed to be no way. His grace is free and available to anyone who asks. My prayer for you is that you ask, seek, and find that strength and courage to become all that you were meant to be to live your best life.

My husband, Jim, the man who can literally do all things! I would not be where I am today without you! You pick up the slack, you jump whenever needed, you clean all the dishes from all the messes I make. You calm my chaos and my Sicilian temper! You are the perfect man God knew I needed and one of the greatest gifts He has given me. I'm so grateful for the life we have together. Thank you for loving me the way you do and always putting the needs of myself and our children above your own.

My children, Joshua, Rebekah, and Jack. You three are my greatest accomplishment! Seeing you all grow into young adults is beyond words, and I am so very proud of all of you. I don't care how old you get; I will always be there rooting for all you do in life, standing with you in anything life throws your way, praying for your protection each day, and, most of all, loving you with all that I have. No matter where you are, whenever you need me, I'll come running, because my favorite and most important job of all is being your momma.

Andrea, not only my best friend but also my trusted and dedicated VA! I know I could not have made the deadline for this book without your tireless effort and precision in everything you do. I am so grateful for our friendship and can't thank you enough for working so hard for me!

The entire Victory Belt team. Your encouragement during the writing process has been wonderful. From the first call with Lance when I pitched my idea for this book, I have been so appreciative of your belief in me and your assistance in helping me put out my best work. To all the designers who made the graphics and made my photos look so beautiful, I am so thankful. Pam, Holly, and Charlotte, my editors, are gifted beyond words and truly made my work shine! Susan, my amazing marketing genius, thank you for making my message stand out and reach so many!

Last, but of course not least, a special thank you to all of you! Thank you for making my recipes and sharing them with your friends and family. Without you, my blog wouldn't be what it is today—I am certain of that! To all my special women who have taken the chance on changing their lives through my online course and VIP membership, thank you for sharing your stories and life with me, and for trusting me that this really could be a sustainable lifestyle. Your testimonies inspire and motivate me to continue to spread the message about sugar freedom! I am forever grateful.

BIBLIOGRAPHY

Burger, K. S., and E. Stice, "Variability in Reward Responsivity and Obesity: Evidence from Brain Imaging Studies," *Current Drug Abuse Reviews* 4, no. 3 (2011): 182–9, https://www.ncbi.nlm.nih.gov/pmc/articles/PMC3462740/.

Cona, L. A., "How Does Fasting Affect Stem Cells?" DVC Stem website, last updated December 21, 2021, https://www.dvcstem.com/post/fasting-and-stem-cells.

Davis, C., "From Passive Overeating to 'Food Addiction': A Spectrum of Compulsion and Severity," *ISRN Obesity* 2013 (2013), https://www.ncbi.nlm.nih.gov/pmc/articles/PMC3901973/.

Dow, M., *The Sugar Brain Fix: The 28-Day Plan to Quit Craving the Foods That Are Shrinking Your Brain and Expanding Your Waistline* (Carlsbad, CA: Hay House, 2020).

Fasano, A., "Zonulin, Regulation of Tight Junctions, and Autoimmune Diseases," *Annals of the New York Academy of Sciences* 1258, no. 1 (2012): 25–33, https://www.ncbi.nlm.nih.gov/pmc/articles/PMC3384703/.

Fromentin, C., D. Tome, F. Nau, L. Flet, C. Luengo, D. Azzout-Marinche, P. Sanders, G, Fromentin, and C. Gaudichon, "Dietary Proteins Contribute Little to Glucose Production, Even Under Optimal Gluconeogenic Conditions in Healthy Humans," *Diabetes* 62, no. 5 (2013): 1435–42, https://pubmed.ncbi.nlm.nih.gov/23274906/.

Fung, J., and J. Moore, *The Complete Guide to Fasting: Heal Your Body Through Intermittent, Alternate-Day, and Extended Fasting* (Las Vegas, NV: Victory Belt Publishing, 2016).

Gailliot, M. T., and R. F. Baumeister, "The Physiology of Willpower: Linking Blood Glucose to Self-Control," *Personality and Social Psychology Review* 11, no. 4 (2007): 303–27, https://pubmed.ncbi.nlm.nih.gov/18453466/.

Gannon, M. C., and F. Q. Nuttall, "Effects of a High-Protein, Low-Carbohydrate Diet on Blood Glucose in People with Type 2 Diabetes," *Diabetes* 53, no. 9 (2004): 2375–82, https://diabetes.diabetesjournals.org/content/53/9/2375.

Greenberg, J. A., and A. Geliebter, "Coffee, Hunger, and Peptide YY," *Journal of the American College of Nutrition* 31, no. 3 (2012): 160–6, https://pubmed.ncbi.nlm.nih.gov/23204152/.

Greger, M., "Are Sugary Foods Addictive?" NutritionFacts.org 15 (2013), https://nutritionfacts.org/video/are-sugary-foods-addictive.

Kerndt, P. R., J. L. Naughton, C. E. Driscoll, and D. A. Loxterkamp, "Fasting: The History, Pathophysiology and Complications," *The Western Journal of Medicine* 137, no. 5 (1982): 379–99, https://pubmed.ncbi.nlm.nih.gov/6758355/.

Kinney, K., "Is It Safe to Cook with Olive Oil?" last updated June 28, 2019, https://chriskresser.com/is-it-safe-to-cook-with-olive-oil/.

Kolata, G., "Low-Salt Diet Ineffective, Study Finds. Disagreement Abounds," *New York Times,* May 3, 2011, https://www.nytimes.com/2011/05/04/health/research/04salt.html.

Lally, P., C. H. M. van Jaarsveld, H. W. W. Potts, and J. Wardle, "How Are Habits Formed: Modelling Habit Formation in the Real World," *European Journal of Social Psychology* 40, no. 6 (2010): 998–1009, https://onlinelibrary.wiley.com/doi/10.1002/ejsp.674.

Meule, A., and A. Kubler, "Food Cravings in Food Addiction: The Distinct Role of Positive Reinforcement," *Eating Behaviors* 13, no. 3 (2012): 252–5, https://pubmed.ncbi.nlm.nih.gov/22664405/.

Naiman, T., Burn Fat Not Sugar website, accessed January 11, 2022, https://burnfatnotsugar.com/macros.html.

Phinney, S., "How Much Protein Should I Eat on a Ketogenic Diet?" Virta Health website, accessed January 11, 2022, https://www.virtahealth.com/faq/protein-ketogenic-diet.

Phinney, S., "Is Fasting Safe?" Virta Health website, accessed January 20, 2022, https://www.virtahealth.com/faq/is-fasting-safe.

Pilcher, J. J., D. M. Morris, J. Donnelly, and H. B. Feigl, "Interactions Between Sleep Habits and Self-Control," *Frontiers in Human Neuroscience* 9 (2015): 284, https://www.ncbi.nlm.nih.gov/pmc/articles/PMC4426706/.

PKD Foundation, "Hunger vs. Thirst: Tips to Tell the Difference," PKD Foundation blog, accessed January 13, 2022, https://pkdcure.org/hunger-vs-thirst/.

Pursey, K. M., P. Stanwell, R. J. Callister, K. Brain, C. E. Collins, and T. L. Burrows, "Neural Responses to Visual Food Cues According to Weight Status: A Systematic Review of Functional Magnetic Resonance Imaging Studies," *Frontiers in Nutrition* 1 (2014): 7, https://pubmed.ncbi.nlm.nih.gov/25988110/.

Pursey, K. M., P. Stanwell, A. N. Gearhardt, C. E. Collins, and T. L. Burrows, "The Prevalence of Food Addiction as Assessed by the Yale Food Addiction Scale: A Systematic Review," *Nutrients* 6, no. 10 (2014): 4552–90, https://www.ncbi.nlm.nih.gov/pmc/articles/PMC4210934/.

Roszkowska, A., M. Pawlicka, A. Mroczek, K. Bałabuszek, and B. Nieradko-Iwanicka, "Non-Celiac Gluten Sensitivity: A Review," *Medicina (Kaunas)* 55, no. 6 (2019): 222, https://www.ncbi.nlm.nih.gov/pmc/articles/PMC6630947/.

Schulte, E. M., N. M. Avena, and A. N. Gearhardt, "Which Foods May Be Addictive? The Roles of Processing, Fat Content, and Glycemic Load," *PLOS One* 10, no. 2 (2015): e0117959, https://journals.plos.org/plosone/article?id=10.1371/journal.pone.0117959.

Schwartz, J. M., and S. Begley, *The Mind and the Brain: Neuroplasticity and the Power of Mental Force* (New York: ReganBooks, 2002).

Simopoulos, A. P., "The Importance of the Ratio of Omega-6/Omega-3 Essential Fatty Acids," *Biomedicine & Pharmacotherapy* 56, no. 8 (2002): 365–79, https://pubmed.ncbi.nlm.nih.gov/12442909/.

Symons, T. B., M. Sheffield-Moore, R. R. Wolfe, and D. Paddon-Jones, "A Moderate Serving of High-Quality Protein Maximally Stimulates Skeletal Muscle Protein Synthesis in Young and Elderly Subjects," *Journal of the American Dietetic Association* 109, no. 9 (2009): 1582–6, https://pubmed.ncbi.nlm.nih.gov/19699838/.

Wolf, R., *Wired to Eat: Turn Off Cravings, Rewire Your Appetite for Weight Loss, and Determine the Foods That Work for You* (New York: Harmony, 2017).

Yan-Do, R., and P. E. MacDonald, "Impaired 'Glycine'-mia in Type 2 Diabetes and Potential Mechanisms Contributing to Glucose Homeostasis," *Endocrinology* 158, no. 5 (2017): 1064–73, https://pubmed.ncbi.nlm.nih.gov/28323968/.

RECIPE QUICK REFERENCE

RECIPE	PAGE	🥛	🥚	🥜	🍳	🫙
Apple Pie Dutch Baby	94			O	●	
Asparagus Salad with Avocado Dressing	96	O	●	●		
Bacon Bourbon Burgers	98	O		●		
Breakfast Sausage Patties	100	●	●	●	●	
Brown Butter Crispy Chicken Thighs	102		●	●	●	
Buffalo Chicken Salad Wraps	104			●		
Buffalo Wings	106	O	●	●	●	
Buffalo Wing Sauce	108		●	●		
Cabbage Roll Skillet	110	●	●	●	●	
Cauliflower Rice	112	●	●	●	●	
Cheddar and Bacon–Stuffed Burgers	114		●	●		O
Chicken Cauliflower Fried Rice	116	●		●	●	
Chicken Chili Stuffed Peppers	118	O	●	●		
Chicken Kiev Meatballs	120			●		
Chicken Mushroom Skillet	122		●	●	●	
Chimichurri	124	●	●	●		
Cloud Bread Rolls	126	●		●		
Cobb Ranch Salad	128	O		●		
Corned Beef Hash Skillet with Eggs	130	O		●		
Creamy Cilantro Lime Slaw	132	●		●		
Crispy Broccoli	134	●	●	●	●	O
Crustless Ham and Cheese Quiches	136			●		
Crustless Skillet Supreme Pizza	138		●	●	●	
Dairy-Free Mini Waffles	140	●		●		
Deviled Eggs	142	●		●		
Easy Bacon	144	●	●	●	●	O
Easy-Peel Hard-Boiled Eggs	146	●		●		
Egg Foo Young	148	●		●		
Egg Noodles	150	O		●	●	
Egg Salad	152	●		●		
Eggs Benedict	154			●		
Fish Taco Bowl	156	●		●	●	
French Onion Meatballs	158			●		
Garlic Butter Mushrooms	160		●	●	●	
Garlic Butter Steak Bites	162		●	●	●	
German "Potato" Salad	164	●	●	●		
Grilled Romaine Salad	166		●	●		
Homemade Ketchup	168	●	●	●		
Jambalaya	170	●	●	●	●	
Low-Carb Marinara Sauce	172	●	●	●	●	
Mashed Roasted Cauliflower	174		●	●	●	
Momma's Italian Dressing	176	●	●	●		
Monte Cristo Waffle Sandwiches	178			●		
Open-Face Tuna Chaffles	180	O		●		
Palmini Rice	182	●	●	●	●	

RECIPE	PAGE	🧂	🥚	🌰	🍳	🍱
Pan-Seared Lemon Butter Salmon	184		●	●	●	
Philly Cheesesteak Stir-Fry	186	O	●	●	●	
Pizza Chaffles	188			●		
Protein Pancakes	190			●	●	
Reverse-Seared Rib Eye with Chimichurri	192		●	●		
Roasted Balsamic Vegetables	194	●	●	●	●	
Rutabaga Fries	196	●	●	●	●	O
Sausage Egg Cups	198	●		●	●	
Sausage Zucchini Skillet	200	O	●	●	●	
Sautéed Summer Squash	202	O	●	●	●	
Scotch Eggs	204	●		●	●	
Sheet Pan Chicken Fajitas	206	●	●	●	●	
Sheet Pan Shrimp with Crispy Pepperoni	208	O	●	●	●	
Shirataki Rice	210	O	●	●	●	
Shrimp Linguine in Garlic Butter Sauce	212		●	●	●	
Simple Skillet Chili	214	●	●	●	●	
Smoked Salmon Omelet Roll-Ups	216			●	●	
Smoky Grilled Pork Chops	218	●	●	●		
Soft Scrambled Eggs	220			●	●	
Spicy Mayo	222	●		●		
Spicy Smoked Salmon Wrap	224	●		●		
Spring Roll Chicken Salad with Creamy Asian Dressing	226	●	●	O		
Stuffed Chicken Thighs	228		●	●	●	
Sugar-Free BBQ Sauce	230	●	●	●		
Sugar-Free Maple Syrup	232	O	●	●	●	
Taco Seasoning	234	●	●	●		
Taco Soup	236	●	●	●	●	
Tuna Salad	238	●		●		
2-Minute English Muffins	240	O		O		
Waffle Breakfast Sandwich	242			●		
Zucchini Noodles with Roasted Garlic Cream Sauce	244		●	●		
Berry Fluff	248		●	●		
Brownie in a Mug	250			O		
Keto Chocolate Lava Cakes for Two	252			O		
Keto Dalgona Coffee	254	●	●	O		
Deep Dish Chocolate Chip Cookie	256	O		O		
Egg Custard	258			O		
Keto Electrolyte Drink—Three Ways	260	●	●	●		
No-Churn Vanilla Ice Cream	262			●		
Panna Cotta	264		●	O		
Raspberry Clafoutis	266			O		
Scrambled Egg Chocolate Pudding	268	O		O		
Sugar-Free Whipped Cream	270		●	●		
Tiramisu for Two	272			●		

RECIPE INDEX

Breakfast

94

Apple Pie
Dutch Baby

100

Breakfast Sausage
Patties

130

Corned Beef Hash
Skillet with Eggs

136

Crustless Ham and
Cheese Quiches

140

Dairy-Free
Mini Waffles

144

Easy Bacon

146

Easy-Peel
Hard-Boiled Eggs

154

Eggs Benedict

190

Protein Pancakes

198

Sausage Egg Cups

216

Smoked Salmon
Omelet Roll-Ups

220

Soft Scrambled
Eggs

240

2-Minute
English Muffins

242

Waffle Breakfast
Sandwich

Salads

96
Asparagus Salad with Avocado Dressing

128
Cobb Ranch Salad

152
Egg Salad

164
German "Potato" Salad

166
Grilled Romaine Salad

226
Spring Roll Chicken Salad with Creamy Asian Dressing

238
Tuna Salad

Beef & Pork

98
Bacon Bourbon Burgers

110
Cabbage Roll Skillet

114
Cheddar and Bacon–Stuffed Burgers

138
Crustless Skillet Supreme Pizza

158
French Onion Meatballs

162
Garlic Butter Steak Bites

178
Monte Cristo Waffle Sandwiches

186
Philly Cheesesteak Stir-Fry

188
Pizza Chaffles

192
Reverse-Seared Rib Eye with Chimichurri

200
Sausage Zucchini Skillet

204
Scotch Eggs

214
Simple Skillet Chili

218
Smoky Grilled Pork Chops

236
Taco Soup

Chicken

Brown Butter Crispy
Chicken Thighs
102

Buffalo Chicken
Salad Wraps
104

Buffalo Wings
106

Chicken Cauliflower
Fried Rice
116

Chicken Chili
Stuffed Peppers
118

Chicken Kiev
Meatballs
120

Chicken Mushroom
Skillet
122

Egg Foo Young
148

Sheet Pan
Chicken Fajitas
206

Stuffed
Chicken Thighs
228

Fish & Seafood

Fish Taco Bowl
156

Jambalaya
170

Open-Face
Tuna Chaffles
180

Pan-Seared Lemon
Butter Salmon
184

Sheet Pan
Shrimp with
Crispy Pepperoni
208

Shrimp Linguine in
Garlic Butter Sauce
212

Spicy Smoked
Salmon Wrap
224

Sides

Cauliflower Rice

Cloud Bread Rolls

Creamy Cilantro Lime Slaw

Crispy Broccoli

Deviled Eggs

Egg Noodles

Garlic Butter Mushrooms

Mashed Roasted Cauliflower

Palmini Rice

Roasted Balsamic Vegetables

Rutabaga Fries

Sautéed Summer Squash

Shirataki Rice

Zucchini Noodles with Roasted Garlic Cream Sauce

Sauces & Seasonings

Buffalo Wing Sauce

Chimichurri

Homemade Ketchup

Low-Carb Marinara Sauce

Momma's Italian Dressing

Spicy Mayo

Sugar-Free BBQ Sauce

Sugar-Free Maple Syrup

Taco Seasoning

Desserts & Beverages

248

Berry Fluff

250

Brownie in a Mug

252

Keto Chocolate
Lava Cakes for Two

254

Keto Dalgona
Coffee

256

Deep Dish Chocolate
Chip Cookie

258

Egg Custard

260

Keto Electrolyte
Drink—Three Ways

262

No-Churn Vanilla
Ice Cream

264

Panna Cotta

266

Raspberry
Clafoutis

268

Scrambled Egg
Chocolate Pudding

270

Sugar-Free
Whipped Cream

272

Tiramisu for Two

GENERAL INDEX

A

abstaining, 276–277

addiction, to hyperpalatable foods, 22–23

"after" pictures, 25

aftertaste, reducing, 54

air fryer, 79

alcohol, 50

alfredo sauce, brand recommendations, 288

almond milk

Egg Custard, 258–259

Keto Dalgona Coffee, 254–255

Panna Cotta, 264–265

Scrambled Egg Chocolate Pudding, 268–269

alternate-day fasting, 62

Apple Pie Dutch Baby recipe, 94–95

"Are Sugary Foods Addictive" (Greger), 276

artificial sweeteners, on food labels, 27–28. See also sweeteners

Asparagus Salad with Avocado Dressing recipe, 96–97

aspartame, 61

avocado oil mayonnaise, brand recommendations, 288

avocados

Asparagus Salad with Avocado Dressing, 96–97

Cobb Ranch Salad, 128–129

Fish Taco Bowl, 156–157

Sheet Pan Chicken Fajitas, 206–207

Smoked Salmon Omelet Roll-Ups, 216–217

Spicy Smoked Salmon Wrap, 224–225

Taco Soup, 236–237

B

bacon

Bacon Bourbon Burgers, 98–99

Easy Bacon, 144–145

German "Potato" Salad, 164–165

Stuffed Chicken Thighs, 228–229

Bacon Bourbon Burgers recipe, 98–99

Bacon's Heir brand, 288

basil

Egg Noodles, 150–151

Orange Basil Keto Electrolyte Drink, 260–261

Roasted Balsamic Vegetables, 194–195

bathroom scale, 25, 42–43, 291

bean sprouts

Egg Foo Young, 148–149

beef

Bacon Bourbon Burgers, 98–99

Cabbage Roll Skillet, 110–111

Cheddar and Bacon–Stuffed Burgers, 114–115

Corned Beef Hash Skillet with Eggs, 130–131

Garlic Butter Steak Bites, 162–163

Philly Cheesesteak Stir-Fry, 186–187

Reverse-Seared Rib Eye with Chimichurri, 192–193

Simple Skillet Chili, 214–215

Taco Soup, 236–237

"before" pictures, 25

bell peppers

Chicken Chili Stuffed Peppers, 118–119

Crustless Skillet Supreme Pizza, 138–139

Jambalaya, 170–171

bell peppers *(continued)*
    Philly Cheesesteak Stir-Fry, 186–187
    Roasted Balsamic Vegetables, 194–195
    Sheet Pan Chicken Fajitas, 206–207
    Simple Skillet Chili, 214–215
    Taco Soup, 236–237
Bennett, Brenda, personal story of, 7, 9–11
berries. *See also* raspberries
    Berry Fluff, 248–249
    Dairy-Free Mini Waffles, 140–141
    Egg Custard, 258–259
    Keto Chocolate Lava Cakes for Two, 252–253
    Panna Cotta, 264–265
    Protein Pancakes, 190–191
Berry Fluff recipe, 248–249
Better Than Sugar brand, 288, 290
beverages, 48–50
Bifidobacterium, 32
bloating, 59
blood glucose, 72–73
blue cheese
    Cobb Ranch Salad, 128–129
bone broth
    about, 49
    brand recommendations, 288
    Brown Butter Crispy Chicken Thighs, 102–103
    Chicken Mushroom Skillet, 122–123
    Corned Beef Hash Skillet with Eggs, 130–131
    Egg Noodles, 150–151
    French Onion Meatballs, 158–159
    Garlic Butter Mushrooms, 160–161
    Jambalaya, 170–171
    Simple Skillet Chili, 214–215
    Taco Soup, 236–237
bourbon
    Bacon Bourbon Burgers, 98–99
boxed mixes, shopping guide for, 289
Breakfast Sausage Patties recipe, 100–101
breathing, cravings and, 66

broccoli
    Crispy Broccoli, 134–136
    Roasted Balsamic Vegetables, 194–195
Brown Butter Crispy Chicken Thighs recipe, 102–103
Brownie in a Mug recipe, 250–251
Buffalo Chicken Salad Wraps recipe, 104–105
Buffalo Wings recipe, 106–107
Buffalo Wing Sauce recipe, 108–109
    Buffalo Chicken Salad Wraps, 104–105
    Buffalo Wings, 106–107
butternut squash, carbs in, 26

C

cabbage
    Cabbage Roll Skillet, 110–111
    Creamy Cilantro Lime Slaw, 132–133
    Fish Taco Bowl, 156–157
    Spring Roll Chicken Salad with Creamy Asian Dressing, 226–227
Cabbage Roll Skillet recipe, 110–111
caffeine, 48
cage-free poultry, 46
calcium magnesium powder
    Keto Electrolyte Drink—Three Ways, 260–261
Cali'flour Foods Pizza Crusts, 289
Canadian bacon
    Eggs Benedict, 154–155
carbs
    reasons for craving, 17–23
    reintroducing, 278–280
    testing, 279
Carnivore Crisps, 289
carrots
    Chicken Cauliflower Fried Rice, 116–117
cauliflower rice, carbs in, 26
Cauliflower Rice recipe, 112–113
    Chicken Cauliflower Fried Rice, 116–117
    Mashed Roasted Cauliflower, 174–175
    Roasted Balsamic Vegetables, 194–195

celery
  Jambalaya, 170–171
Cheddar and Bacon–Stuffed Burgers recipe,
  114–115
cheddar cheese
  Bacon Bourbon Burgers, 98–99
  Buffalo Chicken Salad Wraps, 104–105
  Cheddar and Bacon–Stuffed Burgers,
    114–115
  Chicken Chili Stuffed Peppers, 118–119
  Crustless Skillet Supreme Pizza, 138–139
  Open-Face Tuna Chaffles, 180–181
  Simple Skillet Chili, 214–215
  Taco Soup, 236–237
  Waffle Breakfast Sandwich, 242–243
cheese. See specific types
chicken
  Brown Butter Crispy Chicken Thighs,
    102–103
  Buffalo Chicken Salad Wraps, 104–105
  Buffalo Wings, 106–107
  cage-free vs. free-range, 46
  Chicken Cauliflower Fried Rice, 116–117
  Chicken Chili Stuffed Peppers, 118–119
  Chicken Kiev Meatballs, 120–121
  Chicken Mushroom Skillet, 122–123
  Cobb Ranch Salad, 128–129
  Egg Foo Young, 148–149
  Sheet Pan Chicken Fajitas, 206–207
  Spring Roll Chicken Salad with Creamy
    Asian Dressing, 226–227
  Stuffed Chicken Thighs, 228–229
Chicken Cauliflower Fried Rice recipe, 116–117
Chicken Chili Stuffed Peppers recipe, 118–119
Chicken Kiev Meatballs recipe, 120–121
Chicken Mushroom Skillet recipe, 122–123
Chimichurri recipe, 124–125
  Reverse-Seared Rib Eye with Chimichurri,
    192–193
chocolate
  brand recommendations, 288
  Brownie in a Mug, 250–251

Deep Dish Chocolate Chip Cookies,
    256–257
  Keto Chocolate Lava Cakes for Two,
    252–253
ChocZero Chocolate Bark, 289
Chomps Jerky, 289
Chosen Foods brand, 288
cilantro
  Chimichurri, 124–125
  Creamy Cilantro Lime Slaw, 132–133
  Sheet Pan Chicken Fajitas, 206–207
  Simple Skillet Chili, 214–215
  Taco Soup, 236–237
Cloud Bread Rolls recipe, 126–127
  Bacon Bourbon Burgers, 98–99
  Eggs Benedict, 154–155
  Tiramisu for Two, 272–273
  Tuna Salad, 238–239
Cobb Ranch Salad recipe, 128–129
cocoa powder
  Brownie in a Mug, 250–251
  Scrambled Egg Chocolate Pudding,
    268–269
  Simple Skillet Chili, 214–215
  Tiramisu for Two, 272–273
coconut aminos
  Chicken Cauliflower Fried Rice, 116–117
  Egg Foo Young, 148–149
  Philly Cheesesteak Stir-Fry, 186–187
  Spring Roll Chicken Salad with Creamy
    Asian Dressing, 226–227
coconut milk
  Smoked Salmon Omelet Roll-Ups,
    216–217
coconut water
  Keto Electrolyte Drink—Three Ways,
    260–261
Coconut Wraps, 289
cod
  Fish Taco Bowl, 156–157
coffee
  about, 49

coffee *(continued)*
>   Keto Chocolate Lava Cakes for Two, 252–253
>   Keto Dalgona Coffee, 254–255
>   Tiramisu for Two, 272–273

coleslaw mix
>   Spring Roll Chicken Salad with Creamy Asian Dressing, 226–227

combating cravings, 57, 63–66

comfort eating, 69–70

The Complete Guide to Fasting (Fung), 61–62

condiments. *See also* sauces
>   Homemade Ketchup, 168–169
>   in meal plans, 76
>   prepared, shopping guide for, 288
>   Spicy Mayo, 222–223

consistency, cravings and, 66

constipation, 59, 63

Corned Beef Hash Skillet with Eggs recipe, 10–131

cravings
>   combating, 57, 63–66
>   for sugar and carbs, 17–23

cream cheese
>   Berry Fluff, 248–249
>   Chicken Kiev Meatballs, 120–121
>   Protein Pancakes, 190–191
>   Smoked Salmon Omelet Roll-Ups, 216–217
>   Tiramisu for Two, 272–273

Creamy Cilantro Lime Slaw recipe, 132–133

Crispy Broccoli recipe, 134–136

Crustless Ham and Cheese Quiches recipe, 136–137

Crustless Skillet Supreme Pizza recipe, 138–139

cucumber
>   Spring Roll Chicken Salad with Creamy Asian Dressing, 226–227

D

daikon radish
>   Corned Beef Hash Skillet with Eggs, 130–131
>   German "Potato" Salad, 164–165

dairy, in meal plans, 77. *See also specific types*

Dairy-Free Mini Waffles recipe, 140–141
>   Monte Cristo Waffle Sandwiches, 178–179
>   Waffle Breakfast Sandwich, 242–243

Deep Dish Chocolate Chip Cookies recipe, 256–257

Defy Foods Cheddar Crackers, 289

dehydration
>   dizziness and, 59
>   symptoms of, 48

desserts. *See also specific recipes*
>   about, 247
>   in meal plan, 77
>   sugar-free, 55

Deviled Eggs recipe, 142–143

DEXA scan, 43

diet soda, 49

dill pickles
>   Open-Face Tuna Chaffles, 180–181

distraction, from cravings, 64

dizziness, 58–59, 63

doctor visits, 24

dopamine, 23, 40

Dow, Mike, *The Sugar Brain Fix*, 23

E

Easy Bacon recipe, 144–145
>   Cheddar and Bacon–Stuffed Burgers, 114–115
>   Cobb Ranch Salad, 128–129
>   Crustless Skillet Supreme Pizza, 138–139

Easy-Peel Hard-Boiled Eggs recipe, 146–147
>   Cobb Ranch Salad, 128–129
>   Deviled Eggs, 142–143
>   Egg Salad, 152–153

Egg Custard recipe, 258–259

Egg Foo Young recipe, 148–149

egg noodles, carbs in, 26

Egg Noodles recipe, 150–151

Egg Salad recipe, 152–153

Egglife Egg White Wraps, 289

eggs

Apple Pie Dutch Baby, 94–95

Brownie in a Mug, 250–251

Chicken Cauliflower Fried Rice, 116–117

Chicken Kiev Meatballs, 120–121

Cloud Bread Rolls, 126–127

Corned Beef Hash Skillet with Eggs, 130–131

Crustless Ham and Cheese Quiches, 136–137

Dairy-Free Mini Waffles, 140–141

Deep Dish Chocolate Chip Cookies, 256–257

Easy-Peel Hard-Boiled Eggs, 146–147

Egg Custard, 258–259

Egg Foo Young, 148–149

Egg Noodles, 150–151

Eggs Benedict, 154–155

French Onion Meatballs, 158–159

Keto Chocolate Lava Cakes for Two, 252–253

Monte Cristo Waffle Sandwiches, 178–179

No-Churn Vanilla Ice Cream, 262–263

Open-Face Tuna Chaffles, 180–181

Pizza Chaffles, 188–189

Protein Pancakes, 190–191

Raspberry Clafoutis, 265–266

Sausage Egg Cups, 198–199

Scotch Eggs, 204–205

Scrambled Egg Chocolate Pudding, 268–269

Smoked Salmon Omelet Roll-Ups, 216–217

Soft Scrambled Eggs, 220–221

2-Minute English Muffins, 240–241

Waffle Breakfast Sandwich, 242–243

Eggs Benedict recipe, 154–155

electrolyte drinks, homemade, 49, 260–261

electrolytes, 48–50

Epic brand, 288, 289

equipment, kitchen, meal plans and, 79

erythritol, 53

espresso/espresso powder

Brownie in a Mug, 250–251

Tiramisu for Two, 272–273

Everly brand, 50

Evolved Keto Almond Butter Cups, 289

exceptions, 65

exercise, 41–42

extra-virgin olive oil, 51

F

fabric tape measure, 25

farm-raised fish and seafood, 47

fasting. *See* intermittent fasting

fat fasting, 61–62

Fat Snax brand, 289

fats and oils, 50–52

Fbomb Nut Butter Packets, 289

fennel

Breakfast Sausage Patties, 100–101

feta cheese

Asparagus Salad with Avocado Dressing, 96–97

fish and seafood

Fish Taco Bowl, 156–157

Jambalaya, 170–171

Pan-Seared Lemon Butter Salmon, 184–185

Sheet Pan Shrimp with Crispy Pepperoni, 208–209

Shrimp Linguine in Garlic Butter Sauce, 212–213

Smoked Salmon Omelet Roll-Ups, 216–217

Spicy Smoked Salmon Wrap, 224–225

Tuna Salad, 238–239

wild-caught vs. farm-raised, 47

Fish Taco Bowl recipe, 156–157

5:2 intermittent fasting, 62

flaxseed

    Chicken Kiev Meatballs, 120–121

folate, 20

Folios Cheese Wraps, 289

Fond brand, 288

food journaling, 24, 40–41, 66

food scale, 24, 279

4-5-7 breathing technique, 66

4505 Chicharrones, 289

Fox Hill Kitchen "Bagelz" and "Bunz," 289

free-range poultry, 46

french fries, low-carb swaps for, 26

French Onion Meatballs recipe, 158–159

Fresno chili peppers

    Bacon Bourbon Burgers, 98–99

    Chimichurri, 124–125

Frontier Co-Op brand, 288

fruits, low-carb, 56. *See also specific types*

full single-day fasting, 62

Fung, Jason, *The Complete Guide to Fasting,*
61–62

G

garlic

    Asparagus Salad with Avocado Dressing,
96–97

    Brown Butter Crispy Chicken Thighs,
102–103

    Cabbage Roll Skillet, 110–111

    Cauliflower Rice, 112–113

    Chicken Cauliflower Fried Rice, 116–117

    Chicken Chili Stuffed Peppers, 118–119

    Chicken Kiev Meatballs, 120–121

    Chicken Mushroom Skillet, 122–123

    Chimichurri, 124–125

    Egg Foo Young, 148–149

    Fish Taco Bowl, 156–157

    French Onion Meatballs, 158–159

    Garlic Butter Mushrooms, 160–161

    Garlic Butter Steak Bites, 162–163

    German "Potato" Salad, 164–165

    Homemade Ketchup, 168–169

    Jambalaya, 170–171

    Low-Carb Marinara Sauce, 172–173

    Momma's Italian Dressing, 176–177

    Palmini Rice, 182–183

    Pan-Seared Lemon Butter Salmon,
184–185

    Reverse-Seared Rib Eye with Chimichurri,
192–193

    Roasted Balsamic Vegetables, 194–195

    Sausage Zucchini Skillet, 200–201

    Sheet Pan Shrimp with Crispy Pepperoni,
208–209

    Shrimp Linguine in Garlic Butter Sauce,
212–213

    Simple Skillet Chili, 214–215

    Spicy Mayo, 222–223

    Spring Roll Chicken Salad with Creamy
Asian Dressing, 226–227

    Stuffed Chicken Thighs, 228–229

    Taco Soup, 236–237

    Zucchini Noodles with Roasted Garlic
Cream Sauce, 244–245

Garlic Butter Mushrooms recipe, 160–161

Garlic Butter Steak Bites recipe, 162–163

gas, 59

gelatin powder

    Dairy-Free Mini Waffles, 140–141

    Panna Cotta, 264–265

German "Potato" Salad recipe, 164–165

ginger

    Chicken Cauliflower Fried Rice, 116–117

    Lemon Ginger Keto Electrolyte Drink,
260–261

glucomannan

    Egg Foo Young, 148–149

    Egg Noodles, 150–151

    Jambalaya, 170–171

    Raspberry Clafoutis, 265–266

    Sugar-Free Maple Syrup, 232–233

Zucchini Noodles with Roasted Garlic
Cream Sauce, 244–245
gluten, 279–280
glycine, 60
Good Dee's brand, 289
grains, 279–280
grass-fed proteins, 46
green chilies
Chicken Chili Stuffed Peppers, 118–119
Greger, Michael, "Are Sugary Foods Addictive,"
276
Grilled Romaine Salad recipe, 166–167
Gruyère cheese
Monte Cristo Waffle Sandwiches,
178–179
gut health, 60

H

habit hunger, compared with true hunger, 292
habits, building new, 36–37
halloumi, carbs in, 26
ham
Crustless Ham and Cheese Quiches,
136–137
Crustless Skillet Supreme Pizza, 138–139
Jambalaya, 170–171
Monte Cristo Waffle Sandwiches, 178–179
Waffle Breakfast Sandwich, 242–243
hamburger bun pan, 79
hangry, 57
headaches, from intermittent fasting, 63
heart of palm pasta and rice, 288. *See also*
Palmini rice
heartburn, 59, 63
heavy cream
Apple Pie Dutch Baby, 94–95
Berry Fluff, 248–249
Brownie in a Mug, 250–251
Chicken Mushroom Skillet, 122–123
Crustless Ham and Cheese Quiches,
136–137
Egg Custard, 258–259

Eggs Benedict, 154–155
Monte Cristo Waffle Sandwiches, 178–179
No-Churn Vanilla Ice Cream, 262–263
Panna Cotta, 264–265
Raspberry Clafoutis, 265–266
Soft Scrambled Eggs, 220–221
Sugar-Free Whipped Cream, 270–271
Zucchini Noodles with Roasted Garlic
Cream Sauce, 244–245
herbal tea, 49
high-carb vegetables, 56
HighKey mixes, 289
high-protein meal plans, committing to, 65
Homemade Ketchup recipe, 168–169
Sugar-Free BBQ Sauce, 230–231
"honesty pants" test, 43
human growth hormone (HGH), 61
Hunger or Habit? worksheet, 292
hydration, 48–50, 65
hydrochloric acid, 59
hyperpalatable foods, addicted to, 22–23

I

ingredients, optional, 76
Instant Pot, 79
insulin, 56–57, 61
intermittent fasting
about, 60–61
allowances between meals, 61–62
meal plan and, 78
options for, 62–63
Italian sausage
Sausage Zucchini Skillet, 200–201
It's Skinny Pasta brand, 288

J

jalapeño peppers
Bacon Bourbon Burgers, 98–99
Simple Skillet Chili, 214–215
Taco Soup, 236–237
Jambalaya recipe, 170–171

journaling
  about, 24, 40–41
  cravings and, 66

K

ketchup
  brand recommendations, 288
  Homemade Ketchup, 168–169
keto, compared with low-carb, 29–30
Keto and Co Banana Caramel Muffin, 289
Keto Chocolate Lava Cakes for Two recipe, 252–253
Keto Dalgona Coffee recipe, 50, 254–255
Keto Electrolyte Drink—Three Ways recipe, 260–261
ketone testing, 72–73
Kettle & Fire brand, 50, 288
Kiss My Keto Bread, 289
kitchen
  cleaning out, 24
  equipment for meal plan, 79
Kresser, Chris, 51

L

labels, reading, 27–28
Lakanto brand, 288
Lemon Ginger Keto Electrolyte Drink recipe, 260–261
lemons
  Asparagus Salad with Avocado Dressing, 96–97
  Cauliflower Rice, 112–113
  Eggs Benedict, 154–155
  Lemon Ginger Keto Electrolyte Drink, 260–261
  Pan-Seared Lemon Butter Salmon, 184–185
  Shrimp Linguine in Garlic Butter Sauce, 212–213
  Tuna Salad, 238–239

lettuce
  Buffalo Chicken Salad Wraps, 104–105
  Cobb Ranch Salad, 128–129
  Grilled Romaine Salad, 166–167
  Spicy Smoked Salmon Wrap, 224–225
  Tuna Salad, 238–239
Lily's brand, 288, 289
Lime Mint Keto Electrolyte Drink recipe, 260–261
limes
  Brown Butter Crispy Chicken Thighs, 102–103
  Cauliflower Rice, 112–113
  Creamy Cilantro Lime Slaw, 132–133
  Egg Salad, 152–153
  Eggs Benedict, 154–155
  Fish Taco Bowl, 156–157
  Lime Mint Keto Electrolyte Drink, 260–261
  Sheet Pan Chicken Fajitas, 206–207
  Spicy Mayo, 222–223
  Spicy Smoked Salmon Wrap, 224–225
  Spring Roll Chicken Salad with Creamy Asian Dressing, 226–227
lipolysis, 61
liquid extracts, 288
LMNT brand, 50
low-carb diet, compared with keto, 29–30
low-carb fruits, 56
Low-Carb Marinara Sauce recipe, 172–173
  Cabbage Roll Skillet, 110–111
  Chicken Chili Stuffed Peppers, 118–119
  Crustless Skillet Supreme Pizza, 138–139
  Pizza Chaffles, 188–189
low-carb sweeteners. *See* sweeteners
low-carb vegetables, 55
low-carb whole foods, 20, 26

M

magnesium, 20

magnesium glycinate

    supplementing with, 32

    for relief of constipation, 59

maltitol, 53

maple syrup, brand recommendations, 288

marinara sauce, brand recommendations, 288

mascarpone cheese

    Tiramisu for Two, 272–273

mashed cauliflower, carbs in, 26

mashed palmini, carbs in, 26

mashed potatoes, low-carb swaps for, 26

Mashed Roasted Cauliflower recipe, 174–175

mashed turnip, carbs in, 26

MCT oil, 59

meal plan

    about, 76

    condiments in, 76

    dairy in, 77

    days 1–7, 82–83

    days 8–15, 84–85

    days 16–23, 86–87

    days 24–30, 88–89

    desserts during, 77

    intermittent fasting during, 78

    kitchen equipment needed for, 79

    nuts in, 77

    optional ingredients, 76

    recipes for, 91–273

    shopping lists for, 79–89

melatonin, 32

Mexican cheese

    Sheet Pan Chicken Fajitas, 206–207

mini waffle maker, 79

mint

    Lime Mint Keto Electrolyte Drink, 260–261

Miracle Noodle brand, 288

moderation, eating in, 276–277

molasses

    Sugar-Free Maple Syrup, 232–233

Momma's Italian Dressing recipe, 176–177

    Tuna Salad, 238–239

monk fruit, 53, 290

monounsaturated fats, 51

Monte Cristo Waffle Sandwiches recipe, 178–179

Monterey Bay Aquarium Seafood Watch, 47

Monterey Jack cheese

    Chicken Kiev Meatballs, 120–121

movement, cravings and, 64

mozzarella cheese

    Crustless Ham and Cheese Quiches, 136–137

    Crustless Skillet Supreme Pizza, 138–139

    French Onion Meatballs, 158–159

    Open-Face Tuna Chaffles, 180–181

    Philly Cheesesteak Stir-Fry, 186–187

    Pizza Chaffles, 188–189

    Sausage Zucchini Skillet, 200–201

    Stuffed Chicken Thighs, 228–229

mushrooms

    Chicken Mushroom Skillet, 122–123

    Garlic Butter Mushrooms, 160–161

    Philly Cheesesteak Stir-Fry, 186–187

N

Naiman, Ted, 45

natural sugar-free sweeteners, 52–57

No-Churn Vanilla Ice Cream recipe, 262–263

non-celiac gluten sensitivity (NCGS), 280

Nush Foods Keto Snack Cakes, 289

nut butter

    Deep Dish Chocolate Chip Cookies, 256–257

    Spring Roll Chicken Salad with Creamy Asian Dressing, 226–227

Nutpods Dairy-Free Creamer, 289

nuts, in meal plans, 77

O

olive oil, 51

omega-3 fats and oils, 51

omega-6 fats and oils, 51–52

one meal a day (OMAD), 62

onions

    Bacon Bourbon Burgers, 98–99

    Buffalo Chicken Salad Wraps, 104–105

    Cabbage Roll Skillet, 110–111

    Chicken Chili Stuffed Peppers, 118–119

    Corned Beef Hash Skillet with Eggs, 130–131

    Crustless Skillet Supreme Pizza, 138–139

    Egg Salad, 152–153

    French Onion Meatballs, 158–159

    German "Potato" Salad, 164–165

    Jambalaya, 170–171

    Philly Cheesesteak Stir-Fry, 186–187

    Roasted Balsamic Vegetables, 194–195

    Sausage Zucchini Skillet, 200–201

    Sautéed Summer Squash, 202–203

    Sheet Pan Chicken Fajitas, 206–207

    Sheet Pan Shrimp with Crispy Pepperoni, 208–209

    Simple Skillet Chili, 214–215

    Taco Soup, 236–237

    Tuna Salad, 238–239

OOOFlavors brand, 288

Open-Face Tuna Chaffles recipe, 180–181

Orange Basil Keto Electrolyte Drink recipe, 260–261

P

packaged proteins, 47

Paleovalley Beef and Turkey Sticks, 289

Palmini brand, 288

Palmini noodles, carbs in, 26

Palmini rice

    carbs in, 26

    Chicken Chili Stuffed Peppers, 118–119

    Palmini Rice, 182–183

Palmini Rice recipe, 182–183

Panna Cotta recipe, 264–265

Pan-Seared Lemon Butter Salmon recipe, 184–185

pantry staples, 81, 288, 289

Parmesan cheese

    Crustless Skillet Supreme Pizza, 138–139

    Grilled Romaine Salad, 166–167

    Sautéed Summer Squash, 202–203

    Zucchini Noodles with Roasted Garlic Cream Sauce, 244–245

parsley

    Breakfast Sausage Patties, 100–101

    Brown Butter Crispy Chicken Thighs, 102–103

    Buffalo Wings, 106–107

    Cabbage Roll Skillet, 110–111

    Cauliflower Rice, 112–113

    Chicken Chili Stuffed Peppers, 118–119

    Chicken Kiev Meatballs, 120–121

    Chicken Mushroom Skillet, 122–123

    Chimichurri, 124–125

    Cobb Ranch Salad, 128–129

    Corned Beef Hash Skillet with Eggs, 130–131

    Crustless Ham and Cheese Quiches, 136–137

    Crustless Skillet Supreme Pizza, 138–139

    Deviled Eggs, 142–143

    Egg Noodles, 150–151

    Eggs Benedict, 154–155

    French Onion Meatballs, 158–159

    Garlic Butter Mushrooms, 160–161

    Garlic Butter Steak Bites, 162–163

    German "Potato" Salad, 164–165

    Jambalaya, 170–171

    Momma's Italian Dressing, 176–177

    Open-Face Tuna Chaffles, 180–181

    Palmini Rice, 182–183

    Pan-Seared Lemon Butter Salmon, 184–185

    Pizza Chaffles, 188–189

Sausage Egg Cups, 198–199
Sausage Zucchini Skillet, 200–201
Sautéed Summer Squash, 202–203
Scotch Eggs, 204–205
Shirataki Rice, 210–211
Shrimp Linguine in Garlic Butter Sauce, 212–213
Smoked Salmon Omelet Roll-Ups, 216–217
Soft Scrambled Eggs, 220–221
Spicy Smoked Salmon Wrap, 224–225
Stuffed Chicken Thighs, 228–229
Tuna Salad, 238–239
Zucchini Noodles with Roasted Garlic Cream Sauce, 244–245
pasta, low-carb swaps for, 26
pasture-raised proteins, 46
peanut butter
  Deep Dish Chocolate Chip Cookies, 256–257
peanuts
  Spring Roll Chicken Salad with Creamy Asian Dressing, 226–227
pepper Jack cheese
  Chicken Kiev Meatballs, 120–121
pepperoni
  Crustless Skillet Supreme Pizza, 138–139
  Pizza Chaffles, 188–189
  Sheet Pan Shrimp with Crispy Pepperoni, 208–209
Perfect Keto Bars, 289
Philly Cheesesteak Stir-Fry recipe, 186–187
Phinney, Stephen, 45
Pique Tea brand, 50
Pizza Chaffles recipe, 188–189
polyunsaturated fats, 51
pork
  Breakfast Sausage Patties, 100–101
  Crustless Skillet Supreme Pizza, 138–139
  French Onion Meatballs, 158–159
  Sausage Egg Cups, 198–199
  Scotch Eggs, 204–205

Smoky Grilled Pork Chops, 218–219
  Stuffed Chicken Thighs, 228–229
Pork King Good brand, 288
pork rinds
  brand recommendations, 288
  Chicken Kiev Meatballs, 120–121
  French Onion Meatballs, 158–159
  Scotch Eggs, 204–205
poultry, cage-free vs. free-range, 46. See also chicken; turkey
prepared foods, shopping guide for, 289
Primal Kitchen brand, 28, 288
processed proteins, 47
proteins
  about, 44–45
  cage-free vs. free-range poultry, 46
  grass-fed and pasture-raised, 46
  processed and packaged, 47
  prioritizing, 44–47, 65
  wild-caught vs. farm-raised fish and seafood, 47
Protein Pancakes recipe, 190–191
protein powder
  Cloud Bread Rolls, 126–127
  Protein Pancakes, 190–191

Q–R
quiche dishes, 79
radishes
  Asparagus Salad with Avocado Dressing, 96–97
  carbs in, 26
Rao's brand, 288
raspberries. See also berries
  Monte Cristo Waffle Sandwiches, 178–179
  Raspberry Clafoutis, 265–266
Raspberry Clafoutis recipe, 265–266
Realgood Foods Bacon-Wrapped Stuffed Chicken, 289
Redmond Real Salt brand, 58

reintroducing carbs, 278–280

replenishing sodium, 49

Reverse-Seared Rib Eye with Chimichurri
recipe, 192–193

rice, low-carb swaps for, 26

Roasted Balsamic Vegetables recipe, 194–195

romaine lettuce. *See* lettuce

rosemary

        Reverse-Seared Rib Eye with Chimichurri,
192–193

rutabaga, carbs in, 26

Rutabaga Fries recipe, 196–197

S

salad dressings

        Avocado Dressing, 96–97

        brand recommendations, 288

        Creamy Asian Dressing, 226–227

        Momma's Italian Dressing, 176–177

        Ranch Dressing, 128–129

salads

        Asparagus Salad with Avocado Dressing,
96–97

        Buffalo Chicken Salad Wraps, 104–105

        Cobb Ranch Salad, 128–129

        German "Potato" Salad, 164–165

        Grilled Romaine Salad, 166–167

        Spring Roll Chicken Salad with Creamy
Asian Dressing, 226–227

        Tuna Salad, 238–239

salmon

        Pan-Seared Lemon Butter Salmon,
184–185

        Smoked Salmon Omelet Roll-Ups,
216–217

        Spicy Smoked Salmon Wrap, 224–225

salsa

        Sheet Pan Chicken Fajitas, 206–207

        Simple Skillet Chili, 214–215

salt. *See* sodium

saturated fats, 51

sauces. *See also* condiments

        Buffalo Wing Sauce, 108–109

        Low-Carb Marinara Sauce, 172–173

        prepared, shopping guide for, 288

Sugar-Free BBQ Sauce, 230–231

Sausage Egg Cups recipe, 198–199

Sausage Zucchini Skillet recipe, 200–201

Sautéed Summer Squash recipe, 202–203

scale

        bathroom, 25, 42–43

        food, 24, 279

        worksheet, 291

scallions

        Chicken Cauliflower Fried Rice, 116–117

        Corned Beef Hash Skillet with Eggs,
130–131

        Egg Foo Young, 148–149

        Jambalaya, 170–171

        Spicy Smoked Salmon Wrap, 224–225

        Spring Roll Chicken Salad with Creamy
Asian Dressing, 226–227

Scotch Eggs recipe, 204–205

Scrambled Egg Chocolate Pudding recipe,
268–269

seafood. *See* fish and seafood

self-care, serotonin and, 18–20

serotonin

        about, 18

        activities for increasing, 19

        low-carb whole foods and, 20

        self-care and, 18–20

        sleep and, 21–22

        sunlight and, 20

sesame seeds

        Cloud Bread Rolls, 126–127

        Egg Foo Young, 148–149

        Spring Roll Chicken Salad with Creamy
Asian Dressing, 226–227

shallots

        Chimichurri, 124–125

        Garlic Butter Mushrooms, 160–161

Sheet Pan Chicken Fajitas recipe, 206–207

Sheet Pan Shrimp with Crispy Pepperoni recipe, 208–209

shirataki noodles

brand recommendations, 288

carbs in, 26

Shrimp Linguine in Garlic Butter Sauce, 212–213

shirataki rice

brand recommendations, 288

Cabbage Roll Skillet, 110–111

carbs in, 26

Jambalaya, 170–171

Shirataki Rice, 210–211

Spicy Smoked Salmon Wrap, 224–225

Shirataki Rice recipe, 210–211

shopping guide, 288–289

shrimp

Jambalaya, 170–171

Sheet Pan Shrimp with Crispy Pepperoni, 208–209

Shrimp Linguine in Garlic Butter Sauce, 212–213

Shrimp Linguine in Garlic Butter Sauce recipe, 212–213

Siete Foods Grain-Free Taco Shells, 289

silicone hamburger bun pan, 79

Simple Skillet Chili recipe, 214–215

sleep, serotonin and, 21–22

Smoked Salmon Omelet Roll-Ups recipe, 216–217

Smoky Grilled Pork Chops recipe, 218–219

snacks

during Days 1–7 of the meal plan, 56–57

shopping guide for, 289

soda, 49

sodium

for combating cravings, 64

dizziness and, 58–59

as electrolyte, 49

Soft Scrambled Eggs recipe, 220–221

sorbitol, 53

soups and stews

Simple Skillet Chili, 214–215

Taco Soup, 236–237

sour cream

Chicken Mushroom Skillet, 122–123

Sheet Pan Chicken Fajitas, 206–207

Simple Skillet Chili, 214–215

Taco Soup, 236–237

spaghetti squash noodles, carbs in, 26

sparkling water

about, 49

Keto Electrolyte Drink—Three Ways, 260–261

Spicy Mayo recipe, 222–223

Spicy Smoked Salmon Wrap recipe, 224–225

spinach

Sausage Egg Cups, 198–199

Spring Roll Chicken Salad with Creamy Asian Dressing recipe, 226–227

Sriracha sauce

Spicy Mayo, 222–223

stevia, 53, 290

stevia glycerite, 53, 290

stress, serotonin and, 18

Stuffed Chicken Thighs recipe, 228–229

substitutions, low-carb whole foods as, 26

sucralose, 61

sugar

on labels, 27–28

reasons for craving, 17–23

The Sugar Brain Fix (Dow), 23

Sugar-Free BBQ Sauce recipe, 230–231

Bacon Bourbon Burgers, 98–99

sugar-free desserts, 55. See also specific recipes

Sugar-Free Maple Syrup recipe, 232–233

Dairy-Free Mini Waffles, 140–141

Protein Pancakes, 190–191

Sugar-Free BBQ Sauce, 230–231

Sugar-Free Whipped Cream recipe, 270–271
    Egg Custard, 258–259
    Keto Chocolate Lava Cakes for Two, 252–253
    Panna Cotta, 264–265
    Raspberry Clafoutis, 265–266
sunflower seed butter
    Spring Roll Chicken Salad with Creamy Asian Dressing, 226–227
sunlight, serotonin and, 20
supplements, 31–33
sweet potatoes, carbs in, 26
sweeteners
    brand recommendations, 288
    conversion chart, 290
    natural sugar-free, 52–55
SweetLeaf Water Drops brand, 50
Swerve brand, 288, 290
Swerve Cake Mixes, 289
Swiss cheese
    Open-Face Tuna Chaffles, 180–181

T

Taco Seasoning recipe, 234–235
    Fish Taco Bowl, 156–157
    Taco Soup, 236–237
Taco Soup recipe, 236–237
tahini
    Spring Roll Chicken Salad with Creamy Asian Dressing, 226–227
tape measure, 25
tea, herbal, 49
testimonials, 284–287
testing carbohydrates, 279
30-Day Sugar Elimination Diet
    about, 15–16
    after completing, 281–282
    basics of, 38–43
    days 1–7, 48–57
    days 8–15, 58–66
    days 16–23, 67–71

days 24–30, 72–73
    prioritizing protein during, 65
    not making exceptions, 65
    preparing for, 24–28
thyme
    Reverse-Seared Rib Eye with Chimichurri, 192–193
    Sheet Pan Shrimp with Crispy Pepperoni, 208–209
Tiramisu for Two recipe, 272–273
tomato paste
    Homemade Ketchup, 168–169
    Taco Soup, 236–237
tomato puree
    Homemade Ketchup, 168–169
    Low-Carb Marinara Sauce, 172–173
tomatoes
    Buffalo Chicken Salad Wraps, 104–105
    Cabbage Roll Skillet, 110–111
    Cobb Ranch Salad, 128–129
    Fish Taco Bowl, 156–157
    Grilled Romaine Salad, 166–167
    Jambalaya, 170–171
    Sheet Pan Shrimp with Crispy Pepperoni, 208–209
    Simple Skillet Chili, 214–215
    Taco Soup, 236–237
Trader Joe's Fresh Cauliflower Thins, 289
trigger foods, identifying, 68–69
troubleshooting, 70–71
tryptophan, 20
Tuna Salad recipe, 238–239
    Open-Face Tuna Chaffles, 180–181
turkey
    Egg Foo Young, 148–149
2-Minute English Muffins recipe, 240–241

V

vegetables, 55–56. *See also specific types*
vitamin B, 20
vitamin C, 20

vitamin D, 33
Volek, Jeff, 45

W

Waffle Breakfast Sandwich recipe, 242–243
waffle maker, 79
water, drinking, 48, 59. *See also* sparkling
    water
weight loss, low-carb or keto diet for, 30
Whisps Cheese Crisps, 289
Wholesome brand, 288
wild-caught fish and seafood, 47
Wired to Eat (Wolf), 23
Wolf, Robb, *Wired to Eat*, 23
worksheets
    hunger or habit, 292
    scale, 291

X

xanthan gum
    Egg Foo Young, 148–149
    Egg Noodles, 150–151
    Jambalaya, 170–171
    Raspberry Clafoutis, 265–266
    Sugar-Free Maple Syrup, 232–233
    Zucchini Noodles with Roasted Garlic
        Cream Sauce, 244–245
xylitol, 53

Y

yacón syrup
    about, 53
    Homemade Ketchup, 168–169
    Sugar-Free BBQ Sauce, 230–231
    Sugar-Free Maple Syrup, 232–233
yellow squash
    Sautéed Summer Squash, 202–203

Z

Zevia brand, 50
zinc, 20, 33
zucchini
    Roasted Balsamic Vegetables, 194–195
    Sausage Zucchini Skillet, 200–201
    Sautéed Summer Squash, 202–203
    Zucchini Noodles with Roasted Garlic
        Cream Sauce, 244–245
zucchini noodles, carbs in, 26
Zucchini Noodles with Roasted Garlic Cream
    Sauce recipe, 244–245